More information about this subseries at http://www.springer.com/series/7409

Andrea Kö · Enrico Francesconi ·
Gabriele Kotsis · A Min Tjoa ·
Ismail Khalil (Eds.)

Electronic Government and the Information Systems Perspective

10th International Conference, EGOVIS 2021
Virtual Event, September 27–30, 2021
Proceedings

 Springer

Editors
Andrea Kö (iD)
Corvinus University Budapest
Budapest, Hungary

Gabriele Kotsis
Johannes Kepler University of Linz
Linz, Austria

Ismail Khalil
Johannes Kepler University of Linz
Linz, Austria

Enrico Francesconi
National Research Council
and European Parliament
Florence, Italy

A Min Tjoa
Vienna University of Technology
Vienna, Austria

ISSN 0302-9743 ISSN 1611-3349 (electronic)
Lecture Notes in Computer Science
ISBN 978-3-030-86610-5 ISBN 978-3-030-86611-2 (eBook)
https://doi.org/10.1007/978-3-030-86611-2

LNCS Sublibrary: SL3 – Information Systems and Applications, incl. Internet/Web, and HCI

This Springer imprint is published by the registered company Springer Nature Switzerland AG
The registered company address is: Gewerbestrasse 11, 6330 Cham, Switzerland

Preface

The 10th International Conference on Electronic Government and the Information Systems Perspective, EGOVIS 2021, originally planned to be held in Linz, Austria, took place online on September 27–30, 2021. The conference belongs to the 32nd DEXA conference series.

The international conference EGOVIS focuses on information systems and ICT aspects of e-government. Information systems are a core enabler for e-government/governance in all its dimensions: e-administration, e-democracy, e-participation, and e-voting. EGOVIS brings together experts from academia, public administrations, and industry to discuss e-government and e-democracy from different perspectives and disciplines, i.e., technology, policy and/or governance, and public administration.

The Program Committee accepted 13 papers from recent research fields such as artificial intelligence, machine learning, e-identity, e-participation, open government and e-government architectures for e-government, intelligent systems and semantic technologies for services in the public sector. Beyond theoretical contributions, the papers cover e-government practical applications and experiences.

These proceeding are organized into three sections according to the conference sessions' about e-government theoretical background, e-government cases - data and knowledge management; identity management and legal issues; and artificial intelligence and machine learning in e-government context.

Chairs of the Program Committee wish to thank all the reviewers for their valuable work; the reviews raised several research questions discussed at the conference. We would like to thank Ismail Khalil for the administrative support and helping us with proper scheduling.

We wish pleasant and beneficial learning experiences for the readers and we hope that the discussion will continue after the conference between the researchers, contributing to building a global community in the field of e-government.

September 2021

Enrico Francesconi
Andrea Kő

Organization

Program Committee Chairs

Andrea Kő   Corvinus University Budapest, Hungary
Enrico Francesconi   Italian National Research Council, Italy,
                           and European Parliament, Belgium

Steering Committee

Gabriele Kotsis   Johannes Kepler University Linz, Austria
A Min Tjoa   Technical University of Vienna, Austria
Robert Wille   Software Competence Center Hagenberg, Austria
Bernhard Moser   Software Competence Center Hagenberg, Austria
Ismail Khalil   Johannes Kepler University Linz, Austria

Program Committee

Francesco Buccafurri   Mediterranea University of Reggio Calabria, Italy
Alejandra Cechich   Universidad Nacional del Comahue, Argentina
Wojciech Cellary   Poznan University of Economics and Business, Poland
Wichian Chutimaskul   King Mongkut's University of Technology Thonburi,
                           Thailand
Flavio Corradini   University of Camerino, Italy
Peter Cruickshank   Edinburgh Napier University, UK
Csaba Csáki   Corvinus University of Budapest, Hungary
Vytautas Čyras   Vilnius University, Italy
Ivan Futo   Multilogic Ltd., Hungary
Andras Gabor   Corvinno Technology Transfer Center Nonprofit Public
                           Ltd., Hungary
Fernando Galindo   University of Zaragoza, Spain
Francisco Javier García   University of Zaragoza, Spain
   Marco
Stefanos Gritzalis   University of Piraeus, Greece
Henning Sten Hansen   Aalborg University, Denmark
Christos Kalloniatis   University of the Aegean, Greece
Nikos Karacapilidis   University of Patras, Greece
Evangelia Kavakli   University of the Aegean, Greece
Bozidar Klicek   University of Zagreb, Croatia
Hun Yeong Kwon   Kwangwoon University, South Korea
Herbert Leitold   Secure Information Technology Center Austria, Austria
Javier Nogueras Iso   University of Zaragoza, Spain
Aljosa Pasic   Atos Origin, France

Andrea Polini	University of Camerino, Italy
Aires Rover	Universidade Federal de Santa Catarina, Brazil
Luis Alvarez Sabucedo	Universidade de Vigo, Spain
Erich Schweighofer	University of Vienna, Austria
A Min Tjoa	Vienna University of Technology, Austria
Julián Valero-Torrijos	University of Murcia, Spain
Costas Vassilakis	University of the Peloponnese, Greece
Robert Woitsch	BOC Asset Management, Austria
Chien-Chih Yu	National ChengChi University, Taiwan

Organizers

Contents

Artificial Intelligence and Machine Learning in E-Government Context

e-Government Theoretical Background and Cases

Government as a Platform? Constitutive Elements of Public Service Platforms

Benedict Bender[1]([✉]) [iD] and Moreen Heine[2] [iD]

[1] University of Potsdam, August-Bebel-Str. 89, 14482 Potsdam, Germany
bbender@wi.uni-potsdam.de
[2] Universität zu Lübeck, Ratzeburger Allee 160, 23562 Lübeck, Germany

Abstract. Digital platforms, by their design, allow the coordination of multiple entities to achieve a common goal. Motivated by the success of platforms in the private sector, they increasingly receive attention in the public sector. However, different understandings of the platform concept prevail. To guide the development and further research a coherent understanding is required. To address this gap, we identify the constitutive elements of platforms in the public sector. Moreover, their potential to coordinate partially autonomous entities as typical for federal organized states is highlighted.

This study contributes through a uniform understanding of public service platforms. Despite constitutive elements, the proposed framework for platforms in the public sector may guide future analysis. The analysis framework is applied to platforms of federal states in the European Union.

Keywords: Public service platforms · Digital platforms · Government as a platform · Public sector · Platform economy · Federal states

1 Introduction

A central e-government objective is to make public services and contacts with administrations as convenient as possible for citizens and businesses. Without knowledge of official structures and responsibilities, requests should be able to be processed easily at a single point. This concept has long been discussed under the term one-stop government [1]. One-stop government creates the need for joint decisions and joint development efforts, especially, but not only, in federal states. The responsibilities are split between central and local authorities and the provincial diets have the constitutional right of legislation [2]. Previous articles have already drawn attention to the challenges arising from the claim to simplify access to public services regardless of the responsibilities in the federal state: The doctrines of federalism and separation of powers must be taken into account [3]. Holistic e-government offerings, whether in federal or centralized states, require the involvement of many different actors, which is reminiscent of digital platforms in the private sector.

Digital platforms by their architecture and governance allow the coordination of multiple entities to achieve a common goal [4]. Platforms are accompanied by a powerful

© Springer Nature Switzerland AG 2021
A. Kö et al. (Eds.): EGOVIS 2021, LNCS 12926, pp. 3–20, 2021.
https://doi.org/10.1007/978-3-030-86611-2_1

ecosystem that involves various actors that participate on the platform. Platform users benefit from the combination of the functionality provided by the platform core itself and the contributed third-party functionalities [5]. Through the integration of third-parties, platforms are able to provide more functionality than a single entity could realize [6]. Well-known examples are platforms for mobile devices such as Google Android or Apple iOS [5]. For multi-sided platforms, the coordination of multiple entities through standardization is fundamental to platform scalability and success [7].

Several structural similarities between digital platforms and service provision in the public sector exist. It seems worthwhile to transfer the organizational principles and technical elements, that constitute a digital platform, to the public sector and thereby aim to benefit from the effective and efficient organization that platforms allow for. Especially in federal systems, many different entities provide various services that need to be integrated, to offer the citizens a one-stop shop for their belongings [8]. E-Government has to promote the horizontal and vertical integration of the branches of government within the framework of the constitutionally guaranteed autonomy [3]. Whereby these specialized services, are to be offered by the different entities to account for the government's organization and specialization, many services are needed throughout all processes. This corresponds to the idea of micro-services in the context of service-oriented platform architectures [5, 9]. The platform logic can be used to provide commonly needed features centrally (such as identification services or payments) which are supplemented by specialized services from local entities as well as to link processes in the sense of a workflow. Thereby many of the aspired contextual targets such as one-stop shop [8] could be achieved.

So far, different *understandings* of the *platform* concept in the public sector context exist [10]. Among these are the provision of single services and a holistic platform, that orchestrates different services. *Individual services* are considered a platform since multiple players can participate. In contrast, the holistic concept of *government as a platform* describes the orchestration of services using digital technologies. The platform orchestrates the public service portfolio at a single access point [11]. We argue that individual services do not fulfill the requirements of the platform concept. However, to guide future research a consistent understanding is required. To shed light on this discussion, constitutive elements of a public service platform are identified by this paper:

RQ1: Which elements constitute a public service platform?

In addition to theoretic components, the status-quo concerning public platforms is of interest. Indeed, the UN E-Government Survey 2020 shows that some states and municipalities have included new principles and fields of action in their strategy papers, including the provision of services according to Government as a Platform [12]. The very broad and varying use of the term platform within the UN report (e.g., participation platforms, e-procurement platforms, or collaboration platforms) shows that a precise definition of the term is necessary to examine the specifics of digital platforms. We thrive to provide a first notion on the level of platform realization in public service provision. Using example cases, we aim to illustrate:

RQ2: Are constitutive elements of digital platforms recognizable in current digital government approaches?

This study contributes through a uniform understanding of the platform term in the public context. Despite constitutive elements, the proposed framework for public service platforms may guide the assessment of current concepts.

To develop related artifacts, the Design Science Research Methodology (DSRM) is adopted [13]. The paper is structured accordingly. First, a brief overview of recent research on digital platforms in the public sector is given in Sect. 2, which identifies the problem, in that different understandings prevail (problem-oriented). The design objective (Sect. 3) is to conceptualize the constituting elements of public service platforms through the transfer of private platform research to the public domain. More than a definition, constitutive elements are operationalized in the public context. Section 4 serves as the demonstration in which federal platform approaches are evaluated against the conceptualized elements. Section 5 discusses the results and section six concludes the paper.

2 Related Literature

Prior research did consider various aspects of digital platforms. Different research perspectives on digital platforms were highlighted by [14]. While the engineering perspective focuses on platforms as technical architectures, the economics perspective focuses on platforms as markets. Regarding the platform scope, [15] differentiate company-specific (internal) from industry-wide (external) platforms. Prior research analyzed different platform domains. In the context of software-based platforms, platforms for mobile devices, browsers, and enterprise software were considered [16, 17].

We consider the group of software platforms to be most similar to platforms for public service provision. Software platforms, such as platforms for public service provision, provide services for customers whereby multiple entities are involved in the provisioning process. Both platform types have similar characteristics (e.g., coherent infrastructure) and targets (e.g., single point of service access). The domain of software platforms is well-developed in research. This does not apply to public platforms. As such, the domain of software platforms is suitable to guide the conceptualization of public service platforms.

For problem identification as a first phase of the DSRM approach, we reviewed the literature on public sector and platforms. Literature was identified through database queries on Google Scholar, Web of Science, and JStor. To gather recent findings on public service platforms we focused on sources from 2010 on. For this study, we focused on influential and important contributions. Completeness was not aimed for. For highly influential contributions for- and backward search were used to identify underlying principles and subsequent adoptions of the concepts.

2.1 Digital Platforms in Public Sector Service Provision

Given the different stakeholders being involved in the context of platforms and the surrounding ecosystem, governments may occur in different roles in the platform context [18]. These involve: as a user, as a platform provider, as a service provider, and as a regulator. Governments may act as a user if they purchase services over a platform [18].

Governments may act as service providers when they provide services for specific life events [19]. As regulators, states issue legal frameworks for platforms that are not bound to the public environment [20]. For instance, platforms related to the sharing economy received attention regarding regulatory aspects [21]. While previous studies predominately focus on the government as a platform provider, [18] discuss the advantages and disadvantages of governments in the different roles. This contribution focuses on the role of the government as a platform provider.

The concept of digital platforms gains importance in the public sector [11, 22]. The Government as a platform (GaaP) concept initially proposed by [11] incorporates the idea to integrate external parties in governmental processes. Seven guidelines are proposed to successfully support the GaaP approach using recent technology and related lessons. A definition is not provided.

While earlier studies focused on the conceptual development of platforms in the public context [11], more recent studies focus on concrete implementations. Thereby, platform concepts in different countries have been examined. Among these are the United Kingdom (UK) platform, the Estonian platform [23], the Italian platform [10], and the Finish platform [24, 25]. Furthermore, approaches in less developed countries are studied [26]. While different platforms (at least in terms of individual services) may exist within one state, the notion of the central platform (GaaP) focuses the platform with the broadest, integrated service portfolio available.

Different aspects of public platforms have been discussed. With a focus on the value dimension, [19] analyzed business models in four services domains of the Swedish platform. Thereby, the emerging view describes the incorporation of different stakeholders and new opportunities concerning the financing aspects for service provision. In the traditional view, service provision is financed by public agencies. The adoption of platforms is illustrated in different examples. Using the example of the American platform challenge.gov [27] identifies the drives and barriers of such solutions. Open innovation approaches aim to access the knowledge from outsiders, e.g., citizens, for the platform's advantage [28, 29].

Platform Understandings
Previous research has shown that there are different understandings of the platform concept in the public sector context (see Table 1) [10]. The most common are the provision of *single services* and the provision of a *holistic platform (government as a platform)* integrating different services – which we use for this article.

The holistic concept of the government as a platform focuses on the use of digital technologies to integrate different services. Thereby, the platform orchestrates the public service portfolio, whereby the government acts as a platform provider with the different authorities to provide different services. Basic services and the infrastructural environment are usually provided from a central instance (e.g., the government) whereby the individual services are provided by different actors (e.g., public authorities or NGOs) [11]. The platform provides a central access point for public services using digital technologies. Whereas [11] discusses success factors, a definition is not provided. However, [30] proposes a definition with a technical focus that fits the nature of software platforms: *Reorganizing the work of government around a network of shared APIs and components, open-standards and canonical datasets, so that civil servants, businesses and others can deliver radically better services to the public, more safely, efficiently and accountably.*

Table 1. Existing platform understandings in the public domain (own presentation)

Platform concept	Individual service platforms	Government as a platform
External innovation	Not necessary	Integrative aspect
Service orchestration	If any, within limited domain scope	Integration of service portfolio from different contexts
Platform rationale	Different players	Different services and their integration

Especially, two aspects are useful to differentiate between the understandings. First, the *involvement of outsiders*. While in the concept of service provision, the platform may serve as technological infrastructure to coordinate processes, it is not required to involve external parties in the value provision. In contrast, the government as a platform concept requires the involvement of different authorities to provide various services. Second, the aspect of *orchestration* is useful to distinguish the approaches [31]. The government as a platform approach integrates the public services provided by the different authorities according to their responsibilities. The orchestration within a single technological infrastructure allows to achieve the benefits related to the platform concept and to fulfill underlying targets of e-government solutions as for instance a one-stop shop [8, 10]. Thereby, the value of the integrated solution is assumed to be more than the sum of the individual service values [31]. The single service approach does not fulfil the integrative aspect of the public service portfolio.

To guide future research, a common understanding of platforms in the public context is of great importance. [32] focus on the separation of platform architecture in core components and complementary peripherals to support variety and an overall evolvable system. The government as a platform approach provides the overall environment with core features and infrastructure whereby the different authorities provide complementary services. However, research lacks an understanding of which elements constitute a platform.

2.2 Constitutive Platform Aspects

To guide further conceptualization, the question of which aspects are constitutive for a public service platform arises. We thrive to combine important aspects of previous platform research and adapt them to the public context. Following [4], we consider the three aspects of the platform ecosystem, the technical platform architecture, and the platform governance as constitutive elements. The ecosystem encompasses the parties involved to provide services on the platform. The technical architecture specifies fundamental platform components. The governance covers mechanisms to govern related dynamics.

First, the group of parties involved in providing the platform is seen as crucial. To identify related parties, the concept of platform *ecosystems* is established. We follow the notion of a platform ecosystem as: "The network of innovation to produce complements that make a platform more valuable" [33]. The category of external platforms involves contributors from outside the provisioning entity (platform owner) [15].

Second, the platform architecture itself needs to fulfill the requirements. Following [4] a (software) platform is recognized as "The extensible codebase of a software-based system that provides core functionality shared by the modules that interoperate with it and the interfaces through which they interoperate". The platform itself provides core functionality in terms of centralized features, that can be accessed by contributed modules. Related interfaces allow to use these features and interact with the platform (core). The extensibility through innovative contributions from the ecosystem is central.

Third, the dynamics that emerge from the external innovation need to be governed to ensure the desired interest of the platform owner. Platform governance subsumes the rules and policies to govern the platform and ecosystem operation [34]. For instance, mechanisms to ensure the quality of complements in terms of requirements and review processes of submitted modules are common in platform environments [35]. Related mechanisms allow the platform owner to control value creation and capture activity.

3   A Public Service Platform Concept

Following [4], we suggest three constitutive aspects for a public service platform: (1) the platform ecosystem that integrates different stakeholders, (2) the platform architecture that provides the technical foundation, (3) the platform governance to coordinate related activities. For each of the elements, respective concepts are identified, and important findings are discussed.

3.1   Platform Ecosystem

Software platforms involve a surrounding ecosystem that is composed of the different players that are involved in the value creation process [15]. Thereby, value creation is not limited to the platform owner as the provisioning entity but is a product of the group of stakeholders involved. Figure 1 depicts value creation in ecosystems. Thereby, the customer gathers functionality from the focal firm platform directly (e.g., basic services) but also benefits from complementary products offered by third parties. The platform itself may involve external components that are aggregated by the owner [36].

In the platform context, different stakeholders with respective roles are to be distinguished that are part of the platform ecosystem [34, 36] (see Fig. 2). The platform owner is the entity that maintains and governs the platform. The group of contributors is the source of external innovation and external input [4, 37]. For public service provision in the public context, the group of contributors can be distinguished in public and non-public contributors. Non-public actors such as private companies may provide additional services to enhance the platform utility for users. Finally, the group of users refers to the group of all those who use services in the public context.

The integration of external innovation distinguishes the holistic platform concept from the concept of individual services. External innovation in the form of added services may be provided by public institutions other than the platform provider or NGOs as well as private companies [10, 11].

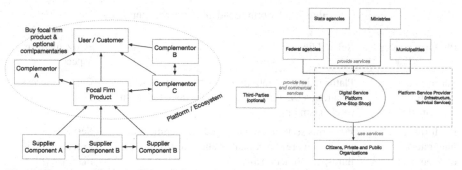

Fig. 1. Ecosystem-based value creation [36]   **Fig. 2.** Public platform concept

The aspect of orchestration and integration distinguishes the platform concept from the provision of individual services. In this regard, the aspects of integration mechanisms and integration environment were identified as requirements for public sector platforms. First, the platform serves as an integration mechanism. Platforms with their inherent interoperability allow for the integration of external functionality [38] or services in the public domain [39]. Second, the platform provides an integrated environment. In contrast to stand-alone features, platforms aim to integrate functionality. Integration in contrast to stand-alone functionality is important to realize synergies from the multiple features available [40]. Correspondingly, the target of a one-stop-shop in the public sector reflects the idea of integration [8].

Platforms typically provide a kind of service directory. Private platforms use marketplaces to categorize available functionality [41]. Marketplaces rely on a pre-defined set of categories to ease users' search process for the desired functionality. In a similar vein, public service offerings are typically structured according to life events [8].

A constituting element of multi-sided platforms is the integration of external innovation. The value of a specific platform is to a large extent determined by the ability and success to integrate external innovation [37]. While a high degree of innovation is not equally relevant as for private sector platforms, public platforms focus on providing necessary services in a resource-efficient way. Public service platforms need to fulfill the three ecosystem aspects. The platform needs to act as a central access point that provides integrated service functionality (integration mechanism, environment). The services provided should combine a portfolio to support a one-stop shop government approach (external innovation resp. contribution). Finally, a less decisive aspect is a service directory that allows navigating the available services (service directory) (Table 2).

3.2 Platform Architecture

Concerning the technical architecture of the platform, two aspects are of importance. First, the platform itself needs to provide functionality in terms of basic features provided by the core [4, 32]. Second, to serve as an environment for external innovation and contribution, platforms provide boundary resources for external parties to provide complements and interfaces to access the core features [35].

Table 2. Platform foundation & ecosystem

Platform concept	Related findings	eGov. platform aspect
Platform as integration mechanism	Platform interoperability forms basis for functional integration [4, 42]; Platforms serve as integration mechanism [40]	Central Access Point [1, 39]
Platforms as integrated environment	Platforms serve as an integrated environment of platform (core) functionality and contributed third-party functionality [43]	Services are executed on the platform [8]
Platform marketplace as service directory	Platform marketplace list available third-party functionality in pre-defined categorizations to allow for the identification of related services [41]	Service overview [8]
External innovation and contribution	Integration of external innovation to provide value on the platform [37] More functionality than a single entity could achieve alone [6]	Involvement of public third parties [44]

Software platforms provide basic functionality with their core features [45] (see Table 3). These allow for an more efficient contribution development than individual realization [4]. For instance, platforms provide account management functionality through a centrally managed ID. Many public services require citizens to identify themselves.

Platform owners provide boundary resources to allow for complements. To allow for the contribution and effective development, platform owners provide software development kits [35]. Developers are keen on well-documented features to deploy related functionality and services effectively [46]. Moreover, the accessibility of learning material is important for new contributors to join the platform [16].

3.3 Platform Governance

Digital platforms show a dynamic development. The interest of the platform owner is to govern related dynamics to achieve its targets [35]. Thereby platform control refers to the formal and informal mechanisms to encourage desirable behaviors by module developers [4]. Related rules and mechanisms are defined by the platform owner (see Table 4). Given the regulated environment in that public platforms work, we see it as essential, that platforms provide mechanisms for assuring service quality. The extent of rules and policies public platforms employ may vary according to their targets.

To ensure that applications and services are in accordance with the rules set by the platform owner, reviews are conducted before their release [16]. Reviews involve multiple aspects such as technical compatibility as well as content screening [49]. Security and privacy are of utmost importance on digital platforms [50]. Platform owners are highly interested to ensure a similar service quality throughout their platform. Typically, platform owners release detailed guidelines and requirements for contributions to ensure a uniform level of quality [49]. For the public context, related service quality in itself might be a target to provide such a platform environment [51].

Table 3. Platform architecture

Platform concept	Related findings	eGov. platform aspect
Core features		
Account management	The platform provides central services for authentication of users. The platform provides the account management component [41]	Citizen ID [42, 47]
Messaging	The platform provides a central messaging infrastructure. This allows services to provide messages, documents in the form of a messaging box	Electronic Post Box [48]
Payment	The platform provides a central payment unit. Services can use the component to handle payments related to service requests (e.g. fee payment) [41]	Payment service [10, 23]
Data storage	Data is a major resource on digital platforms. Data can be provided by the owner as well as complementors. [14]	Document storage, archive [48]
Boundary resources		
Software development kit	Provide resources to develop applications [35]. SDKs develop over time [17]	Form templates [42]
Documentation	Documentation is important for third parties satisfaction and basis for scalability [46]	Resource documentation [42]
Learning material	Learnability of technical standards and technical documentation [16]	Documentation, online resources [42]

Table 4. Platform governance (mechanisms for quality assurance)

Platform concept	Related findings	eGov. platform aspect
Application/Service review	Usually, applications are reviewed prior to their release in the marketplace [16, 41] Platforms differ in their restrictiveness of review process and requirements [49]	Quality Dimensions in eGovernment Services [42, 52]
Security and privacy	Platforms use different methods to ensure security and privacy of customer data [50]. Moreover, users are provided with a control centre to decide which information (such as GPS or photo access) may be accessed by applications [50]	Legal Security and Privacy Regulations, Data Sovereignty [53]
Service quality	Platform guidelines put platform constraints on developers' contributions. Guidelines ensure a uniform service quality throughout the platform and external contributions [39, 49]. Templates as part of SDKs include elements for frontend design to ensure uniformity from a visual perspective	Service Quality in Public Services [52]

4   Public Platforms in Federal States

This section examines the One-Stop-Shops of federal states of the European Union and additionally of the United Kingdom. The question is to what extent they exhibit the characteristics elaborated above and thus correspond to the concept of a platform. While the study gives individual examples, it does not provide a comprehensive platform analysis. The aim is to identify different platform approaches.

First, the federal states of the EU were identified, with the UK still taken into account. Based on this categorization, we consider the national e-government platforms of Austria, Belgium, Germany, Spain, and the UK (https://op.europa.eu/s/oSHU). For identification of the e-government platforms, the e-government factsheets of the European Union were used (https://joinup.ec.europa.eu/collection/nifo-national-interoperability-framework-observatory/digital-government-factsheets-2019). Information on the ecosystem and the architecture was easy to identify in this way. Gaps remained with regard to governance. Therefore, in the third step, we consulted the EU eGovernment Factsheets again and included recent scientific literature. However, some aspects still remained vague. As we do not have access to user accounts, we could not check the exact implementation of concrete services. Thus, results are based on available information and should be regarded as preliminary accordingly. The German platform (named portal network) has not yet been fully implemented and is thus preliminary as well. However, it can be considered as an initiative to realize a government-as-a-platform approach. A table with the detailed results per country can be found in the appendix.

Ecosystem/Foundation. The general goal is to create a central access point despite the different responsibilities in the federal (multi-level) system. In the different platforms, not all services are made available directly in the central instance, sometimes only a small part. Austria and the UK have a clear leading role, as comparatively many services can be carried out directly on the platform. Otherwise, the platforms offer life situation- or topic-oriented directories with information on the available services and links to the corresponding authorities. Users are forwarded to specialized services as required. In terms of third-party involvement, external partners are relevant as development contributors for all platforms. Especially in the UK, great importance is attached to open standards and clear specifications, which means that various development partners can participate but quality requirements are ensured [54]. Furthermore, companies can act as advertising partners with personalized offers (e.g. in Austria).

Architecture. All platforms provide core features, including for example user accounts (with an officially recognized eID), search, messages, folders, and e-payment. Regarding boundary resources, the situation is different. Some platforms offer extensive and detailed resources. The UK, for example, uses GitHub to facilitate development processes and reuse. In some cases, there are complementary initiatives for joint development efforts that are not exclusively related to the One-Stop-Shops (e.g. G-Cloud in Belgium; central development of modules for online applications in Austria; eGovernment platform about the current situation and a directory of solutions in Spain). In Germany, no centrally provided resources for the development of specific services are provided. Only rough process models, for example for user-centered design methods, are available.

Governance. Overall, the cooperation of the federal levels with their administrations within the platforms is characterized by diversity and voluntariness as well as multiple agreements between the players. Control is distributed among the participating units, which are equal partners and cooperate in committees. Applications or standards, such as style guides or quality criteria to be applied, are jointly reviewed (Austria explicitly states this in the platform). However, there are deviating cases where the platform provider (central government) plays a stronger role (e.g. UK). Components or patterns are evaluated by a central unit in terms of usefulness and uniqueness (to ensure reuse). Yet there are gaps in the data on this point. It is unclear, for example, how decisions are made in the joint bodies.

5 Discussion

Regarding digital platforms in the public sector, this paper provides various theoretical contributions. *First*, this paper highlights different prevailing understandings of the platform concept in previous literature. In this regard, individual service platforms are to be differentiated from the holistic government as a platform approach. We argue that only the holistic approach fulfills the requirements and matches the idea of platforms (GaaP). Especially the aspect of orchestration and involvement of contributors are key aspects for platforms. In this regard, this study contributes to a coherent understanding of the platform concept in the public sector.

Second, even though the idea of public service platforms has prevailed for a while [11], research yet misses a concrete understanding of what constitutes a public service platform. More recently, first approaches to define public service platforms were made [10]. Faced with different understandings and a missing operationalization of public service platforms, this study contributes by conceptualizing the constituting elements of a public service platform. Through the operationalization of platform requirements, research question 1 is addressed. Thereby, three elements are essential: platform ecosystem, platform architecture, and platform governance and need to go together for an efficient public service provision [4] and to fulfill related eGovernment targets [10]. The results serve as a basis for future research to be based on a uniform understanding and for the assessment of existing solutions.

This study provides *practical implications* and contributes to the assessment of the state of the art. The results allow assessing platform concepts as well as existing implementations. Through the operationalization, the results enable an assessment of whether a particular solution meets the requirements of a public service platform. Concerning research question 2, this study contributes through the analysis of public service platforms of federal states.

The results indicate that different eGovernment targets, such as one-stop shop, can be realized through a platform approach. In a similar vein, previous studies identified related potentials [10, 11]. For federal states in the EU, related platform approaches were identified. Whereas the approaches are similar in their fundamental idea, differences were found for platform architecture and governance approaches. Future efforts might be devoted to further develop the concept. Thereby, design choices that contribute to the success of government as a platform approaches are of great interest. In this regard, former research highlights the importance of a coherent design of architecture, governance, and the ecosystem [4]. While some aspects suggestions were made [11], their adaptation to government setup is missing. Except for individual approaches, platform initiatives exist on the European level such as CEF Building Blocks [55].

Limitations of this study include the use of a few example cases in Europe and the limited data collection. To further detail the results, quantitative assessments should be conducted (e.g. number of services directly on the platform vs. linked services) and governance structures should be surveyed through interviews. The literature studied for the conceptualization is not exhaustive but focused on important contributions.

6 Conclusion

A central e-government objective is to make public services and contacts with administrations as convenient as possible for citizens and businesses. Thereby, the idea of a one-stop government allows handling all requests at a single point. For federal states, joint decisions and development efforts are required to realize one-stop government. Digital platforms by their design allow the coordination of multiple entities to achieve a common goal. Through the proposed notion of public service platforms, known advantages of the platform economy shall be realized for the public sector. We identify the aspects of the platform ecosystem, platform architecture, and platform governance as essential for a holistic platform concept. Platform approaches were recognized for federal EU states and the UK (Austria, Belgium, Germany, and Spain). Whereas all approaches follow the platform idea, differences were found between their architectures and governance approaches. The examples show that there is still a need for research on the governance of ecosystems. How open should they be to externals? How can quality criteria be enforced effectively and efficiently? What effects do different governance models have on e-government progress? Further analyses, especially based on interviews and quantitative data, can provide important insights here.

Federal States; Platform/URL; Online Availability* (EU eGov Benchmark 2018/2019)	Ecosystem/Foundation (Central Access, Integration, Service Directory, Involvement, Third Parties)	Architecture (Core Features, Identification, Resources, Resource Reuse)	Governance (Governance Structure, Participation, Service Quality, Quality/Reviews)
Austria oesterreich.gv.at 97	Central access with linked websites and few direct services; Service directory for life events; Co-services for specific life events possible (e.g., NGO), advertising and secondary services (e.g., editorial office)	eID, mailbox, search, personalization (relevant services by region); Central development of modules for online applications (open source); Austrian Interoperability Framework for cross-border interoperability; Style guides	Federal government as drawing card [56]; Various participation options, partner from different governmental levels and areas ("active participation of all levels of Government by representatives')
Belgium belgium.be 88	Central access with linked websites and few direct services; Service directory for life events; G-Cloud uses services offered by private companies (beyond the platform); Third Parties not on service level, but according to secondary services (e.g., eID)	eID/single-sign-on (CSAM), mailbox (messages/postbox), search, account settings, assistance for users	All public authorities are equal partners with various participation options; Partly comparable activities (Platform Ecosystems) at regional level – fragmentation in the eGov field [57]; Application review (security, privacy, service quality, compatibility)

(*continued*)

(*continued*)

Federal States; Platform/URL; Online Availability* (EU eGov Benchmark 2018/2019)	Ecosystem/Foundation (Central Access, Integration, Service Directory, Involvement, Third Parties)	Architecture (Core Features, Identification, Resources, Resource Reuse)	Governance (Governance Structure, Participation, Service Quality, Quality/Reviews)
Germany portal network – *in progress* – verwaltung.bund.de 90	Central access as portal network (regional, local and federal network of different portals); All online services can be accessed via any portal or on a separate (linked) website; Service directory for life events; Participation through development of portals and online services through public administrations and consultancies	Minimum requirements for the portals involved: eID, mailbox, search, payment; Interoperable user accounts; Assistance for the creation and integration of services hardly standardized, mainly individual cooperation; In several portals technical components are reused	All participants in the portal network are equal partners; Various options for the Länder to participate in the portal network; Integration of the regional portals is the responsibility of the Länder; Recommended standards in the federal portal (e.g. comprehensible language, accessibility), no corporate design
Spain aministracion.gob.es 96	Central access with most frequent electronic services and linked websites; Service directory for life events	eID, mailbox, search, citizen folder, online webchat; Separate eGovernment Portal as information point about the current eGov situation, directory of applications and solutions to encourage reuse	Ministry of Territorial Policy and Civil Service owns the General Access Point; Various options for participation

(*continued*)

(*continued*)

Federal States; Platform/URL; Online Availability* (EU eGov Benchmark 2018/2019)	Ecosystem/Foundation (Central Access, Integration, Service Directory, Involvement, Third Parties)	Architecture (Core Features, Identification, Resources, Resource Reuse)	Governance (Governance Structure, Participation, Service Quality, Quality/Reviews)
United Kingdom gov.uk 93	Central access with many direct services; Service directory for life events; Contribution by proposing a new component or pattern or developing a component or pattern; Open standards and interoperability to create competition and drive innovation [54]: companies, charities and so on can use the same infrastructure to set up additional services	eID, search, payment; GOV.UK styles, components and patterns	Multiple governance arrangements between central and other administrations; Community-oriented (research, design and development form across government); Reviews by the Design System working group: components and patterns have to be useful and unique

* Online availability: the extent to which selected services are provided online, and via a portal (0 for not online, 100 for online via portal and for automated) – https://digital-strategy.ec.europa.eu/en/library/egovernment-benchmark-2020-egovernment-works-people.

References

1. Wimmer, M.A.: Integrated service modelling for online one-stop government. Electr. Markets **12**, 149–156 (2002)
2. Strejcek, G., Theil, M.: Technology push, legislation pull? E-government in the European Union. Decis. Support Syst. **34**, 305–313 (2003)
3. Jaeger, P.T.: Constitutional principles and e-government: an opinion about possible effects of federalism and the separation of powers on e-government policies. Gov. Inf. Q. **19**, 357–368 (2002)
4. Tiwana, A., Konsynski, B., Bush, A.A.: Platform evolution: coevolution of platform architecture, governance, and environmental dynamics. Inf. Syst. Res. **21**, 675–687 (2010)
5. Ye, H.J., Kankanhalli, A.: User service innovation on mobile phone platforms: investigating impacts of lead userness, toolkit support, and design autonomy. MIS Q. **42**, 165–188 (2018)
6. Eisenmann, T.R., Parker, G., Van Alstyne, M.: Platform envelopment. Strat. Manage. J. **32**, 1270–1285 (2011)
7. Brunswicker, S., Schecter, A.: Coherence or flexibility? The paradox of change for developers' digital innovation trajectory on open platforms. Res. Policy **48** (2019)

8. Scholta, H., Mertens, W., Kowalkiewicz, M., Becker, J.: From one-stop shop to no-stop shop: an e-government stage model. Govern. Inf. Q. **36**, 11–26 (2019)
9. Xue, L., Song, P., Rai, A., Zhang, C., Zhao, X.: Implications of application programming interfaces for third-party new app development and copycatting. Prod. Oper. Manage. **28**, 1887–1902 (2019)
10. Cordella, A., Paletti, A.: Government as a platform, orchestration, and public value creation: the Italian case. Govern. Inf. Q. **36**, 101409 (2019)
11. O'Reilly, T.: Government as a platform. Innov. Technol. Govern. Global. **6**, 13–40 (2011)
12. United Nations: United Nations E-Government Survey (2020)
13. Peffers, K., Tuunanen, T., Rothenberger, M.A., Chatterjee, S.: A design science research methodology for information systems research. J. Manage. Inf. Syst. **24**, 45–77 (2007)
14. Gawer, A.: Bridging differing perspectives on technological platforms: toward an integrative framework. Res. Policy **43**, 1239–1249 (2014)
15. Gawer, A., Cusumano, M.A.: Industry platforms and ecosystem innovation. J. Prod. Innovation Manage. **31**, 417–433 (2014)
16. Benlian, A., Hilkert, D., Hess, T.: How open is this platform? The meaning and measurement of platform openness from the complementors' perspective. J. Inf. Technol. **30**, 209–228 (2015)
17. Eaton, B., Elaluf-Calderwood, S., Sorensen, C.: Distributed tuning of boundary resources: the case of Apple's iOS service system. MIS Q. **39**, 217–243 (2015)
18. Hofmann, S., Saebo, O., Braccini, A.M., Za, S.: The public sector's roles in the sharing economy and the implications for public values. Govern. Inf. Q. **36**, 101399 (2019)
19. Ranerup, A., Henriksen, H.Z., Hedman, J.: An analysis of business models in Public Service Platforms. Govern. Inf. Q. **33**, 6–14 (2016)
20. Lenaerts, K., Beblavý, M., Kilhoffer, Z.: Government Responses to the Platform Economy: Where do we stand? Policy Insights (2017)
21. Ganapati, S., Reddick, C.G.: Prospects and challenges of sharing economy for the public sector. Govern. Inf. Q. **35**, 77–87 (2018)
22. Janssen, M., Estevez, E.: Lean government and platform-based governance-Doing more with less. Govern. Inf. Q. **30**, S1–S8 (2013)
23. Margetts, H., Naumann, A.: Government as a platform: What can Estonia show the world. Research paper, University of Oxford (2017)
24. Yli-Huumo, J., Päivärinta, T., Rinne, J., Smolander, K.: Suomi.fi – Towards Government 3.0 with a National Service Platform. In: Parycek, P., Glassey, O., Janssen, M., Scholl, H.J., Tambouris, E., Kalampokis, E., Virkar, S. (eds.) EGOV 2018. LNCS, vol. 11020, pp. 3–14. Springer, Cham (2018). https://doi.org/10.1007/978-3-319-98690-6_1
25. Hautamäki, A., Oksanen, K.: Digital platforms for restructuring the public sector. In: Smedlund, A., Lindblom, A., Mitronen, L. (eds.) Collaborative Value Co-creation in the Platform Economy. TSS, vol. 11, pp. 91–108. Springer, Singapore (2018). https://doi.org/10.1007/978-981-10-8956-5_5
26. Senyo, P.K., Effah, J., Osabutey, E.L.C.: Digital platformisation as public sector transformation strategy: a case of Ghana's paperless port. Technol. Forecast. Soc. Change **162**, 120387 (2021)
27. Mergel, I.: Open innovation in the public sector: drivers and barriers for the adoption of Challenge.gov. Public Manage. Rev. **20**, 726–745 (2018)
28. Kankanhalli, A., Zuiderwijk, A., Tayi, G.K.: Open innovation in the public sector: a research agenda. Govern. Inf. Q. **34**, 84–89 (2017)
29. Androutsopoulou, A., Karacapilidis, N., Loukis, E., Charalabidis, Y.: Towards an integrated and inclusive platform for open innovation in the public sector. In: Katsikas, S.K., Zorkadis, V. (eds.) e-Democracy 2017. CCIS, vol. 792, pp. 228–243. Springer, Cham (2017). https://doi.org/10.1007/978-3-319-71117-1_16

30. https://medium.com/digitalhks/a-working-definition-of-government-as-a-platform-1fa6ff 2f8e8d
31. Panagiotopoulos, P., Klievink, B., Cordella, A.: Public value creation in digital government. Govern. Inf. Q. **36** (2019)
32. Baldwin, C.Y., Woodard, C.J.: The architecture of platforms: a unified view. In: Platforms, Markets and Innovation, pp. 19–44. Edward Elgar Publishing Ltd. (2009)
33. Gawer, A., Cusumano, M.A.: Platform Leadership: How Intel, Microsoft, and Cisco Drive Industry Innovation. Harvard Business School Press, Boston (2002)
34. Song, P., Xue, L., Rai, A., Zhang, C.: The ecosystem of software platform: a study of asymmetric cross-side network effects and platform governance. MIS Q. **42**, 121–142 (2018)
35. Ghazawneh, A., Henfridsson, O.: Balancing platform control and external contribution in third-party development: the boundary resources model. Inf. Syst. J. **23**, 173–192 (2013)
36. Jacobides, M.G., Cennamo, C., Gawer, A.: Towards a theory of ecosystems. Strat. Manage. J. **39**, 2255–2276 (2018)
37. Helfat, C.E., Raubitschek, R.S.: Dynamic and integrative capabilities for profiting from innovation in digital platform-based ecosystems. Res. Policy **47**, 1391–1399 (2018)
38. Pozzebon, M., Cunha, M.A., Coelho, T.R.: Making sense to decreasing citizen eParticipation through a social representation lens. Inf. Organ. **26**, 84–99 (2016)
39. Meacham, S., Rath, P., Moharana, P., Phalp, K.T., Park, M.S.: One-stop shop e-government solution for South-Korean government multi-ministry virtual employment-welfare plus center system. In: Thirteennth International Conference on Digitial Society and eGovernments, Athens, Greece (2019)
40. Bender, B.: The impact of integration on application success and customer satisfaction in mobile device platforms. Bus. Inf. Syst. Eng. **62**(6), 515–533 (2020). https://doi.org/10.1007/s12599-020-00629-0
41. Ghazawneh, A., Henfridsson, O.: A paradigmatic analysis of digital application marketplaces. J. Inf. Technol. **30**, 198–208 (2015)
42. Lucia Kim, S., Teo, T.S.: Lessons for software development ecosystems: South Korea's e-government open source initiative. MIS Q. Exec. **12** (2013)
43. Tiwana, A.: Evolutionary competition in platform ecosystems. Inf. Syst. Res. **26**, 266–281 (2015)
44. Haraldsen, M., Stray, T.D., Päivärinta, T., Sein, M.K.: Developing e-government portals: from life-events through genres to requirements. In: Proceedings of the 11th Norwegian Conference on Information Systems (2004)
45. Bender, B., Gronau, N.: Coring on digital platforms – fundamentals and examples from the mobile device sector. In: International Conference on Information Systems (ICIS), Seoul, South Korea (2017)
46. Ryu, M.H., Kim, J., Kim, S.: Factors affecting application developers' loyalty to mobile platforms. Comput. Hum. Behav. **40**, 78–85 (2014)
47. Bazarhanova, A., Yli-Huumo, J., Smolander, K.: Love and hate relationships in a platform ecosystem: a case of Finnish electronic identity management. In: Proceedings of the 51st Hawaii International Conference on System Sciences (2018)
48. Sandoval-Almazan, R., Gil-Garcia, J.R.: Are government internet portals evolving towards more interaction, participation, and collaboration? Revisiting the rhetoric of e-government among municipalities. Gov. Inf. Q. **29**, S72–S81 (2012)
49. Schreieck, M., Hein, A., Wiesche, M., Krcmar, H.: The challenge of governing digital platform ecosystems. In: Linnhoff-Popien, C., Schneider, R., Zaddach, M. (eds.) Digital Marketplaces Unleashed, pp. 527–538. Springer, Heidelberg (2018). https://doi.org/10.1007/978-3-662-49275-8

50. Stach, C., Mitschang, B.: Privacy management for mobile platforms--a review of concepts and approaches. In: 2013 IEEE 14th International Conference on Mobile Data Management, vol. 1, pp. 305–313. IEEE (2013)

51. Kuk, G., Janssen, M.: Assembling infrastructures and business models for service design and innovation. Inf. Syst. J. **23**, 445–469 (2013)

52. Papadomichelaki, X., Magoutas, B., Halaris, C., Apostolou, D., Mentzas, G.: A review of quality dimensions in e-government services. In: Wimmer, M.A., Scholl, H.J., Grönlund, Å., Andersen, K.V. (eds.) EGOV 2006. LNCS, vol. 4084, pp. 128–138. Springer, Heidelberg (2006). https://doi.org/10.1007/11823100_12

53. Irion, K.: Government cloud computing and national data sovereignty. Policy Internet **4**, 40–71 (2012)

54. Brown, A., Fishenden, J., Thompson, M., Venters, W.: Appraising the impact and role of platform models and Government as a Platform (GaaP) in UK Government public service reform: towards a Platform Assessment Framework (PAF). Gov. Inf. Q. **34**, 167–182 (2017)

55. https://ec.europa.eu/cefdigital/wiki/display/CEFDIGITAL/CEF+Digital+Home

56. Wimmer, M.A.: Einblick in aktuelle Entwicklungen des E-Governments in Österreich. E-Government und Netzpolitik im europäischen Vergleich 119 (2019)

57. Vandenberghe, H., Macken, M., Simonofski, A.: Towards a prioritization of e-government challenges: an exploratory study in Belgium. 2019 13th International Conference on Research Challenges in Information Science (RCIS), pp. 1–12. IEEE (2019)

A Solution to Support Integrity in the Lawful Interception Ecosystem

Francesco Buccafurri[1]([✉]), Angelo Consoli[2], Cecilia Labrini[1],
and Alice Mariotti Nesurini[2]

[1] University of Reggio Calabria, via dell'Università 25,
Reggio Calabria, Italy
{bucca,cecilia.labrini}@unirc.it
[2] University of Applied Sciences and Arts of Southern Switzerland (SUPSI),
Lugano, Switzerland
{angelo.consoli,alice.mariottinesurini}@supsi.ch

Abstract. In this paper, we present an innovative solution to support integrity in a lawful interception ecosystem. The problem arises from the fact that whatever the interception system is organized, external (potentially untrusted) parties can be involved in the process. Therefore, the need to guarantee completeness, correctness, and freshness of the intercepted contents should be given. Moreover, contents often have to be transferred from law enforcement agencies to Courts or delivered to the defence, also partially. In this work, we design a complex architecture able to support effectively the above needs.

Keywords: Lawful interception · Data integrity · Message authentication code

1 Introduction

The lawful interception ecosystem, not only in the European Union, is characterized by a complex landscape with open issues from both legal and technical points of view [8]. One of the aspects that introduces complexity in interception systems is the fact that intercepted contents, also partially, often have to be transferred from law enforcement agencies to the Court or delivered to the defence. Moreover, in the whole process, even third potentially untrusted parties might be involved. Indeed, it can happen that the high technical expertise and specialization required to perform the interception, enforce the collaboration of external private parties, which materially operate the interception, by also providing tools and IT dedicated infrastructures. This is true both in the case of environmental interception and trojan-based interception. Trojan-based interception [1, 19] is a practice, adopted by some European legal systems (e.g., Italy and Germany), based on the injection of a malware into the (mobile) device of the target, which can capture different data streams, including those extracted from files or deriving from the microphone of the device that the spyware is able

© Springer Nature Switzerland AG 2021
A. Kö et al. (Eds.): EGOVIS 2021, LNCS 12926, pp. 21–33, 2021.
https://doi.org/10.1007/978-3-030-86611-2_2

to turn on. In this field, there is a controversial and difficult equilibrium between conflicting rights [21], but, whatever is the legal system and the established procedures, to give strong cybersecurity guarantees to interception activities, meets any possible ethical and legal perspective. This paper is inspired by this principle. It does not refer to a particular interception ecosystem. It just proposes an innovative methodology applied to both environmental and trojan-based interception. The aim is to provide a support to those activities that require transfers of intercepted contents or extraction of their portions. The proposed approach is inspired by the classical problem of *query integrity*, aimed to guarantee that outsourced data are returned to the data owner (or to another client) completely, correctly, and freshly (i.e., the last version of data is returned). However, we have some specificity to consider. First, in the general case, the client performing queries is a party different from the data owner, so that the adopted techniques should guarantee that it is publicly verifiable that the party in which data are outsourced and execute queries behaves well. In contrast, in the considered use case, the integrity of intercepted contents is threatened by the fact that the data owner (i.e., the public parties involved in the investigation and judicial proceedings) could not have continuous and complete control on data due to the intervention of third parties. Therefore, we do not have the need of public verifiability. Second, to design a solution, we have to take into account how new information is inserted in the database being protected. The dynamics is not standard, because strongly depends on the way the interception is performed (i.e., through a device, a trojan, etc.).

The structure of the paper is the following. In Sect. 2, we review the related literature. In Sect. 3, we provide the reader with some basic concepts needed to better understand the sequel of the paper. The core of the technical solution from the algorithmic point of view is presented in Sect. 4. In Sect. 5, we contextualize the proposed solution within our application setting, by depicting a general architectural solution involving all the parties participating in the interception process and by considering the two cases of environmental and trojan-based interception. The security analysis of our solution is provided in Sect. 6. Finally, in Sect. 7, we draw our conclusions.

2   Related Work

This paper proposes an approach to supporting integrity in the lawful interception ecosystem, which draws inspiration from the approaches used in the classic query integrity problem in the context of data outsourcing. As in the introduction we have contextualized the paper in the application domain (i.e. the lawful interception ecosystem), we devote this section to illustrate the main results available in the literature in the field of query integrity. The query integrity problem [20] occurs when the outsourced data must be returned to the data owner by guaranteeing the properties of *completeness* (no data involved in the query is omitted), *freshness* (the most recent version of the data is returned), *correctness* (the returned data must not be altered). In the literature, the approaches proposed to address the query integrity problem fall into two categories, namely *probabilistic* and *deterministic*. The probabilistic solutions [2,4,23] guarantee a result with a certain degree of confidence. The deterministic solutions [11,18,24] solve the problem with no uncertainty. The party in which data are outsourced, in addition to returning the requested data, provides a number of additional information called *Verification Object* (VO) that allows the verification of the integrity of the data returned. Most deterministic techniques [5,12,16] are based on Merkle Hash tree (MHT) structures [14], which involve logarithmic costs for inserting/deleting data and linear costs for verification. Other approaches propose signature-based schemes [3,15,17] in which each tuple is signed and the cloud returns an aggregated signature. These solutions do not outperform MHT-based techniques, as they require much more computational power. MHTs are designed for static contexts. Therefore, they are not suitable to our application case, in which constant updates are required.

The solution proposed in this paper is inspired by some previous works [6,7] which use the concept of *message authentication code* (MAC). The solution [7] guarantees integrity on highly dynamic outsourced map data by proposing a lightweight message-authentication-code-based approach. This approach satisfies the required requirements better than the solutions found in the literature, according to an analytical cost assessment. In this paper, we specialize the approach to the context of the lawful interception ecosystem, by proposing a concrete solution working for both environmental and trojan-based interceptions.

3   Background

Our paper applies the perspective of query integrity used in the context of data outsourcing to the field of lawful interception. Therefore, it is useful to give some background knowledge about this topic.

In the classical problem of *query integrity*, we consider three actors: the *data owner*, which manages data, the *provider*, which stores data and executes operations on behalf of the owner, and the *client*, which requires the provider to perform operations on data. We have to guarantee the following three properties:

1. *Completeness*: All data involved in the queries have to be returned.
2. *Correctness*: The data returned by the provider have not to be corrupted.
3. *Freshness*: The newest version of data has to be returned.

We denote by $H(x)$, the application of a secure cryptography hash function (e.g., SHA256) on a message x. $HMAC(k, M)$ represents the application of the HMAC function [10] (with any underlying secure cryptographic hash function) with secret key k on a message M.

The state-of-the-art approach for query integrity is based on the concept of *Merkle Hash Tree* (MHT) [14]. It is defined as a tree in which every node (except for the leaves) is labelled with the hashes of its children nodes (or values, in case of leaves). An example of MHT is reported in Fig. 1. $H_{0,0}$ and $H_{0,1}$ are the

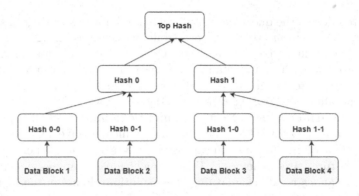

Fig. 1. An example of Merkle Hash Tree.

hash values of the first and the second data blocks D_0 and D_1, respectively. Observe that H_0 can be computed by $H(H_{0,0}||H_{0,1})$, where $||$ represents the concatenation operator. To prove that a given leaf belongs to a MHT requires bottom-up tree traversal until the root, with a logarithm cost on the number of the nodes of the tree. For instance, to authenticate the first data block a user has to be provided with the hash value of the second data block ($H_{0,1}$) together with H_1. Since the client holds the root of the MHT digitally signed by the data owner, she checks if the root is equal to $H(H(H(D_0)||H_{0,1})||H_1)$.

Our solution takes inspiration from some previous papers [6,7] which use the concept of *message authentication code* (MAC). A MAC is a short piece of information, associated with a message, used to assess the integrity and authenticity of the message itself. *HMAC* [10] is a specific kind of MAC constructed from a cryptographic hash function. In particular, $HMAC(K, m) = H\left((K \oplus opad)||H((K \oplus ipad)||m)\right)$ where K is a secret key generated from a master key, m is the message to be authenticated, $||$ denotes the operation of concatenation, $\oplus$ represents the exclusive or (XOR) operation, and *opad* and *ipad* are two kinds of padding, namely outer and inner padding.

4   A Message-Authentication-Code-Based Technique

We represent the intercepted content as a sequence $\langle A_1, ..., A_n \rangle$ of *frames*. As all the contents are streams increasing in the time, the only update we have to consider is the *append* operation. We assume that frames are intercepted with a regular frequency so that time slots can be just indicated as an integer value. In other words, A_1 is intercepted at the time slot 1, A_2 at the slot 2, and so on. A temporal *marker scheme* is set, in such a way that, since the starting time of the interception, the time is divided into *buckets* of equal size. Let denote by $M_0, M_1, \ldots, M_z, \ldots$ be the markers. Let denote by t the number of frames that are included in a bucket. Therefore, between two consecutive markers M_i, M_{i+1}, the frames $A_{i \cdot t}, \ldots A_{i \cdot (t+1)-1}$ are included. We have a special marker, called *final*

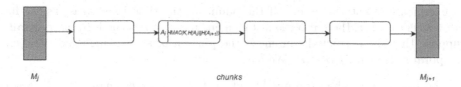

M_j chunks M_{j+1}

Fig. 2. A bucket of the verification object.

marker M_f, which is the highest marker of the list of markers. Therefore, the whole sequence of markers is: $M_0, M_1, \ldots, M_z \ldots M_f$.

The verification object VO for an intercepted content $\langle A_1, \ldots, A_n \rangle$ is composed of:

1. the last frame A_n, and
2. the chain of *chunks*, where a chunk is an element of the form:
   (a) $\langle A_i, \text{HMAC}(K, H(A_i) || H(A_{i+1})) \rangle$, if both A_i and A_{i+1} are internal the corresponding bucket;
   (b) $\langle \text{HMAC}(K, H(M_j) || H(A_{j.t+1})) \rangle$, if the chunk is the initial of a bucket;
   (c) $\langle \text{HMAC}(K, H(A_{j.(t+1)}) || H(M_{j+1})) \rangle$, if it is the final of a bucket;
   (d) $\langle \text{HMAC}(K, H(A_n) || H(M_f)) \rangle$, if it is the final chunk of the chain.

In Fig. 2, the graphical representation of a bucket of the verification object is reported.

We describe now how the update of an intercepted content occurs. Suppose an agent has intercepted the content $\langle A_1, \ldots, A_n \rangle$ at the time slot n. Suppose now that, at the next time slot $n+1$, the agent retrieves a new frame A_{n+1}. The agent has to update the chain of the Verification Object. As the next section will clarify, this operation cannot be performed always by the agent, because it depends on the fact that the agent can securely keep the secret key or not. Anyway, for the purpose of this section, this aspect can be neglected here.

The chain is updated by appending a new chunk and by updating the new last element. Specifically, the chain is changed as follows. The information needed to update the chain is:

1. the secret key K
2. the old last element A_n
3. the new last element A_{n+1}

Recall that the final element of the chain before updating is $\langle \text{HMAC}(K, H(A_n) || H(M_f)) \rangle$. This element is replaced by: $\langle A_n, \text{HMAC}(K, H(A_n) || H(A_{n+1})) \rangle$. Then, a new element is added. This is of the form: $\langle \text{HMAC}(K, H(A_{n+1}) || H(M_f)) \rangle$. Finally, the kept last element becomes A_{n+1}.

Now, we show how a portion of an intercepted content can be extracted in such a way that the integrity of the content can be verified. Intuitively, by considering that an extracted portion corresponds to a temporal interval, the portion of the verification object that is associated with the extraction portion is a sequence of entire buckets. If the bound of the time interval is inside the most recent bucket, then also the last element must be returned. In more detail, suppose that the extracted content is the portion of stream included between temporal slots i and j $(i < j)$. We have to consider two cases:

1. The first case is when the number of buckets is greater than $j/t + 1$. Then the portion of the chain that should be provided with the extracted content is the sequence of buckets bounded by the markers $M_{i/t}$ and $M_{j/t+1}$.
2. Otherwise (if the number of buckets is not greater than $j/t+1$), the extracted content will be returned together with the chain (until the last element) starting from the marker $M_{i/t}$.

Concerning the integrity verification of the extracted content, we can easily realize the following:

1. If we are in the first case above, that is the number of buckets is greater than $j/t + 1$, then the party that has to verify the content needs only the secret K. The verification proceeds by computing, starting from the lowest marker, the sequence of HMACS until the last marker. This is done by taking two consecutive elements A_d, A_{d+1} $(i \le d \le j)$, by computing the hashes $H(A_d)$ and $H(A_{d+1})$ and then by computing $\mathrm{HMAC}(K, H(A_d)\|H(A_{d+1}))$. This value should correspond with the value included in the corresponding chunk of the chain.
2. Otherwise (if the number of buckets is not greater than $j/t+1$), the verification is done in a similar way of the previous case. The only difference is that, in this case, also the last element of the chain must be considered by the party that performs the verification. Indeed, it is needed to check that the extracted content is fresh. It is easy to see that an old version of the chain (and thus an old version of the extracted content), in any case ends with a chunk of the form: $\langle \mathrm{HMAC}\,(K, H\,(A_x)\|H(M_f))\rangle$. Therefore, if $x/t = j/t$, then the last returned marker appears correct, but some final elements of the incomplete bucket could be missing. If the last element is checked, this integrity fault is detected.

5   The Proposed Solution

In this section, we describe our solution, by identifying the actors, the interception scenarios, and the procedures we design to guarantee the integrity of intercepted contents.

The actors of our solution are:

– **The Authority.** With this actor we indicate any party belonging to the State involved in the interception process. Therefore, we refer to both the law enforcement agency directed responsible for the execution of the interception actions and the persons in charge who are part of the Court who are holders of the investigation of the judicial proceeding.

- **The Provider.** The Provider is one or more companies (or, in general entities external to the Authority) which materially executes the interception activities. Independently of the fact that the activities are partially run within buildings of the Authorities, it is common that interception activities are supported by the presence of some specialized companies, which also provide the Authority with the needed tools (devices, software, communication equipment, skilled human resources, etc.).
- **The Client.** The Client is in the Authority itself. Indeed, the Authority, which is actually the *owner* of the intercepted contents, may act, with its different components, as the client. This means that, in various steps of the workflow, a component of the Authority may ask the provider or another component of the Authority to provide a given content or a portion of it.

We give here the notion of intercepted content in a more detailed way. Again, this formalization is quite general, and does not refer to a specific setting, but includes all the basic elements common to any case.

An intercepted content (IC) can be viewed as a triple $\langle I, L, C \rangle$, where:

- I represents the image of the whole digital object placed in some support including all the components needed to access the intercepted content (for example, if the content is stored on a CD, I is the ISO of the CD and could contain also the viewer necessary to open the content).
- L is a list a *events*. The events are elementary elements of the IC. With each event a number of metadata, including the type, are associated. The type is a complex element, indicating the format of the element and the kind of interception (for the purpose of this paper, we are restricting to either environmental interception or trojan-based interception).
- C is a list of integrity chains. We have a chain per event, according to the scheme described in Sect. 4.

The main primitives of the integrity methodology applied to the interception process we propose are the following:

1. *Agent integrity check*
2. *Secret key injection*
3. *Content provision*
4. *Integrity verification*

Agent Integrity Check. This is complex point, whose complete addressing is out of the scope of this paper. We mainly refer to trojan-based interception, in which the role of the agent, is played by the trojan. Indeed, in this case, it appears fundamental to guarantee that the installed software is exactly compliant with the requirements, and that the action it performs are not less and not more those that the holder of the investigation has required, in compliance with the law. This goal should be reached by requiring a preliminary step of certification given by a trusted third party, and by obtaining a signature from this TTP on a fingerprint of the code. On the other hand, the trojan should be designed

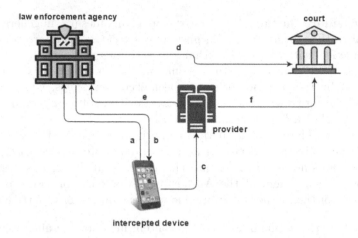

Fig. 3. The architecture of the solution: trojan-based interception.

in such a way that all the possible options that the holder of the investigation can require are configurable, and the software has a function that responds to a C&C of the Authority by exposing (on-demand) the current configuration. Also hardware devices used for environmental interception, must be certified and equipped with a secure smart-card to execute the functions needed for the correct execution of the process, as we will see in the sequel of the section.

Secret Key Injection. As we have seen in Sect. 4, the integrity check is based on the fact that each component of the Authority knows a secret key, that we call MAC secret key, which is not known to the Provider. As this key must be shared among different human subjects of the same entity (belonging to the different components of the Authority), the right way to manage this key is to provide each authorized user with a secure smart card embedding this key (besides the Hardware Security Module that we describe later). The most critical issue is how to inject this secret key in the intercepting agent. Indeed, it is necessary to produce the integrity chains at the source, otherwise we cannot exclude that the contents are compromised just after their acquisition. We have to distinguish the two cases: (1) environmental interception and (2) trojan-based interception.

– In the case of environmental interception, the device must be initialized by the Authority. It should be equipped with suitable interfaces to be connected with a standard computer, in such a way that, prior the installation of the device in the target environment, the Authority is able to inject the MAC secret key. As in this step a malicious behavior of the device could entirely compromise the process, it is very important that the hardware and firmware of the device are certified by the above TTP. The MAC key is injected in a protected memory not allowing reversing.

- In the case of trojan-based interception, the workflow is the following:
  1. The Authority stores its MAC secret key into an Hardware Security Module (HSM) in which the C&C is executed. A Hardware Security Module (HSM) [9,13,22] is a physical computing device that is used for data encryption and decryption performed by one or more cryptographic keys. HSMs are hardware designed to manage and protect digital keys from any type of logical and physical tampering or extraction of cryptographic material. Hence, HSMs have the ability to detect an attack on their surface and securely delete sensitive content stored in their memory. The trojan contacts the C&C at the end of every intercepted frame (see Sect. 4) and sends the corresponding chunk (recall that this is a small piece of information). The C&C computes the new element of the chain and sends back it to the trojan. This process can also happen in asynchronous way if the connectivity is not continuous.
  2. The intercepted content, together with the corresponding integrity chain is transmitted to the provider. Obviously, the destination of this flow is not the previous HSM, which, for its nature, cannot be used for this purpose. In contrast, as it can happen in the current system, the flow is directed towards a server managed by the Provider. Possible encryption of the flow with the public key of the Authority could be allowed. But this is not a conclusive solution (invalidating our MAC-based approach), because always it can happen that the content must be managed by the provider in plaintext and, further, encryption per se does not guarantee completeness of contents but only integrity. Moreover, the problem of the extraction of portions of contents would remain open.

Content Provision. Content provision is done by simply providing the intercepted content or a portion together with any element useful for the verification. This corresponds to the verification object (the portion of chunk chain) described in Sect. 4.

Integrity Verification. Verification can be done only by the Authority or any delegated party on the basis of the knowledge of the secret (as explained in Sect. 4) and the other information needed to check the integrity of the extracted content. It is worth noting that this allows us to have flexibility and modularity when portions of contents should transferred or exposed against the defence, or in any step of the investigation process. The above process in the case of trojan-based interception is summarized in Fig. 3. Therein, both the law enforcement agency and the Court are part of the Authority. Messages a and b represent the messages exchanged to update the Verification Object (i.e., the chunk chain). The content is transferred to the provider thanks to message c. Through message d the key K is exchanged to allow integrity verification. Contents are delivered to the Authority by the Provider through messages e and f.

6   Security Analysis

In this section, we provide the security analysis of our solution in a threat model that does not assume the trustworthiness of the Provider. We start by describing the security model and analyze the security properties we require as security guarantees. We may identify the following properties our system has to assure:

SP1. An extracted content has to be complete, it means that no frame or chunk of the Verification Object is omitted (including *markers*).
SP2. An extracted content has to be fresh. It means that the Client can check whether the newest version of the intercepted content is returned.
SP3. An extracted content has to be correct. It means that the Client can verify that all the frames have not been corrupted, and that no spurious frames have been introduced.

To analyze the security properties above, our threat model includes the following assumptions: **A1.** The interception agent (trojan or device) is trusted. **A2.** A secure communication between the interception agent and the Authority is established. **A3.** Collision, preimage and second preimage attacks on the cryptographic hash function, used by HMAC, are infeasible.

Now, we are ready to show that our approach satisfies the security properties on the basis of the attack model described above.

Compliance with SP1
In this case, our approach has to resist attacks in which the Provider may attempt to return incomplete results. Thanks to assumptions **A1** and **A2**, we may identify four possible ways the Provider can reach this goal:

1. The Provider returns an empty content. In this case, the Client checks whether there exists the last element. In the affirmative case, the attack is detected.
2. The Provider tries to omit some frame of the extracted content. In this case, the Client can check that the result is incomplete by verifying the chain linking between all the result elements inside each bucket (see Sect. 4). Therefore, thanks to Assumption **A3**, this attack is contrasted.
3. The Provider does not return a whole internal bucket. Also this attack is detected because, in the first step of the integrity verification procedure, the data owner identifies the chain head and tail and then verifies the integrity of the entire chain. Therefore, any possible missing bucket is detected because the corresponding links in the chunk chain will be missing too.
4. The Provider does not return elements or buckets at the edges of the extracted content. This attack makes sense only in the case of *unbounded* extracted content, in which one or both interval bounds are not set. Concerning the verification of the left-hand bucket, the Client can identify the first *marker* because this information is previously fixed an known to any party belonging to the Authority (thus, also to the Client). In the case of a right-side unbounded query, the Client can verify the completeness of the result by checking whether the last element of the intercepted content is present (see Sect. 4).

Compliance with SP2

To be compliant with **SP2**, our approach should resist attacks in which the Provider to return an old version of the intercepted content. This kind of attack can always be detected by the data owner because she knows the last element inserted in intercepted content. Indeed, there is only one chunk in the chain of the form $\langle \text{HMAC} (K, H (A_n) \| H(M_f)) \rangle$. Therefore, the correspondence with the last element A_n allows the Client to detect if the extracted content is fresh.

Compliance with SP3

The compliance with **SP3** requires that our approach guarantees data correctness. We may identify two cases:

1. The Provider adds a whole bucket or a single element to the extracted content. However, due to assumptions **A1**, **A2**, and **A3**, no valid HMAC element of a chunk can be generated without the knowledge of the secret key K.
2. The Provider compromises some frames or *markers* in the extracted content. Also this attack cannot succeed because of the above reasoning on HMAC element of the chunks.

7   Conclusions

The lawful interception ecosystem is becoming more and more complex due to the evolution of the technology and the consequent need to involve in the whole interception process also parties external to government and judiciary actors. Moreover, intercepted contents, also not entirely, have to be copied or transferred many times; for this reason strong measures to guarantee and verify data integrity are certainly welcome. The above framework is further complicated by the advent of interceptions based on the injection in the target device of specific trojans, whose development, management, installation, control, introduce further elements of complexity and increase threats on integrity. By taking inspiration from the approaches used in the context of query integrity in data outsourcing, this paper proposes a framework to support integrity in the lawful interception ecosystem, by considering both environmental and trojan-based interception. A detailed security analysis shows the effectiveness of the proposed solution. As a future work, we plan to implement the solution to give a proof of concept and experiment its feasibility in real-life contexts.

Acknowledgement. This paper is partially supported by Project POR FESR/FSE 14/20 Line A (Action 10.5.6).

References

1. Abel, W.: Agents, trojans and tags: the next generation of investigators. Int. Rev. Law Comput. Technol. **23**(1–2), 99–108 (2009)
2. Chen, F., Liu, A.X.: Privacy and integrity preserving multi-dimensional range queries for cloud computing. In: 2014 IFIP Networking Conference, pp. 1–9, June 2014

3. Cheng, W., Tan, K.-L.: Query assurance verification for outsourced multi-dimensional databases. J. Comput. Secur. **17**, 101–126 (2009)
4. De Capitani di Vimercati, S., Foresti, S., Jajodia, S., Paraboschi, S., Samarati, P.: Efficient integrity checks for join queries in the cloud 1. J. Comput. Secur. **24**(3), 347–378 (2016)
5. Devanbu, P., Gertz, M., Martel, C., Stubblebine, S.G.: Authentic data publication over the internet. J. Comput. Secur. **11**(3), 291–314 (2003)
6. Buccafurri, F., Lax, G., Nicolazzo, S., Nocera, A.: Range query integrity in cloud data streams with efficient insertion. In: Foresti, S., Persiano, G. (eds.) CANS 2016. LNCS, vol. 10052, pp. 719–724. Springer, Cham (2016). https://doi.org/10.1007/978-3-319-48965-0_50
7. Buccafurri, F., De Angelis, V., Labrini, C.: Integrity guarantees over highly dynamic outsourced map data. In: Proceedings of the 36th ACM-SIGAPP Symposium on Applied Computing (ACM-SAC), pp. 1691–1694. ACM (2021)
8. Cajani, F.: "All along the watchtower": matters not yet solved regarding communication interception systems and electronic data retained on foreign servers. In: Biasiotti, M.A., Mifsud Bonnici, J.P., Cannataci, J., Turchi, F. (eds.) Handling and Exchanging Electronic Evidence Across Europe. LGTS, vol. 39, pp. 59–71. Springer, Cham (2018). https://doi.org/10.1007/978-3-319-74872-6_5
9. Kim, D., Jeon, Y., Kim, J.: A secure channel establishment method on a hardware security module. In: 2014 International Conference on Information and Communication Technology Convergence (ICTC), pp. 555–556. IEEE (2014)
10. Krawczyk, H., Canetti, R., Bellare, M.: HMAC: keyed-hashing for message authentication (1997)
11. Li, F., Hadjieleftheriou, M., Kollios, G., Reyzin, L.: Authenticated index structures for aggregation queries. ACM Trans. Inf. Syst. Secur. (TISSEC) **13**(4), 32 (2010)
12. Ma, D., Deng, R.H., Pang, H., Zhou, J.: Authenticating query results in data publishing. In: Qing, S., Mao, W., López, J., Wang, G. (eds.) ICICS 2005. LNCS, vol. 3783, pp. 376–388. Springer, Heidelberg (2005). https://doi.org/10.1007/11602897_32
13. Mavrovouniotis, S., Ganley, M.: Hardware security modules. In: Markantonakis, K., Mayes, K. (eds.) Secure Smart Embedded Devices, Platforms and Applications, pp. 383–405. Springer, New York (2014). https://doi.org/10.1007/978-1-4614-7915-4_17
14. Merkle, R.C.: A certified digital signature. In: Brassard, G. (ed.) CRYPTO 1989. LNCS, vol. 435, pp. 218–238. Springer, New York (1990). https://doi.org/10.1007/0-387-34805-0_21
15. Narasimha, M., Tsudik, G.: Authentication of outsourced databases using signature aggregation and chaining. In: Li Lee, M., Tan, K.-L., Wuwongse, V. (eds.) DASFAA 2006. LNCS, vol. 3882, pp. 420–436. Springer, Heidelberg (2006). https://doi.org/10.1007/11733836_30
16. Niaz, M.S., Saake, G.: Merkle hash tree based techniques for data integrity of outsourced data. In: GvD, pp. 66–71 (2015)
17. Pang, H.H., Jain, A., Ramamritham, K., Tan, K.-L.: Verifying completeness of relational query results in data publishing. In: Proceedings of the 2005 ACM SIGMOD International Conference on Management of Data, pp. 407–418. ACM (2005)
18. Pang, H.H., Zhang, J., Mouratidis, K.: Scalable verification for outsourced dynamic databases. Proc. VLDB Endow. **2**(1), 802–813 (2009)
19. Peix, A.: Austrian constitutional court: number plate recognition and 'Trojan Horse' software are unconstitutional. Eur. Data Prot. L. Rev. **6**, 128 (2020)

20. Samarati, P.: Data security and privacy in the cloud. In: Huang, X., Zhou, J. (eds.) ISPEC 2014. LNCS, vol. 8434, pp. 28–41. Springer, Cham (2014). https://doi.org/ 10.1007/978-3-319-06320-1_4
21. Schlehahn, E.: Cybersecurity and the state. In: Christen, M., Gordijn, B., Loi, M. (eds.) The Ethics of Cybersecurity. TILELT, vol. 21, pp. 205–225. Springer, Cham (2020). https://doi.org/10.1007/978-3-030-29053-5_10
22. Sustek, L.: Hardware security module. In: van Tilborg, H.C.A., Jajodia, S. (eds.) Encyclopedia of Cryptography and Security, pp. 535–538. Springer, Boston (2011). https://doi.org/10.1007/978-1-4419-5906-5_509
23. Xie, M., Wang, H., Yin, J., Meng, X.: Integrity auditing of outsourced data. In: Proceedings of the 33rd International Conference on Very Large Data Bases, pp. 782–793. VLDB Endowment (2007)
24. Zheng, Q., Xu, S., Ateniese, G.: Efficient query integrity for outsourced dynamic databases. In: Proceedings of the 2012 ACM Workshop on Cloud Computing Security Workshop, CCSW 2012, pp. 71–82. ACM, New York (2012)

Can Tech4Good Prevent Domestic Violence and Femicides? An Intelligent System Design Proposal for Restraining Order Implementations

Hüseyin Umutcan Ay$^{(\boxtimes)}$, Alime Aysu Öner, and Nihan Yıldırım

İstanbul Technical University, Maslak, Sariyer, 34467 İstanbul, Turkey

Abstract. Domestic violence against women in Turkey is an ongoing problem that the authorities had yet to find solutions to prevent from ever occurring. There exist some technological tools such as the panic button for the women under threat or piloting the ankle bracelets provided for the restraining orders in some regions of Turkey. However, each day's increasing number of femicides shows that those attempts stayed insufficient to bring sustainable solutions to this devastating problem. Most system failures are caused by a system defect concerning inter-institutional information flows and the multi-stakeholder process problem. This multilayered phenomenon requires an integrated approach and intelligent solutions rather than focusing only on a singular failure point in the institutional system of preventing femicides. In this context, this study aims to propose a logical system design framework to integrate crime prediction and prevention solutions into the institutional system. By satisfying prediction, prevention, and protection functions simultaneously, it aims to address most of the existing system's pain points.

Keywords: Domestic violence · Restraining order · Institutional system design · Information systems · Femicides

1 Introduction

Murder of women by men motivated by hatred, envy, and the instinct of possession because they are women as defined femicide [1]. Incidences of femicides are increasing more than incidences of men homicide year after year. Men are still broadly recognized as the essential culprits of femicide, a phenomenon that endures universally, even though it extents contrast by nation. In terms of scholarly circles, legislative issues, backing bunches, and territorial, national, and other authoritative forms at the worldwide level, the occurrence, and scope of femicide proceed to be a subject of wrangle about.

Recently, society has become more aware of violence and endeavors to stop this circumstance have picked up significantly with the evolution of technology, media, non-governmental organizations (NGOs), and various institutions. However, despite the steps taken in regulative and political systems, domestic violence against women has come to disturbing levels, particularly in Turkey. One of the major pieces of evidence of this inefficacy is the substantial number of women subjected to violence even after

© Springer Nature Switzerland AG 2021
A. Kö et al. (Eds.): EGOVIS 2021, LNCS 12926, pp. 34–45, 2021.
https://doi.org/10.1007/978-3-030-86611-2_3

releasing restraining orders to save women. An urgent development in the IT-enabled enforcement systems to protect women's lives under the threat of domestic violence is necessary as an inference of increasing numbers of domestic violence and femicides. Inter-institutional information management is essential for timely intervention to domestic crime incidents. In the current information systems used by law enforcement and legal institutions, the measures and operational processes remained insufficient and inefficient after the restraining orders' issuance. Existing information systems on implementing the restraining orders do not perform crime risk evaluation and prediction, and they also lack digital location tracking tools. However, it is technologically possible to predict and prevent domestic violence and femicides by adapting integrated intelligent systems in the digitalization era.

In this context, our study aims to propose an information system design that multiple actors can use in the inter-institutional restraining order implementation system from Turkey's case. The proposed system comprises prediction, prevention, and protection functions, enabling the timely usage of information for protecting women under domestic violence. After a literature review on this critical social problem, we analyzed the As-Is system by interviewing experts and constructing use cases on the existing systems for restraining order implementation. We defined the improvement needs as kaizen areas by elaborating the pain points on inter-institutional information and process flows map. Corresponding to these improvement needs, we proposed an intelligent system design, including crime prediction, prevention, and protection modules. We constructed use-cases, data flow diagrams, and an entity-relationship diagram for the system's logical structure.

2 Literature Review

2.1 Domestic Violence Against Women

In recent years, femicide is a very critical and noticeable matter all over the world. 87.000 women were killed nastily all over the world in a year [2]. Intimate partners or acquaintances killed 58% of these women. Moreover, this rate has expanded year by year. Femicides are triggered by various social, psychological, ethnic, and economic factors like poverty and immigration experiences. These factors make women more vulnerable to the murderous practice of violence [3].

The numbers of femicides have not been shared by the government since 2014 in Turkey. We Will End Femicide Platform procures the most extensive data source about this subject. The platform collects all of the news about femicides. According to the platform's annual reports, over 2000 women were killed by men in the last five years.

Femicide is seen as an expansion of violence [4]. 37% of women in the East Mediterranean Region, including Turkey, are subjected to violence by their intimate partners [5]. 40.6% of women were killed by their husbands, 22.3% by relatives, and 11.4% by the boyfriends of the victims [6]. On the other hand, the victim and the perpetrator were in a close relationship in 63% of femicides. Most intimate partner murders are based on a long history of violence and the women crave to the conclusion of the relationship. Particularly, risk of being killed increase when women who want to keep away from their abusers [7]. On the other hand, the political climate is working against women's rights and reached its peak with the withdrawal of Turkey from the Istanbul Convention, which it had ratified in 2012 [8]. The Council of Europe Istanbul Convention is a human rights treaty to prevent and combat violence against women and domestic violence, signed by all EC Member States [9]. Ural and Kaya called the femicides a symbolic crisis of political power, referring to Bourdieu's conceptual models [4].

2.2   Femicides Despite Restraining Orders: Location is the Key

The most common way to prevent violence against women is a restraining order. For the femicides of women killed despite having restraining orders, the location of women murders is also a meaningful pattern. Most femicides are committed in the house or residence of victims or perpetrators [2]. In a previous study, Vittes and Sorenson reported that approximately one-five of the femicides were committed in public places such as streets or free fields. They also concluded that the probability of being a homicide victim at home is 14.6 times higher for women with a history of violence. A lower percentage of those killed in a shared house, a higher percentage of those killed in their own home, and a higher percentage of those killed in another indoor place had a restraining order [7]. Similar patterns are observed about femicides in Turkey. 60% of femicides were committed in a house in 2020 [6]. 11 percent of women who lawfully under protection by the restraining orders have been murdered within the last ten years in Turkey. According to the latest domestic violence report of the Ministry of Family and Work in Turkey, the proportion of women who indicated that at any period in her life she had been exposed to physical or sexual violence is 42 percent throughout Turkey. When the marital status of women is evaluated, the most striking result is that the rate of violence is %73 among divorced or separated women [10]. After the restraining order was issued, one-fifth of the women were murdered in 2 days, whereas one-third were murdered in a month [11]. In this context, location tracking of the violator and the victim occur as a critical function in the femicide prediction and prevention systems. The riskiest locations are homes; however, the current safety information systems and location tracking technologies stay short in tracking the potential violator and the potential victims. The current system is based on the "urgent call" of the victim. However, the violator's sudden intrusion into the victim's home prevents the officers' timely calls; hence, the time lag between the intrusion and the arrival of the law enforcement officers to the violent incident location occurs as a system defect causing femicides. The current procedures do not focus on the perpetrator's tracking and do not effectively monitor violent crime risks.

2.3   The Attitude of Violators Against Restraining Orders

Most intimate partner murders are based on a long record of violence and the women's wants to finish the relationship [6]. The violators in jail do not care about the violence they delivered on the women, their quarrels ranging from being an accident to being caused by women's provocation. Instead of accepting the crime, the convicts had appeared a trend towards finding external causes other than themselves. They moreover think that the law is centered on securing the only women whereas neglecting the outside realities that might trigger the murder [12]. A study conducted on the young violators in Canada elaborated some possible effects of electronic monitoring on the violators.

Having visible hardware on their ankles hinders their social lives as most of their friends approach them cautiously. However, this isolation from their immediate environment and the feeling of constantly being watched reduce recidivism rates; they think that the ankle bracelets had kept them in line. The system also affected the violators' mental state, causing higher stress factors than conventional [13]. In previous studies, no other significant physiological or psychological side effects of ankle bracelets or different location tracking wearables have been reported on the convicts with a record of domestic violence against women.

3 Current System in Turkey

Current domestic violence prevention systems have some crucial failures in information-flowing processes between institutions and women exposed to violence. Since the existing systems' connection points with violators are not viable, we interviewed experts from different institutions and NGOs in the As-Is system analysis. In total, we interviewed six experts, including a family court judge, a law enforcement Police Chief, an NGO representative (from We Will Stop Femicides Platform) and a lawyer/attorney specialized in violence against women in Turkey.

The first matter on the restraining order in existing system is that the restraining orders are only issued based on the latest complaint. Nonetheless, before that latest complaint derive from the women the substance of violence could be monitoring. There is no clear risk assessment metrics are supporting the final decision in the system. Standard restraining orders are given to women as a result of lack of objective proofs other than individuals' declarations and will not focus on the previous violence history between two parties. Even if the restraining orders could be issued, currently those orders only protect women on their residence address. They are only offered with protection whenever they report the violation. This procedure creates two distinct issues: The domestic offenders are punishing the women for reporting the violence since they are only provided with protection while they are at home. Secondly, since the women could only notify the police when they face the perpetrator one on one, this creates an issue where the interventions could not be made until it is too late for the victims. Experts also highlighted this issue during the interviews. According to NGOs' experts on women studies, many women are killed despite restraining orders because of late intervention every year in Turkey.

For ensuring the protection of women in Turkey, currently, there are two main implementations. The first of these is the KADES application developed by the Ministry of Interior. It is a basic smartphone application with a panic button where women use it to report domestic violence they have been subjected to by law enforcement officers without a restraining order. However, since the application's effect is dependent on the mobile coverage, it may not be feasible to use in every condition and has some accuracy problems, especially within indoor locations. Besides, a research group from feminist NGOs sampled many cases where timely intervention failed even if the panic button was pressed on time. With the current information system in place within the Turkish governmental system, the victims' location information could not be shared transparently with the law enforcement officers while the information flows through many different stakeholders during the emergency calls, causing late interventions.

The second and most recent implementation is the electronic monitoring system used in the implementation of the restraining order in Turkey that is being piloted within various parts of Turkey. According to interviews with the experts, the electronic monitoring method is the most effective method used in preventing femicide. Previous studies also called this tool as the most effective but the rarest method [14]. In Turkey, the electronic monitoring method is used less than %1 even in the pilot area in domestic violence cases against women due to the ankle bracelets' high prices. Also, the monitoring process for them carries excellent insignificance. The moderators are watching the screen for 7/24 to detect any violations within the orders, which is a labor-intensive process that could easily be solved by installing an efficient information system that investigates the locations without external supervision. Considering all of the factors provided, it is evident that the implementation methods and the precautions methods about preventing violence against women in Turkey are still inefficient and inadequate. The inefficiency of the information flow between institutions causes women to be killed by men every year. The kaizen points indicated on Fig. 1 explains all of those communication failures between institutions on domestic violence.

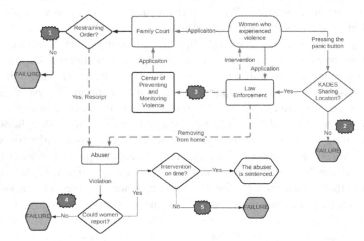

Fig. 1. AS_IS Inter-institutional information and process flow map for preventing domestic violence against women in Turkey

4   An Intelligent System Design Proposal for Predicting and Preventing Domestic Violence Against Women

There is a need for an integrated system satisfying three main functions of prediction, prevention, and protection to ensure that the restraining order implementation provides the safest method for the victims. To solve the current problem areas within the current system, according to the needs determined during the expert interviews for all three phases, which functions the new system should provide to solve current failure points (see Fig. 2).

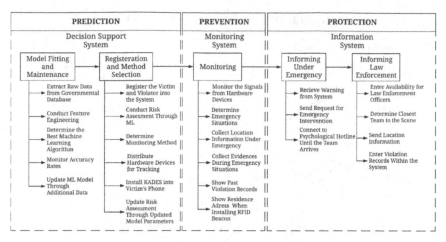

Fig. 2. Block process diagram

The current institutional system lacks a suitable risk assessment mechanism before the execution phase, and the family court issues a standardized restraining order decision regardless of the case's type. Therefore, the system's primary module is designed as a decision support system that runs a predictive algorithm on the offender's criminal records and provides a risk assessment report to assist the family court's decision-making process. Depending on the family court's verdict, the following two modules aim to provide the safest possible option for the victims and decrease the burden of continuous location tracking for potential offenders with low risk of action. To ensure the proposed system's fluent operation, we also provided a guideline on the interventions during the emergencies and the informing procedure for the potential victim and the law enforcement officers. Also, customized user interfaces for both parties will enable a better user experience.

4.1 Use Case Diagrams of the System Modules

As representative logical modules of the system, we designed UML use case diagrams for providing a framework on which actions are performed by the external users and how the system itself will react under those conditions. Each of the use case diagrams are specialized under distinct scenarios, and their interdependencies are also indicated using "extend" and "include" notifications [15].

The model fitting and maintenance module (see Fig. 3) represents the risk assessment algorithm's creation and maintenance process using the existing databases that are available to the governmental officers. According to the expert interviews with law enforcement officers and also the family court judges, it is feasible to follow such method when determining the risk algorithm since the violent behaviors are not a result of a momentary state of delirium but instead occurs within a time period with its violence reflecting to the daily life of the offender. After the initial model is fit, it will also be regularly updated through the close follow-up of the accuracy rates as more domestic violence cases added into the database. Also, the system will be updated according to

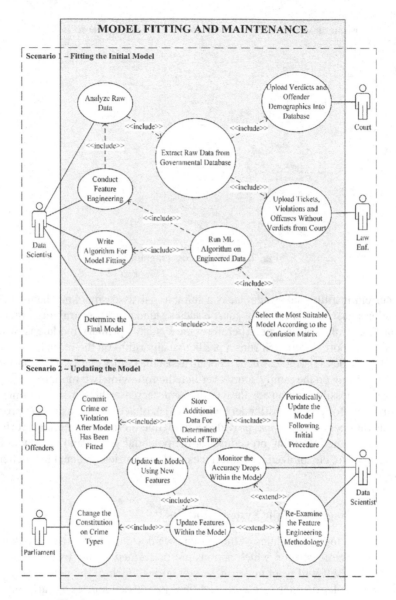

Fig. 3. To-be use case diagram for risk assessment module

the changes within the legislation system and also the recent advancements within the recidivism literature to provide the optimal possible algorithm for risk assessment.

After the risk algorithm reaches a satisfactory level of accuracy, it will then be used as a primary component of a decision support system that will be used on determining the type of the restraining order that will be issued (see Fig. 4). As a procedure, whenever new complaint arrives to the law enforcement and the precautionary measures are taken, officers will then record both the information of offender and victim into the system

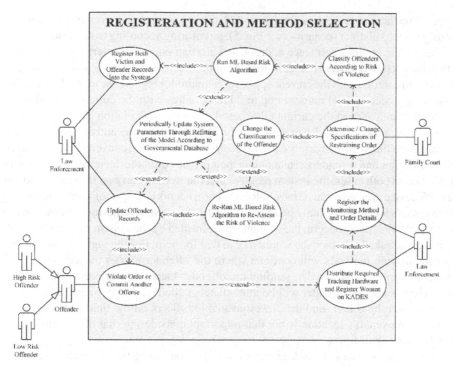

Fig. 4. To-be use case diagram for registration and method selection

alongside with the current details of the most recent complaint. According to the criminal history and the past records of the offender under the law enforcement database, the risk algorithm runs on the features to create a risk assessment report to be used by the family court during decision making process. However, since those algorithms will have natural margin of error basing the final decision for the restraining orders solely on the algorithm is not feasible. That is why the proposed system will only refer to the risk algorithm as one of the supplementary methods for the decision making and will still be dependent on the family court for determining the final details of the order. Depending on the verdict by the court, the tracking hardware will be distributed both to the victim and also the offender to initiate the monitoring process. Here, according to the violence risk of the offender, high risk ones will receive GPS components alongside to their RF bracelets while the low risk offenders will only carry RF bracelets on their ankles. To determine the proximity, the victims will be supplied with RF readers and also will be signed into the redesigned version of KADES application to connect with the law enforcement under emergency. Since the violence after the restraining orders are issued mostly occurs within the residence address of the victim, the houses will be tracked using beacon technology that will be enabled whenever the RF bracelet of the offender gets in range with the beacon itself. While the order is implemented, if the risk classification of the offender changes, the methodology will also be changed accordingly after a throughout consideration by the family court.

After the hardware devices get distributed, the monitoring process happens simultaneously under 3 distinct scenarios (see Fig. 5): monitoring according to variable location, monitoring the victim's residence address, and alerting under the emergency. Our value within the proposed system comes within the application methodology stated in the first scenario. In contrast with the current application methodology, we use an RF linkage that works in a predetermined range set up to 2 km in radius with the current technological constraints compared to the current GPS-based proximity calculation.

Since we propose using RF bracelets on the high-risk offenders and the low-risk ones, relying on RF linkages' proximity calculations yields much more convenient results since both the victims and offenders can maintain their privacy until the devices got linked with each other. In both cases, the system requires that the woman carry an RF reader and not the GPS device to ensure that no psychological harm occurs through constant monitoring. The woman's location will only be important in the low-risk monitoring process. Under the possible violation concern, the woman gets informed by the system through KADES interface and asked whether she would like to call for help. For the high-risk situations, prior monitoring methods will continue where the offender carries an additional GPS device alongside the RF reader, sending the offender location information in violation cases. Here, since the offender will be immediately called whenever he passes a certain proximity threshold and send the closest available officers on the field to his location, tracking the woman's location is not that important considering that the victim carries the RF reader at all times.

The second scenario regarding the module is monitoring the offenders according to the residence address of the victims. The module suggests installing an RF beacon in the victim's house to prevent ambushes from the offender. Within the scenario, RF linkages again determine the offender's proximity to the victim's residence address. The system sends a warning message regarding the violation to the victim's mobile phone. For both scenario 1 and scenario 2, the offenders will be notified about the violation by sending vibrations through bracelets and calling them through GPS devices. Following the scenario, "Alerting Under Emergency" will be executed only after the offender is warned about the violation.

For the last scenario of the combined module, the system sends the emergency alerts to the victims and the law enforcement. Depending on the risk assessment, victims are provided with the option of whether to call law enforcement or not. If the offender has a low risk of committing a violent crime, the offender will be warned about the violation, and after a predetermined time, the victim may contact law enforcement for intervention. However, the officers are obliged to intervene for the high-risk offenders as soon as the offender passes the predetermined proximity threshold. No time allowance will be given for the high-risk offenders since they have a relatively higher risk for committing a violent crime.

Use case diagram also includes processes such as contacting the law enforcement and information sharing with them. For the proposed system, the contacting process relies on determining the closest available team to the location. During the patrol, law enforcement officers indicate their availability on the screen installed on their cars and share their GPS coordinates through their cars' existing GPS devices. The system will track the cars' location and, according to the relative distance and availability, decide

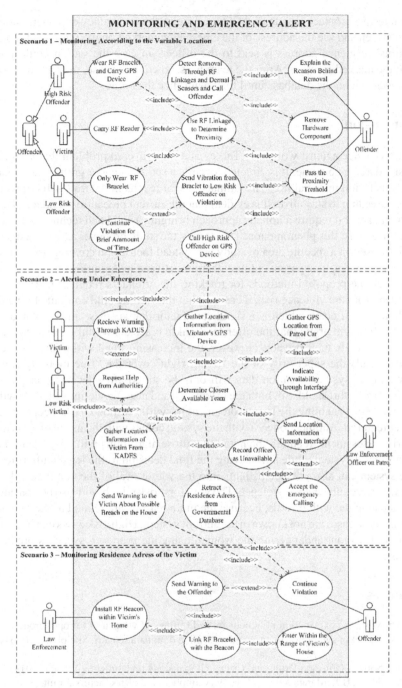

Fig. 5. To-be use case diagram for monitoring and emergency alert

on which team to contact. The team will then receive the emergency explanation on the installed screen and see the address of the emergency marked on the map. Additionally, the victims' residence address is sent to the officers in case the victim could not be found at the marked location. After the team is assigned to the case, they are marked as busy/unavailable on the database until they neutralize the scene.

5 Conclusion

Domestic violence against women in Turkey is a multilayered problem that could also be classified as a hate crime. It is directed towards a specific gender group and threatens women's inclusion in social life. This climate of fear results in the trade-offs of women from their freedom to stay alive. It is evident that the current precautions taken in Turkey are insignificant and require a holistic approach bringing a solid and technological solution to fight against this phenomenon. That is why the study proposes a to-be design that not only focuses on a specific area of study but instead focuses on creating an integrated system that provides transparent communication between its modules.

Although the proposed methods for tracking the offenders require an RF bracelet independent from the violence risk, it ensures that the victim could continue living their life without fear of death which is a significant factor that keeps women isolated from society. Some might argue that the offenders' ankle bracelets would restrict their right to travel and violate their privacy. However, the increasing trend within the number of femicides recalls the superiority of the "living right" over the "free mobility rights". Also, within the system, location data will only be stored after the offender passes a certain proximity threshold. So, both the offender's and also the victim's privacy will be secured while still enabling the law enforcement to swiftly respond to the scene of crisis whenever required. Another concern with the system comes with the usage of algorithms for the risk assessment. It should be noted that those algorithms will only be used as a decision support system while still leaving the final decision to the legal authorities.

The system can also provide insights into the withdrawal of the complaints by the women who were subjected to violence. The violators' risk rate should also be considered when evaluating the withdrawals, because the main reasons are related to the violators' threats and these cases are not known in the current system. High-risk cases can be defined and followed without endangering the woman using the proposed system's prediction mechanism.

References

1. Grzyb, M.A.: An explanation of honour-related killings of women in Europe through Bour-dieu's concept of symbolic violence and masculine domination. Curr. Sociol. **64**, 1036–1053 (2016)
2. United Nations Office on Drugs and Crime. Global study on homicide, Vienna (2019)
3. Walton-Moss, B.J., Manganello, J., Frye, V., Campbell, J.C.: Risk factors for intimate partner violence and associated injury among urban women. J. Commun. Health **30**(5), 377–389 (2005). https://doi.org/10.1007/s10900-005-5518-x
4. Ural, H., Çabuk Kaya, N.: Kadın cinayetlerinde sembolik iktidarın krizi. Sosyoloji Araştırmaları Dergisi **21**, 356–382 (2018)

5. Sen, S., Bolsoy, N.: Violence against women: prevalence and risk factors in Turkish sample. BMC Women's Health **100**, 2–9 (2017)
6. Taştan, C., Yıldız, K.A.: Report of femicides in Turkey and in the word: data and analyzes between 2016 and 2018. J. Police Acad. **68** (2019). Report no. 21
7. Vittes, K.A., Sorenson, S.B.: Restraining orders among victims of intimate partner homicide. Inj. Prev. **14**, 191–195 (2008)
8. Anadolu Agency (AA): Turkey Withdraws from Istanbul Convention. Anadolu Ajansı. https://www.aa.com.tr/en/turkey/turkey-withdraws-from-istanbul-convention/2182168. Accessed 2 May 2021
9. EU: Istanbul Convention Action against violence against women and domestic violence (2021). https://www.coe.int/en/web/istanbul-convention/home
10. Ministry of Family, Labor and Social Services: Women in turkey report, Ankara (2020)
11. We Will End Femicides Platform Reports (2015–2020). http://kadincinayetlerinidurduracagiz.net/kategori/veriler. Accessed Nov 2020
12. Hacettepe University Institute of Population Studies. Research on Domestic Violence against Women in Turkey. Ankara: Republic of Turkey Ministry of Family and Social Policies (2015). http://www.hips.hacettepe.edu.tr/eng/english_main_report.pdf
13. Willoughby, A., Nellis, M.: 'You cannot really hide': experiences of probation officers and young offenders with GPS tracking in Winnipeg, Canada. J. Technol. Hum. Serv. **34**(1), 63–81 (2016). https://doi.org/10.1080/15228835.2016.1139919
14. Gies, S.V., et al.: Monitoring high-risk sex offenders with GPS technology: an evaluation of the California supervision program. Final report. PsycEXTRA Dataset (2012). https://doi.org/10.1037/e566812012-001
15. Gornik, D.: Entity relationship modeling with UML. International business machine: a technical discussion on modelling with UML (2003)

Toward Smart City Architecture Principles: A Cornerstone in the Case of Smart City Duisburg

Peder Bergan(✉), Kevin Rehring, Michel Muschkiet, Frederik Ahlemann, and Léonie Hackemann

University of Duisburg-Essen, Essen, Germany
peder.bergan@uni-due.de

Abstract. Developing smart city (SC) solutions often requires complex collaboration between diverse organizations and systems. Given that SC initiatives face certain challenges comparable to that of traditional enterprises, existing SC architectures are often based on generic enterprise architecture (EA) frameworks. However, the resulting SC architectures tend to suffer from several weaknesses and existing research does not detail the process of developing SC EA principles. We address this gap by reporting on a collaboration with an SC initiative in a medium-sized European city and by presenting two artifacts we developed in that initiative: architecture principles and the related roles and structures. Corresponding to our involvement in the initiative, our work has been guided by the action design research approach. We expect that other SC initiatives can learn from our results and challenges and that transferring our approach to these initiatives will reduce their required effort for SC EA principles development.

Keywords: Smart city · Architecture principles · Governance · Enterprise architecture management · Action design research

1 Introduction

55% of the world's population currently lives in cities, and by 2050 the share of urban citizens is expected to increase to 68% [1]. Partly due to the rapid urban population growth, most resources worldwide are consumed in cities. This contributes to their economic and environmental performance [2]. Besides many positive effects, including potential economic improvement and new job opportunities [3], these circumstances generate a variety of technical, social, economic, and organizational problems [4]. Some are characterized by environmental and infrastructural issues, and have an impact on citizens' quality of life [5], as in air pollution, traffic congestion, and waste disposal [3, 6]. Another set of challenges, from a social and organizational point of view, are associated with multiple diverse stakeholders, high levels of interdependence, competing values, and social as well as political complexity [5].

In this context, digital transformation has been identified as leading the way in cities' movement toward sustainability and in providing the most effective solutions to

© Springer Nature Switzerland AG 2021
A. Kö et al. (Eds.): EGOVIS 2021, LNCS 12926, pp. 46–60, 2021.
https://doi.org/10.1007/978-3-030-86611-2_4

the challenges of urban development [7]. The urgency of cities' problems has moved local public governments, companies, non-profit organizations, and citizens to make cities smarter by embracing the idea of using new information and communication technologies (ICT) and other innovations [8]. In the recent years, the concept of *smart city* (SC) has received increasing attention, eventually providing a new dimension to ICT's role in urban environments [6, 9, 10]. Although there is still no general consensus on the definition of the term SC, there is wide agreement that SCs are characterized by stakeholders attempting to make better use of their resources by implementing ICT [4], and SCs often aim to establish a more sustainable and livable city [6, 11, 12]. In Europe, there are about 240 cities with a population of more than 100,000 that show SC characteristics [13].

Although SC initiatives are characterized by unique challenges resulting from their multidimensionality and thus high complexity [14, 15], an SC shares some characteristics with the concept of the *enterprise*. First, an SC can be seen as a collection of various initiatives and organizations. Second, those organizations, like enterprises, generally have common goals. Third, cities compete with each other, e.g. in terms of being economically attractive [16]. Finally, both enterprises and cities often struggle to adopt digital innovations [17, 18]. Apart from the similarities, there are also significant differences between enterprises and SCs. SC initiatives overall are characterized by significantly more complexity and diversity than ordinary IT projects in private companies, and many cities struggle to implement their SC initiative due to technical, managerial, and governance challenges [15]. This is partly because SC initiatives characteristically have a high degree of partnerships and collaborations with third parties [19] including public administration, state-owned business and private business. Depending on the use case, different (combinations of) stakeholders are in charge. Such stakeholders have different organizational cultures, information system (IS) capabilities, and to some extent, goals [14]. Further, the public sector consists of many layers of authority, often influenced by political factors, which could negatively influence the speed and efficiency of the SC implementation [14].

In order to address these challenges, researchers have proposed several frameworks to describe SC architectures. Some works are based on the assumption that the *enterprise* concept can be transferred to an SC, and thus they propose that *enterprise architecture management* (EAM) approaches could direct and guide a city's digital transformation [16, 20]. EAM, in this context, can be understood as a management practice that "establishes, maintains and uses a coherent set of guidelines, architecture principles and governance regimes that provide direction for and practical help with the design and development of an enterprise's architecture in order to achieve its vision and strategy" [21]. As such, an *enterprise architecture* (EA) fundamentally describes the structures of an enterprise and follows the idea of modelling the enterprise's most important artefacts and its relationships including principles [22]. Due to the unique challenges of SCs mentioned above, researchers and practitioners have proposed various types of EA for SCs, some of which are extended from generic EA frameworks [16, 19, 23–25]. Some of these SC EA efforts suffer from a lack of alignment with the corresponding SC strategies or a focus on technical and data aspects without sufficiently considering managerial and organizational challenges [26].

The EA literature has established reasonably well that an organization should particularly consider its strategic and business goals in developing an EA [21]. According to Greefhorst and Proper [27], *principles* can be seen as the cornerstones of EA, as they fill the gap between high-level strategic intent and concrete design. Thus, we argue that it is more fruitful for an SC initiative to focus first on the process of developing EA principles, and subsequently EA organizational structures, to increase the chances of the EA properly fitting the characteristics of the city, its stakeholders, and their goals. Considering all the above, there is a research gap in that SC EA principles and the process of creating such principles have not been thoroughly examined yet. Therefore, our *research goal* is to report on the process we developed in collaborating with a medium-sized European city to create SC EA principles and related organizational structures and roles, and to explain how these principles help to address the SC initiative's strategic intents and challenges, which may serve as a timely contribution forward for EAM for SCs. Hence, we present two artefacts in this paper, which we developed based on action design research (ADR): SC architecture principles and the related organizational structures and roles. The focus of the developed principles is on the area of SC governance. In describing the development process and various challenges regarding the implementation of these principles, this paper will also contribute an overview of several architecture and governance issues in the context of SCs as well as a practical case study that can help practitioners involved with designing and managing SC initiatives deal with these challenges.

In the following section, we delve deeper into our conceptual foundations. Subsequently, we describe our action design research approach (Sect. 3.1) and the case city (Sect. 3.2). Thereafter, we report on our results in Sect. 4. Finally, Sect. 5 includes our discussion and conclusion.

2   Conceptual Foundations

In the following subsections we go through the key concepts of smart cities and architecture principles as a foundation for our research and to begin to highlight how, in theory, a sound use of architecture principles could aid the implementation of a city's SC goals.

2.1   Smart Cities and Digital Transformation

While recognizing that the term "smart city" is not consensually defined, we rely on Caragliu, del Bo and Nijkamp's [28] definition, because it can be closely adapted to the strategic orientation of this paper's case initiative and has gained somewhat widespread use. The authors state: "we believe a city to be smart when investments in human and social capital and traditional (transport) and modern (ICT) communication infrastructure fuel sustainable economic growth and a high quality of life, with a wise management of natural resources, through participatory governance" [28]. As explained in Sect. 1, SCs consist of networks of diverse, legally distinct stakeholders [11] who have some shared and some competing objectives, as well as complex and slow decision-making procedures [18]. Additionally, public sectors are subject to legal and formal constraints and, partly due to this, tend to avoid technology that has not already been firmly established in the market [18]. Some of these challenges can arguably be addressed through organizational and IT governance mechanisms, especially in areas lacking controlled and coordinated action [29].

Following from the goals and challenges mentioned above, a factor of successful SC initiatives is having city leaders who develop a social infrastructure for collaborations across boundaries of jurisdictions and sectors [30]. In the same vein, a smarter city would be one functioning as a network which attends to linking the city's different subsystems (e.g. electrical grid, waste management, or public transportation) to the improved intelligence (e.g. an SC platform, an information dashboard, or to each other directly) [6]. To increase the chances of successful IT initiatives, public management needs to be involved in shaping the direction of IT efforts according to organizational and operational imperatives [31]. This relates closely to EA because the "readiness for business model and enterprise architecture is an important capability for innovation toward a smart city" [5], as we shall detail below.

2.2 Architecture Principles

Greefhorst and Proper [32] describe architecture as the high-level fundamental structure of the system that guides the people that design and build it. EA can be characterized by five key elements: concerns, models, views, architecture principles, and frameworks [27]. Architecture principles can be defined as "an organization's basic philosophies that guide the development of the architecture" [33]. They provide rationales for the constant examination and re-evaluation of technology plans. As principles are the most stable elements of an architecture, they have the most far-reaching and significant impact on organizations [33]. Thus, architecture principles are used as a fundamental description of how an enterprise will use and deploy IT resources and assets [34]. Although researchers have proposed some enterprise architectures for smart cities (see chapter 1), we have not found prior works specifically about smart city-related architecture principles. To ensure the effectiveness of our architecture principles, we rely on the five characteristics for effective architecture principles listed by the Open Group [34]: understandability, robustness (applicability even in potentially controversial situations), completeness, consistency, and stability (durability, including an ability to accommodate changes).

3 Research Design

In the following subsections, we describe our research design. Moving toward the research goal of this paper, action design research was used and applied to the Smart City Duisburg initiative. After presenting our research design, we will introduce the case itself, and then present our research results.

3.1 Our Action Design Research Approach

Action design research (ADR) is a design science research approach that draws on action research [35]. ADR has been developed to investigate the consequences of changes within a specific domain [35–37], such as SC. Its research approaches seek to generate design

knowledge through building and evaluating ensemble IT artifacts with a practical problem in an organizational setting [35], which is what we were asked to do for the case city.
In this paper, we use an approach similar to Mullarkey and Hevner's [38] ADR research
that adapted and complemented Sein et al.'s [35] approach. Mullarkey and Hevner recognized that the emergent iterative cycle of researcher-practitioner intervention could
best be presented as a sequence of iterative cycles in four different stages, i.e. diagnosis, design, implementation, and evolution. Instead of implementing all design activities
within one single stage, as proposed by Sein et al. establishing the BIE (building, intervention and evaluation) stage [35], each ADR cycle moves through activities of problem
formulation, artefact creation, evaluation, reflection, and learning [38].

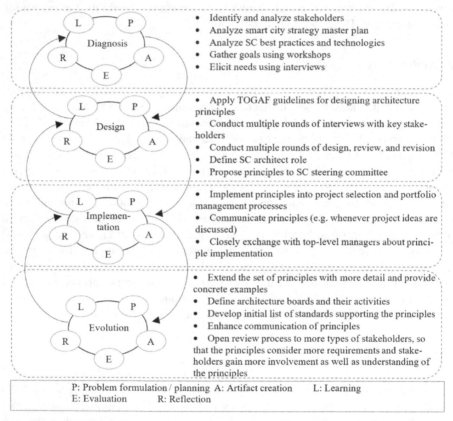

Fig. 1. Overview of our research approach in line with Mullarkey and Hevner [38]

Like Mullarkey and Hevner's [38] approach, we conducted four iterative design
cycles and use these to sequentially report the development of our artifacts in a researcher-
practitioner collaboration. We consider this type of model to be suitable for our research
design because of how well it aligns with our work in the case of SCs. Specifically,
our research goal is to develop two artefacts – the principles and the associated roles
and organizational structures of SC architecture. Considering the general characteristics

of SCs (see Sect. 2.1) and the specific characteristics of our SC case (see Sect. 3.2), we aimed to address the organizational need for intervention, working closely with the respective SC stakeholders through iterative process stages, from problem diagnosis to artefact design, implementation, and evolution. In Fig. 1, we show the ADR model with the related steps implemented. Each stage of the model consists of multiple iterations of the ADR intervention cycle, each with problem formulation/action planning, artifact creation, evaluation, reflection, and formalization of learning [38], and these are explained in detail below.

The diagnosis stage is characterized by the description of the problem and the identification of most relevant theories which can help to solve it [38]. In this stage, we gain insight in the specific problem domain, the conditions of the SC's use case as well as its strategic orientation and goals. In the design stage, the proposed artifact design is identified and conceptualized [38]. As we intended to derive architecture principles and define the SC architect role, we seek to consider existing findings from the EAM discipline. We aimed to base our development on industry independent EAM frameworks due to the heterogeneity of possible SC use cases. Considering the vast amount of frameworks [39], we chose the well-known TOGAF framework as a starting point for designing architecture principles [34]. TOGAF provides a generic introduction to architecture principles, a guideline to their development, as well as proposes four components to describe them [34]. Moreover, TOGAF provides a list of needed skills of various types of EAM roles that we considered as well [34]. In an iterative collaborative process with key stakeholders and the SC's steering committee, we developed, reviewed, and revised the principles and defined an SC architect role. For this process, we conducted interviews with seven business and IT managers of the city and two city-owned companies, as well as six researchers with expertise in both EA and SC.

The third stage, i.e. the implementation phase, aims to support the "instantiation of artifacts" [38]. In our work, this cycle was characterized by the actions of implementing the designed principles and developing an architecture management process, including the key roles responsible for architecture government. The principles were officially approved and enacted by the steering committee of the SC initiative. Subsequently, we cooperated with the SC initiative managers to communicate the principles and their underlying reasoning to stakeholders conducting SC projects.

In the final stage of evolution, we considered and addressed changes in the problem environment, and developed artefacts to meet these changes [38]. We used this stage to extend the elaborated architecture principles with more detail, considering more requirements and concrete application examples. We intensified communication and involved more stakeholders to spread an understanding of the set of principles. In order to support the principles, we defined architecture boards and their activities, and drew up an initial list of architecture standards. Each principle can be linked to more than one of these standards, depending on the respective topic.

3.2 The Case of Smart City Duisburg

Our research shows findings from the SC initiative of the city of Duisburg, located in the western part of Germany. With nearly 500,000 inhabitants, Duisburg can be classified as a medium to large-sized European city [40], which has been identified as the most important class of cities in Europe in terms of its demographic conditions [41]. Duisburg is confronted with the kinds of industrial, economic, and environmental challenges that are typical for medium-sized cities. With the largest inland port of Europe, and its harbor as the economic hub, Duisburg has undergone a structural change from relying on heavy industry to becoming a modern and service-oriented city. In light of current technology advances, the city's lord mayor, the city council, and their associates had a political mandate to explore and oversee the city's digital transformation. As a result, an SC initiative, named Smart City Duisburg, that aims to increase the quality of life, economic attractiveness, and sustainability, has been established. This initiative is defined in a strategic master plan, as reported separately [42], which aims to define a common understanding of the SC's purpose, its main goals and application domains. Duisburg classifies its SC activities according to different domains, namely smart economy, smart mobility, smart living, smart education, broadband, smart infrastructure, and e-government. The SC initiative focuses on a close collaboration between the city, local and city-owned companies, and research institutions.

The close involvement of this paper's authors enabled integrating research knowledge in the field of IS with the SC initiative. To support Duisburg's transformation, we followed the research approach described above and, among other activities, designed and implemented SC architecture principles and related deliverables [42]. These principles were intended to serve as a common baseline for an alignment between the strategic orientation of the SC initiative and the deployment of SC solutions.

4   Results

In this section, we describe our research results comprising the SC architecture principles, the SC architect role, and the SC EA structures we designed and implemented.

4.1   Architecture Principles

Following the approach described in Sect. 3.1, we developed architecture principles in close collaboration with the stakeholders of the SC initiative. Overall, we observed that to an even larger extent that when establishing architecture principles in companies, we have a specific and strong need to establish consensus about SC architecture principles between stakeholders. In the present case, we noted that most stakeholders are highly experienced administrative specialists or managers with limited EA and IT knowhow. We realized a high need to take care that all stakeholders thoroughly understand the principles and the rationale behind each principle. Based on these observations, we argue that for SC initiatives, first, building consensus and, second, implementing architectural thinking [43] seems to be more important and a crucial factor of success than in a company environment. Hence, when adding shared fundamental apps and services for the SC, it is crucial to first establish consensus about how these relate to and support the SC EA principles. If not, the principles may be weakened and the partners are less likely to adhere to the them.

In the case city a central theme for these principles is the goal to establish a common platform for SC related application that can be used by a variety of users, such as citizens as well as political, business and administrative players. In line with TOGAF, we classified each architecture principle as relating to either the business, data, application, or technology layer. We described each principle by the suggested categories of name, statement, rationale, and implications. Table 1 contains an overview of all SC architecture principles with a short description of each.

For the case city, the principles of the business domain are primarily focused on the development of an integrated SC platform that can be used by a variety of user groups and are compliant with the master plan. Therefore, a goal-oriented architecture development and an efficient centralized control is required. To ensure that all parties adhere to these long-term goals, we specified that organizations using the SC platform must comply with the principles. Exceptions from considering one or many principles are possible but must be approved by an architecture board. The principles of the business domain also cover the decision to run the SC platform on a locally settled data center and that employees but also SC applications needs to be certified to prove their compliance with the principles. Furthermore, our interviews revealed the need for a high SC platform stability, SC service availability, as well as minimizing costs for developing and operating SC applications. As an example, this can be achieved by modularization of standard components that can be reused via application programming interfaces (APIs). Modularization and reutilization increases resource efficiency, module quality, and reduces the complexity of contracts and transaction costs [26]. Principle three clarifies that an SC architect (see Sect. 4.2) must analyze risks, in particular information security risks, for SC applications and that each application requires an emergency plan fitting with the sensitivity of the application. Based on our observations, we argue that especially the first principle (stating that architecture principles are obligatory) and the sixth principle (SC certification of employees) are key for SC initiatives in the sense that these principles help address the need for consensus building and development of architectural thinking.

In addition, three main goals about data usage in the SC initiative have been derived from our workshops and interviews. First, a unified data access should be provided to support the development of innovative SC projects. Hence, users only need one account (with varying authentication mechanisms depending on security need) to log in to any SC application running on the platform. It also helps ensure compliance with data protection and security regulations. This demand is addressed by providing users the possibility to control which SC application has access to personal data. Second, an integrated data basis was required to maximize data quality and reuse. This way, updates in the case of changing data values are conducted automatically which can lead to a reduction of incorrect and redundant data input. An example is a change in the postal address of a citizen that only has to be made once. Third, a monitoring cockpit including the status of all SC applications as well as information about the city (e.g. environmental data, live traffic data) should be in place. Hence, all SC applications need an API for this. An integrated data platform can provide reduced development times for SC applications and enable efficient centralized control of operation data [44]. In particular, in principle 11 states that data must to an extent, based on the application context and type of data, be shared through interfaces to the Duisburg's Open Data portal and potentially to other SC applications. Such functionality strongly relates to data security and privacy choices, so principle 12 underlines that each SC application must afford transparent data usage and relevant data choices for users. For the case city it was a goal that such transparency and control would go beyond the regulatory requirements stemming from the General Data Protection Regulation (GDPR).

Principles in the application dimension are focused on providing user-friendly SC applications to ensure a high participation rate and satisfaction level of citizens. In the case city, the principles in this dimension were by some of the partners perceived as being fundamentally different to familiar working environments and revealed some tensions both regarding working practices of the city administration and other stakeholders and regarding the needs for modern user-oriented solution development in SC initiatives. Principle 13, for instance, includes usage of a local cloud operator which enables strict data protection and security and thus may increase user acceptance of SC applications. In an interview this was underlined by an IT manager of one of the city-owned companies who emphasized the need for advanced security measures and a high degree of control to protect user data at all cost. The resulting establishment of a centralized database (principle 9) likewise challenges current processes as the departments usually exchange data to a very limited extent. In addition, an important requirement demanded by the city's stakeholders was to ensure that all applications work on mobile devices – independently of the types of devices used. Following this principle, an emphasis should be on the usability of SC applications to minimize user effort and frustration [45]. This should be further supported by using a consistent design for SC applications. Thus, a unified user interface style guide is needed [46].

The technology principles are designed to offer guidance for making decisions on the technologies which should be implemented. An important requirement of the overarching SC initiative is to ensure that the communication of all SC applications is conducted through open and standardized APIs. This aims to reduce dependencies to specific manufacturers as well as avoid isolated applications and data sets. Following this requirement, it simplifies the integration of future applications, services and external products but also enable performance analysis of the architecture and platform [47]. Further simplification with regard to the interoperability of hardware and software components and the usage of existing know-how is supported by favoring technology partners for the development and operation of applications. However, SC applications should be independent from suppliers' product portfolios and the best available market solution should be chosen for each case. In this sense, competition between suppliers is intended to avoid strong dependencies on providers.

4.2 Smart City Architect Role

We supported the stakeholders in defining the architecture role that will enforce the principles and support partners in terms of architecture topics. Tasks, responsibilities, as well as the overall corresponding profile of the SC architect role were proposed.

The primary responsibility of the architect is to design and further develop the SC platform, as well as to translate strategic requirements into architectural guidelines. Another key task is to provide conceptual support and consultancy in the development and implementation of SC applications, and subsequently to monitor compliance with architecture principles and standards through certifying SC applications. Hence, the architect must revise and propose new SC principles and technical standards, as needed.

Table 1. SC architecture principles implemented in Smart City Duisburg

Business principles
1. Architecture principles are obligatory: The architecture principles pertain to all organizations deploying SC applications on the local cloud platform. (Violation of principles leads to no operation on the joint platform; exceptions handled by the SC architecture board.)
2. Operation of SC applications on the local cloud platform: The local cloud platform serves as the central focal point for users, facilitates the coordination of SC projects, and enables ensuring the other principles.
3. Risk evaluation & recovery plan of SC applications: The SC architect analyses and evaluates the risks and potential impacts of the SC applications. (Critical components need emergency guides.)
4. Support of modularization: Coherent components can be provided for other applications and services via interfaces. For standard components the modularization is obligatory.
5. Consequent reutilization: Software components must be reused whenever possible to reduce costs, unify efforts to improve software, and make the user experience coherent. (Exceptions: generally, avoid replacing already provided services or components with redundant services)
6. SC certification of employees: Employees must be certified as equipped to use the SC platform to ensure its development and security as intended.
7. Certification of SC applications: The applications running on the SC platform must follow its standards and principles and will be certified through the SC architect and the Architecture Board.

Data principles
8. Warranty of data security: Authorization concepts and prohibiting unauthorized access ensure the security and integrity of data. A data governance organization will be established to ensure compliance with the EU General Data Protection Regulation, national legislation, and the existing data security regimes of the city.
9. Integrated database: A central database or data lake integrates the data of single source systems and offers an automatic update when changes take place. Data security, as well as technical and economic framework conditions will be considered.
10. Central overview of information and steering: All SC applications shall connect with a central cockpit through programming interfaces. Integrating city-wide information enables a holistic view of Duisburg and the steering of urban applications.
11. Enabling open data: Compiled and merged data on the SC platform should be delivered for common use through interfaces or a separate open data portal.
12. Transparent data usage: The users of SC applications can examine the data which is ascertained by applications, and then assess how they will be processed further.

Application principles
13. Usage of a local cloud operator: A common cloud operator with a central data center and increased safety precautions (TÜV level 3) for the SC applications is favored. This local data center enables compliance with German and European data protection regulations and increases trust and user acceptance of data processing and the related SC solutions.
14. Mobile usage of SC applications: All SC applications are available via mobile devices and work independently of the device type of the end-user.
15. Usability and intuitive handling of SC applications: The SC applications show a consistent and a self-explaining interactivity so that applications can be used in an effective, efficient, and satisfying way, and are accessible for people with disabilities.
16. User interface (UI) style guide for SC applications: All SC applications follow a consistent UI style guide to ensure the applications are familiar in appearance and behavior.

(continued)

Table 1. (*continued*)

Technology principles
17. Communication across open and network-based interfaces: Open, standardized, and network-based interfaces enable communication and integration of all delivered SC applications.
18. Considering technology-business partnerships: Existing technology partnerships are preferentially considered regarding the development and operation of applications on the SC platform.
19. Independence from technology and software providers: Notwithstanding principle 18, SC applications use the best available technologies and applications, regardless of vendors ("best of breed"), to ensure competitiveness and independence.

Collaborating with the leaders on the program level and the respective project leaders, the architect must analyze and evaluate risks of SC applications and cooperate in developing corresponding emergency plans. The architect must monitor the SC architecture regularly and continuously to ensure early identification and elimination of performance and availability issues. The architect must also report regularly to the SC Architecture Board. As needed, the architect should define and further develop the EAM methods and related tool landscape to be used. Finally, the architect must evaluate new technologies and assess their applicability in the city's SC architecture.

4.3 Smart City Enterprise Architecture Governance Structures

It became evident that organizational structures are needed for planning and controlling SC architecture. Above all, a committee for the development of architecture with strategic guidelines and principles is indispensable. We aimed to find a balance between too little and too much control, so that the SC projects could be carried out quickly and flexibly. At the same time, the connection to already existing plans and structures of the city had to be maintained. In this context, the SC Architecture Board and the SC Architecture Forum were introduced. The SC Architecture Board directly supports the program administrators' work and monitors compliance with architecture principles and standards. It receives strategic guidelines from the SC Steering Committee at the portfolio level but can also submit its own recommendations and reports to the Steering Committee. The SC Architecture Forum serves as an exchange platform for interested stakeholders who want to be more involved in the SC architecture or want to write new proposals for the Architecture Board. The SC architect is organizationally affiliated at the program level of the Smart City Duisburg initiative. The corresponding responsible (R), accountable (A), consulted (C), and informed (I) of the roles SC architect (A), SC project managers (M), and SC project employees (E) are depicted in Fig. 2.

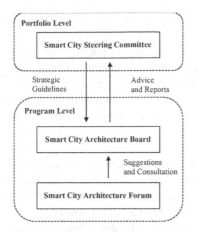

	A	M	E
Revision of architectural principles	R	C	I
Revision of architectural standards	R	C	I
Examination of the SC projects regarding their compliance to SC architecture principles	R	A	
Validation and approval of exceptions regarding architectural principles	R	A	
Certification of SC applications	R	A	
Analysis and evaluation of SC application risks	R	I	
Creation of emergency guides for SC applications	R	I	I

Fig. 2. SC architecture structures in Duisburg

5 Discussion and Conclusion

In the previous sections, we described the process of deriving SC architecture principles, as well as the principles themselves and the corresponding architect role and structures for the specific case of Duisburg. Using the ADR approach, we closely collaborated with the city and its SC partners in four cycles to come up with and implement the principles and structures that address their goals for the SC initiative, including a centralized SC platform.

The research presented in this paper constitutes a valuable contribution to the SC literature, given that existing literature largely neglects the importance of architecture principles for developing an SC EA. This paper does not only present such principles and corresponding roles, but also illuminates the process of creating these principles and roles in the course of an actual SC initiative. Given the representative characteristics of this case – including, for instance, the city's size as well as the economic, environmental, and social challenges it faces – we expect that other SC initiatives can learn from our approach and adopt it in order to develop specific principles for their respective initiatives.

Therefore, it is valuable to discuss the implementation and application of the SC EA principles in the case of Duisburg and how this did not take place without complications. One of these complications occurred during the implementation phase, where we observed that stakeholders' awareness of the principles was not as high as we had hoped, i.e., about half of them were not aware of the content of the principles. Others did not understand the principles in the degree required for adherence to them. Thus, in order to fully realize the potential benefits of SC architecture principles as mediators between high-level strategy and concrete design, these principles must be clearly and thoroughly communicated, ideally through many types of activities, such as architecture boards, the constant work of an SC architect, top managers acting as champions for the principles, and built-in reviews in the project portfolio process. Another problem was that no standards for the practical implementation of the principles had been defined. As a result, the principles were seen by some as esoteric and inconvenient. Defining a set of standards is likely to improve the stakeholders' understanding of the content and usefulness of the principles.

Our research certainly has some limitations. One such limitation consists in the fact that the presented artifacts resulted from the experience of a single case. For cities with divergent characteristics, such as small, very large cities, or cities with an entirely different legal structure, issues will arise that have not been fully covered in the context of our research, and a transfer of our results to such initiatives will require further considerations. Given our participatory role as researchers in this initiative, it was a natural choice to concentrate our observations on this single case. But future work should replicate our case study, identify differences regarding various contextual factors with respect to our study, thereby examining the actual role of these factors as well as the degree of transferability of the artifacts presented in this paper. In particular, it might be beneficial to adapt and apply the presented process in other medium-sized European cities and compare the resulting SC EA principles and their transferability between cities. Further, like other SC literature, our work is based on the general assumption that EAM is essentially applicable to the construct of SC, though this assumption has still to be sufficiently justified. Therefore, future work should be focused on conducting a detailed comparison between traditional enterprises and SC initiatives. Critical factors need to be identified that can be used to assess the applicability of EAM to the SC context, and possible alternative architecture approaches should as well be contemplated. Finally, while we believe our work to define SC architecture principles and structures is a step forward towards EAM for SCs, there is opportunity for research with both different approaches and related to other components of EAM in the SC context.

References

1. United Nations: World Urbanization Prospects: The 2018 Revision (2018)
2. Albino, V., Berardi, U., Dangelico, R.M.: Smart Cities: definitions, dimensions, performance, and initiatives. J. Urban Technol. **22**, 3–21 (2015). https://doi.org/10.1080/10630732.2014.942092
3. Cocchia, A.: Smart and digital city: a systematic literature review. In: Dameri, R.P., Rosenthal-Sabroux, C. (eds.) Smart City. PI, pp. 13–43. Springer, Cham (2014). https://doi.org/10.1007/978-3-319-06160-3_2
4. Neirotti, P., De Marco, A., Cagliano, A.C., Mangano, G., Scorrano, F.: Current trends in Smart City initiatives: some stylised facts. Cities **38**, 25–36 (2014). https://doi.org/10.1016/j.cities.2013.12.010
5. Nam, T., Pardo, T.A.: Smart city as urban innovation: focusing on management, policy, and context. In: Proceedings of the 5th International Conference on Theory and Practice of Electronic Governance, pp. 185–194. ACM, Washington, DC (2011)
6. Nam, T., Pardo, T.A.: Conceptualizing smart city with dimensions of technology, people, and institutions. In: Proceedings of the 12th Annual International Digital Government Research Conference: Digital Government Innovation in Challenging Times, pp. 282–291. ACM, New York (2011). https://doi.org/10.1145/2037556.2037602
7. Federal Institute for Building, U.A. and S.D.: Smart City Charter. https://www.bbsr.bund.de/BBSR/DE/Veroeffentlichungen/Sonderveroeffentlichungen/2017/smart-city-charta-de-eng-dl.pdf?__blob=publicationFile&v=v. Accessed 29 Aug 2018

8. Dameri, R., Rosenthal-Sabroux, C.: Smart city and value creation. In: Dameri, R.P., Rosenthal-Sabroux, C. (eds.) Smart City. PI, pp. 1–12. Springer, Cham (2014). https://doi.org/10.1007/978-3-319-06160-3_1

9. Alawadhi, S., et al.: Building understanding of smart city initiatives. In: Scholl, H.J., Janssen, M., Wimmer, M.A., Moe, C.E., Flak, L.S. (eds.) EGOV 2012. LNCS, vol. 7443, pp. 40–53. Springer, Heidelberg (2012). https://doi.org/10.1007/978-3-642-33489-4_4

10. Hollands, R.G.: Will the real smart city please stand up?: Intelligent, progressive or entrepreneurial? City. **12**, 303–320 (2008). https://doi.org/10.1080/13604810802479126

11. Chourabi, H., et al.: Understanding smart cities: an integrative framework. Presented at the Proceedings of the 45th Hawaii International Conference on System Sciences, January 2012. https://doi.org/10.1109/HICSS.2012.615

12. Simonofski, A., Asensio, E.S., Smedt, J.D., Snoeck, M.: Citizen participation in smart cities: evaluation framework proposal. In: IEEE Conference on Business Informatics, pp. 227–236. IEEE, Thessaloniki (2017). https://doi.org/10.1109/CBI.2017.21

13. EURACTIV: How many smart cities are there in Europe? https://www.euractiv.com/section/digital/infographic/how-many-smart-cities-are-there-in-europe/. Accessed 29 Aug 2018

14. Campbell, J., McDonald, C., Sethibe, T.: Public and private sector IT governance: identifying contextual differences. Austr. J. Inf. Syst. **16** (2010)

15. Ojo, A., Curry, E., Janowski, T.: Designing next generation smart city initiatives - harnessing findings and lessons from a study of ten smart city programs. In: ECIS 2014 Proceedings, p. 15. Tel Aviv (2014)

16. Mamkaitis, A., Bezbradica, M., Helfert, M.: Urban enterprise: a review of Smart City frameworks from an Enterprise Architecture perspective. In: 2016 IEEE International Smart Cities Conference (ISC2), pp. 1–5 (2016). https://doi.org/10.1109/ISC2.2016.7580810

17. Christensen, C.: The Innovator's Dilemma: When New Technologies Cause Great Firms to Fail. Harvard Business Review Press, Boston (2013)

18. Sethibe, T., Campbell, J., McDonald, C.: IT governance in public and private sector organisations: examining the differences and defining future research directions. In: ACIS 2007 Proceedings, p. 118 (2007)

19. Mamkaitis, A., Bezbradica, M., Helfert, M.: Urban Enterprise Principles development approach: a case from a European City. In: Thirty Seventh International Conference on Information Systems, Dublin, Ireland, p. 9 (2016)

20. Bastidas, V., Bezbradica, M., Helfert, M.: Cities as enterprises: a comparison of smart city frameworks based on enterprise architecture requirements. In: Alba, E., Chicano, F., Luque, G. (eds.) Smart Cities. Smart-CT 2017. LNCS, vol. 10268, pp. 20–28. Springer, Cham (2017). https://doi.org/10.1007/978-3-319-59513-9_3

21. Ahlemann, F., Stettiner, E., Messerschmidt, M., Legner, C.: Strategic Enterprise Architecture Management: Challenges, Best Practices, and Future Developments. Springer, Berlin (2012)

22. Aier, S., Riege, C., Winter, R.: Unternehmensarchitektur – Literaturüberblick und Stand der Praxis. Wirtschaftsinformatik **50**, 292–304 (2008)

23. Anthopoulos, L., Fitsilis, P.: Exploring architectural and organizational features in smart cities. In: 16th International Conference on Advanced Communication Technology, pp. 190–195 (2014). https://doi.org/10.1109/ICACT.2014.6778947

24. Anthopoulos, L.: Defining smart city architecture for sustainability. In: Proceedings of 14th Electronic Government and 7th Electronic Participation Conference (IFIP 2015), pp. 140–147 (2015)

25. Bawany, N.Z., Shamsi, J.A.: Smart city architecture: vision and challenges. Int. J. Adv. Comput. Sci. Appl. (IJACSA) **6**, 246–255 (2015)

26. Cavalcanti, J.C.: Effects of IT on Enterprise Architecture, Governance, and Growth. IGI Global (2015)

27. Greefhorst, D., Proper, E.: Architecture Principles: The Cornerstones of Enterprise Architecture. Springer, New York (2011)
28. Caragliu, A., Del Bo, C., Nijkamp, P.: Smart cities in Europe. J. Urban Technol. **18**, 45–59 (2011). https://doi.org/10.1080/10630732.2011.601117
29. Weill, P., Ross, J.W.: IT Governance: How Top Performers Manage IT Decision Rights for Superior Results. Harvard Business Review Press, Boston (2004)
30. Moss Kanter, R., Litow, S.S.: Informed and Interconnected: a Manifesto for Smarter Cities. SSRN Electr. J. (2009). https://doi.org/10.2139/ssrn.1420236
31. Brown, M.M., Brudney, J.L.: Public sector information technology initiatives: implications for programs of public administration. Admin. Soc. **30**, 421–442 (1998)
32. Greefhorst, D., Koning, H., van Vliet, H.: The many faces of architectural descriptions. Inf. Syst. Front. **8**, 103–113 (2006)
33. Richardson, G.L., Jackson, B.M., Dickson, G.W.: A principles-based enterprise architecture: lessons from Texaco and Star enterprise. MIS Q. **14**, 385–403 (1990)
34. The Open Group: The Open Group, TOGAF^{TM} Version 9. USA: ©2009 The Open Group. The Open Group, USA (2009)
35. Sein, M.K., Henfridsson, O., Purao, S., Rossi, M., Lindgren, R.: Action design research. MIS Q. **35**, 37–56 (2011)
36. Recker, J.: Scientific Research in Information Systems - A Beginner's Guide. Springer, Heidelberg (2013)
37. Susman, G.I., Evered, R.D.: An assessment of the scientific merits of action research. Adm. Sci. Q. **23**, 582 (1978). https://doi.org/10.2307/2392581
38. Mullarkey, M.T., Hevner, A.R.: An elaborated action design research process model. Eur. J. Inf. Syst. **28**, 6–20 (2019). https://doi.org/10.1080/0960085X.2018.1451811
39. Matthes, D.: Enterprise Architecture Frameworks Kompendium. Springer, Heidelberg (2011)
40. Organisation for Economic Cooperation and Development: Population by region - Urban population by city size - OECD Data. http://data.oecd.org/popregion/urban-population-by-city-size.htm. Accessed 22 May 2019
41. Giffinger, R., Fertner, C., Kramar, H., Kalasek, R., Pichler-Milanovic, N., Meijers, E.: Smart Cities: Ranking of European Medium-Sized Cities (2007)
42. Bergan, P., Mölders, A.-M., Rehring, K., Ahlemann, F., Decker, S., Reining, S.: Towards Designing Effective Governance Regimes for Smart City Initiatives: The Case of the City of Duisburg. Presented at the January 7 (2020). https://doi.org/10.24251/HICSS.2020.283
43. Winter, R.: Architectural thinking. Bus. Inf. Syst. Eng. **6**(6), 361–364 (2014). https://doi.org/10.1007/s12599-014-0352-2
44. Date, C.J.: An Introduction to Database Systems. Pearson, Upper Saddle River (2003)
45. Kahraman, Z.: Using user-centered design approach in course design. 2071–2076 (2010)
46. Nielsen, J.: Coordinating User Interfaces for Consistency. Morgan Kaufman, San Francisco (2002)
47. Iyer, B., Dreyfus, D., Gyllstrom, P.: A network-based view of enterprise architecture. In: Saha, P. (ed.) Handbook of Enterprise Systems Architecture in Practice (2007)

Analysing the Surface Urban Heat Island Effect with Copernicus Data

Lorenza Apicella$^{(\boxtimes)}$ [iD], Alfonso Quarati [iD], and Monica De Martino$^{(\boxtimes)}$ [iD]

Institute for Applied Mathematics and Information Technologies - National
Research Council, Genoa, Italy
{lorenza.apicella,alfonso.quarati,monica.demartino}@ge.imati.cnr.it
http://www.imati.cnr.it

Abstract. To ensure that the great opportunities of Copernicus satellite data offered, in open and free mode, are fully grasped, a major awareness of them must be widespread among European citizens, companies, and public administrations. To this end, initiatives such as the EO-UPTAKE Ligurian regional project aim at studying application scenarios centered on the use of Copernicus data and the dissemination of their outcomes to citizens and local authorities. As an example of this activity, the paper focuses on an application scenario for monitoring the Urban Heat Island (UHI) effect, considered among the most impacting effects on urban ecosystems, analyzed in the metropolitan area of Genoa. We discuss some strengths and weaknesses in the use of Copernicus satellite data and services, intending to provide a preliminary set of guidelines, useful not only for analyzing the UHI phenomenon in other urban contexts but also as a concrete example of exploitation of the Copernicus ecosystem.

Keywords: Copernicus uptake · Sentinel-3 · Open data · Surface urban heat island

1 Introduction

The climatic phenomenon Urban Heat Island (UHI), affecting urban areas that tend to have a higher temperature than the surrounding rural areas, caused by urbanization and industrialization processes, represents one of the main anthropogenic alterations of Earth environments [17]. It is seen as one of the main ecological problems in the 21st century due to the rapid urbanization and global warming, with dramatic effects on human health and well-being, rise in energy consumption, and mortality rates increase. The identification and the management of UHI contributing and mitigating factors is an open challenge, addressed by urban development strategies and policies aimed at making cities inclusive, safe, resilient and sustainable. Therefore, the need to understand the UHI phenomenon has aroused an increasing worldwide research interest since 2005 [8,17].

UHI may be quantified from the air temperature or from the land surface temperatures (LST) [23]. The atmospheric UHIs are assessed with in situ sensors or model data which provide air temperature information [6,7,16], while

© Springer Nature Switzerland AG 2021
A. Kö et al. (Eds.): EGOVIS 2021, LNCS 12926, pp. 61–72, 2021.
https://doi.org/10.1007/978-3-030-86611-2_5

the surface UHIs (SUHI) are measured by airborne or satellite remote sensing platforms which detect LST [22, 27, 29]. In particular, satellites provide thermal LST data with high spatial and temporal coverage, allowing the employment of such data for urban planning and surface temperature-based heat island effect monitoring [28].

Through a constellation of six Sentinel satellites, the Copernicus Programme, developed by the European Space Agency (ESA) and the European Union (EU) following the Open Data strategy, provides free data and information derived from Earth Observation (EO) satellite images, covering Europe and almost all of Earth. It aims at supporting the environmental and health protection policies of European public administrations and promote economic growth in Europe [9]. The environmental information obtained by the Sentinel satellites consists of thermal, optical, and high-frequency radar images useful for atmospheric, oceanic, and terrestrial monitoring. The S-3 thermal images delivered since 2017 by the Sentinel-3 mission are appropriate to study the SUHI phenomenon as provide ready to use LST measurement[1] [12].

Despite its undeniable potential, the enormous amount of data, up to 12 terabytes per day, collected by Copernicus satellites runs the risk, common to other public Open Data resources [5, 18–21], to be little or no used. To prevent the benefits of Copernicus data from being lost, the European Commission launched a user dissemination strategy [2] in 2016, promoting various initiatives to raise awareness among users to increase competitiveness and dissemination of skills. Among these, the EO-UPTAKE project[2], funded by the Liguria Region, Italy, in 2019, promotes the development and dissemination of skills and competencies linked to the exploitation of Copernicus data and services and their integration with other (local) datasets and applications.

The paper has as its primary objective the exemplification, through the discussion of an application scenario, of the opportunities offered by the Copernicus ecosystem in responding to the needs of public administrations in terms of public health and environmental protection. As such, we present the workflow to evaluate the SUHI effect in the metropolitan area of Genoa (Italy) during the summer of 2020 using the S-3 images as the primary source of information. We also provide some guidelines relating to the information resources and tools used for calculating SUHIs, evaluating their strengths and weaknesses compared to other technological solutions.

2   Copernicus-Based UHI Analysis

2.1   Application Scenario

The metropolitan city of Genoa, the capital of the Liguria Region, with a population of about 800,000 inhabitants, represents the largest and most densely populated urban agglomeration in the Region, whose territory, narrow by the

---

[1] https://sentinel.esa.int/web/sentinel/technical-guides/sentinel-3-slstr.
[2] http://www.gisig.eu/projects/eouptake/.

Mediterranean Sea and the steep hills of the hinterland, over the centuries has undergone an upheaval of its natural landform as a result of human activities, such as modifications of the drainage network, excavations, and filling, building and street constructions, particularly intensified in the 1960s and 1970s [11]. Considering the climatic, demographic, and orographic specificities that differentiate Genoa from other European cities, such as London, Athens, and Stockholm, whose UHI effects have already been studied through the use of Copernicus S-3 satellite data [14, 22, 24, 25], we deemed it appropriate to investigate the adoption of Copernicus resources to analyze the SUHI effect on the Genoese territory.

The SUHI intensity is computed as the LST difference between an urban and its surrounding rural area. Copernicus LST data are measured by the SLSTR (Sea and Land Surface Temperature Radiometer) S-3 sensor, whose mission is characterised by a two-satellites (S-3A in orbit since 2016, S-3B since 2018) constellation [10]; the main objectives are to support the ocean forecasting systems, the environment and the climate monitoring with the measurements of sea surface features (*e.g.* topography and colour), land surface colour and the LST. The spatial resolution of this band is $1 \, \text{km}^2$, and the revisit time of S-3 on the area of interest is one day.

The UHI calculation process also integrated Copernicus data with other Open Data sources. On the one hand, to delimit the study area, we used the vector layers that describe the provincial boundaries and the contour lines provided by the Geoportal of the Liguria Region[3], that allows free access to the updated and structured catalog of geo-referenced regional map data. Furthermore, for the determination of rural surfaces and rural areas, we have integrated the CORINE Land Cover map layer[4] (2018), which provides geographical information on land cover at a 100 m spatial resolution with different land cover categories [1,4], made available by the Copernicus Land Monitoring Service (CLMS).

2.2   Genoa SUHI Workflow

The territory of the municipality of Genoa extends for $240.28 \, \text{km}^2$ and about thirty kilometres along the coastline. The municipal territory has numerous valleys that descend towards the sea from the Ligurian-Po watershed, with mountain reliefs at altitudes between 400 and 1200 m high, which are located between 6 and 10 km from the sea. The orography of the metropolitan area locates Genoa among the Italian metropolitan cities with the greatest variety of climate types. Specifically, the coastline presents the greatest climate differentiation. The area of interest (AOI) for this application scenario is bounded by the borders of the province of Genoa.

We analysed 40 S-3 images acquired in the period between June 21st and September 22nd 2020, which defines the summer season. Figure 1 summarizes the SUHI workflow steps. Firstly, we downloaded from Copernicus Open Access Hub[5] 4-night and 4-day images respectively for June and September, 6-night

---

[3] geoportal.regione.liguria.it/.

[4] land.copernicus.eu/pan-european/corine-land-cover.

[5] scihub.copernicus.eu/dhus/#/home.

and 6-day images for July and August; the time step between the acquisitions is about 5 days. This variability is due to the presence of images affected by cloud cover.

The resources provided by Copernicus are accessible to users through tools[6] such as the Copernicus Open Access Hub. In most cases, data and information can be browsed/discovered without prior registration, but registration is required for downloading and/or for loading a personal cart. User login allows the access to all Sentinel Missions data with an interactive graphical user interface. The procedure starts selecting a target area, setting the parameters of interest (e.g. Orbit, data format, period of interest, etc.) and searching for Sentinel data.

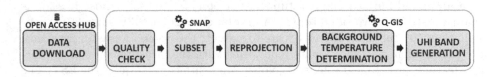

Fig. 1. Processing workflow for SUHI assessment with S-3 image.

Then the data pre-processing is performed with the Sentinel Application Platform (SNAP[7]) provided by ESA. Once the S-3 images are imported on SNAP the first step consists of the cloud cover quality check to discard the partially cloudy images and the ones out of the area of interest (AOI). SNAP allows to batch-process multiple images:

1. to perform the precise AOI subset to reduce its original extent;
2. to reduce the number of bands selecting only the bands LST and x_in, y_in, lat_x, lon_x (for geographical referencing);
3. to reproject the S-3 image to an appropriate map projection by a Reference System assignment;
4. to export the raster products in .BIGTiff format.

We used Quantum-GIS (Q-GIS[8]) to perform the SUHI band computation. The first step creates, for each month, the average LST raster of the AOI, for both the day and night acquisition. Subsequently, the background rural mean temperature, *i.e. the LST mean value of pixels covering rural areas,* is computed.

Owing to Genoa's very complex morphology in the distribution of urban agglomerations, for the highly variable orography and proximity to the sea, the different areas of the municipality have different average temperatures due to the altitude thermal gradient. It is, therefore, necessary to select the rural areas below a given elevation, to avoid considering temperature-affecting factors that are not pertinent to the purpose of the study. With the boundaries of the administrative borders and the contour lines for the AOI, the selection of the areas

---

[6] https://scihub.copernicus.eu/.

[7] step.esa.int/main/toolboxes/snap.

[8] qgis.org/it/site/.

from which to calculate the average background rural temperature is constrained by two criteria: i) the first criterion constrains the non-overlapping and non-adjacency with urban areas, as defined by Corine Land Cover 2018; ii) the other constrains the altitude to lower values at 140 m above sea level, which represents the altimetric belt where most of the urban agglomerates are present, as shown in Fig. 2.

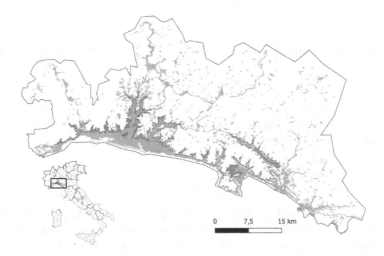

Fig. 2. Sample rural areas for the background rural temperature retrieval in the AOI: Sample rural areas (Light Green) are selected owing to the height above sea level (< 140 m, red line) in absence of impervious surfaces (grey areas). (Color figure online)

Once the rural areas are selected, the mean monthly temperature value for rural areas is retrieved to derive the average day and night monthly SUHI, following Eq. 1:

$$SUHI = LST - BackgroundRuralTemperature \tag{1}$$

Figure 3 reports the resulting average SUHI effect for day and night in summer 2020. It shows Genoa urban areas where the difference in temperature to the surrounding rural area is on average higher (up to 4° during the day) during the summer season. The differences between the daily and nightly seasonal patterns are mainly due to the nature of the SUHI effect: active solar radiation on the Earth's surface increases the LST of particularly reflective surfaces, such as large urban areas during the daytime, thus raising maximum values. The nightly SUHI effect, as explained by Lu et al. [15], owing to the absence of active solar radiation, is less intense in term of temperature variations but more widespread. Positive anomalies in temperature variation are detectable in the urban areas.

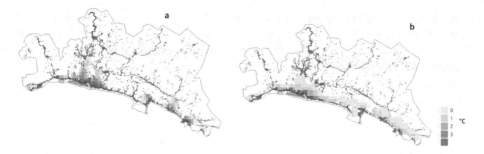

Fig. 3. SUHI daily (a) and nightly (b) average for summer 2020 in Genoa metropolitan area.

Figure 4 reports the same behavior, where the SUHI trend along Genoa's coastline is shown concerning land cover classes, urban or rural; a wide variability in the seasonal daily trend is detectable.

3   Discussion

Some strengths, possible criticalities, and limitations of the information resources and application tools related to the Copernicus ecosystem emerged from the SUHI scenario development. On that basis, in the following, we summarize a preliminary set of guidelines aimed at users with low expertise in the use of satellite data that are interested in creating added-value applications with the open data made available by Copernicus.

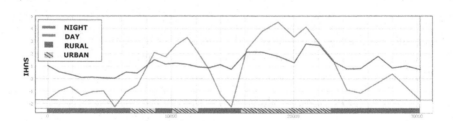

Fig. 4. Daily (red line) and nightly (blue line) SUHI seasonal profile for summer 2020 along Genoa central coastline (1 km wide, 30 km long), in relation to urban (grey) and rural (green) land cover classes (Corine Land Cover) of the same profile. (Color figure online)

Copernicus Data and Resources - Satellite images are produced at various levels, allowing users to choose the level of processing that best suits their purposes. These processing levels may vary depending on the satellite, although generally are considered four levels, each bearing different information. Level 0 products are full resolution raw data as measured by the satellite sensor(s), while at higher levels, raw data is converted to more usable parameters and formats. In particular, the S-3 SLSTR data is supplied into three processing levels[9]:

- Level-0 data, which are not disseminated to Sentinel-3 users;
- Level-1 data, for which radiometric and geographic positioning corrections are made on each pixel;
- Level-2 data (L2), derived from Level-1 products, which contains computed bands for sea surface temperature, LST and fire radiative power.

SUHI assessments result indeed particularly eased with the use of LST band from S-3 Level 2 data since the retrieval of the required band is performed upstream data distribution through specific algorithms.

The EO data is conveyed by Copernicus also through a set of 'Core Services' that rework and convert the data of the above levels into more immediately usable layers, which provide, generally free of charge, variables and ready-to-use parameters specific to the theme. Although these resources are more easily exploited by non-expert users, they do not always perfectly meet the objectives and requirements of the application. Regarding the study of the UHI effect, this is the case of the Copernicus Climate Change Monitoring Service (C3S), which provides two types of resources (see Table 1).

Table 1. C3S resources for UHI intensity.

Resource	Pro	Cons
UHI intensity layer	High spatial resolution (100 m)	Low temporal resolution (from 2008 to 2017)
	Ready to use	Available only for 100 european cities
ERA-5 (T2m)	High temporal resolution (1 h, available since 1981)	Low spatial resolution (4 km)
	Ready to use	

The first is a collection of day and night UHI intensity time-series, relative to 100 European cities[10], including Genoa, supplied as annual maps showing the average summer and winter values, covering the period between 2008 and 2017 with a spatial resolution of 100 m. Since our study relates to 2020 we have not made use of this resource. The second, UHI related, C3S resource is the ERA-5[11] dataset that provides a temperature layer of 2m (T2m) on an hourly scale for the whole of Europe from 1981 to today. Although this resource is suitable for the atmospheric evaluation of the UHI effect, it is not usable for the calculation of SUHI as presented in Sect. 2.

---

[9] sentinels.copernicus.eu/web/sentinel/user-guides/Sentinel-3-slstr/processing-levels.
[10] cds.climate.copernicus.eu/cdsapp#!/Software/app-health-urban-heat-islands-current-climate?tab = app.
[11] cds.climate.copernicus.eu/cdsapp#/Dataset/reanalysis-era5-land?Tab=overview.

Spatial and Temporal Resolution Trade-Off - The thermal infrared remote sensing sensors, widely used to derive LST, are currently characterised by the limited spatial resolution or temporal coverage (yearly, seasonal, diurnal, and nocturnal) [8, 17]. In the current satellite images, a high spatial resolution usually corresponds to a low temporal resolution: the most popular Open Data source is Landsat-8 which provides a measurement of about every 16 days at 100 m for Europe (see Table 2). Other satellite sources, with limited use, are MODIS with 4–6 measurements in near real-time at 1 km and ASTER with measurement about every 16 days at 90 m [30].

Table 2. Landsat 8 S-3 thermal data features comparison.

Satellite Data	Pro	Cons
S-3 Level 2	High temporal resolution (1 day, since 2017)	Low spatial resolution (1 km)
	Ready to use LST band	Offline data archiving (LTA)
	Daily and nightly acquisitions	
Landsat-8 Level 2	High spatial resolution (100 m, since 2013)	Low temporal resolution (16 days for Europe)
		Only daily acquisition

Recently, the release of Copernicus S-3 mission data has improved temporal coverage, especially for the European continent. For this area, comparing to Landsat-8, S-3 has the advantage of having a better temporal resolution, with a revisit cycle of less than one day at the middle latitudes. Moreover, it is worth mentioning that S-3 images are available for both daytime and night-time, providing the opportunity to assess SUHI day-night variation. The high temporal resolution allows also to overcome the cloud-cover issue, which affects the quality of thermal images; in fact, variable weather conditions could result in a significant missing-data problem with lower acquisition frequencies.

On the other hand, the S-3 LST band is at 1 km^2 grid-scale, which is quite a coarse value for monitoring high-variability local phenomena such SUHIs. This aspect may be compensated by applying downscaling algorithms proposed in the literature [3, 13, 26, 30], which consist in re-sampling processes that convert remote sensing low resolution data in high spatial resolution layers through the information extracted from higher spatial resolution satellite data. E.g., combining Sentinel's daily acquisitions and LANDSAT-8 finer scale is possible to obtain daily-nightly accurate thermal images for SUHI local assessment.

A further reason that made us select the Copernicus data instead of the Landsat one, is that the S-3 images have a ready-to-use LST band, with an accuracy of 1° K (even higher at night when the differential surface heating is absent[12]). Conversely, LST information is provided implicitly in Landsat-8 data, thus requiring a more complex SUHI processing workflow.

Data Integration - The opportunity to integrate other data sources makes the implementation of applications based on Copernicus resources more effective. In the SUHI case, we used the resources provided by the CLMS service and the the Liguria region geoportal.

The Liguria Region geoportal, following the accessibility and interoperability objectives of the INSPIRE[13] and OGC standards[14], provides free of charge all the map layers of the Regional Information System through Web Map Services (WMS), to be exploited by GIS applications supporting the use of Web Feature Services (WFS). It is possible to access and browse the catalog of Geoportal maps directly from the GIS platform or, through a Web Viewer. After authentication to the portal and a request via e-mail we received a special link to download the layers of our interest for the SUHI scenario: the shapefiles of the administrative boundaries and the contour lines of the Genoa metropolitan area.

The Corine Land Cover provided by the Copernicus CLMS service supplies a vector-based dataset including 44 land cover and land use classes. It is highly reliable, and the last update on the land cover layer was carried out following the standards of "EEA Technical Guidelines[15] in 2018. Indeed, the small land cover changes which may occur in two years are not substantial for the objectives of this work focused on 2020. We integrated this layer with the land cover to derive the rural background temperature (see Fig. 2).

Performance Issues - To manage and batch process multiple satellite images for the creation of time series, it is necessary to have hardware with minimum performance requirements. For example, the SNAP guidelines recommend having at least 4 Gb of RAM and 10 GB of free memory, although, in our experience, this basic equipment has not been free from performance problems. An alternative solution is provided by the free and open cloud platform Research And User Support (RUS[16]), which hosts a suite of open-source toolboxes pre-installed on virtual machines, which allow registered users to manage and process data derived from the Copernicus Sentinel satellite constellation. After a trial period, deemed necessary to become familiar with the Copernicus ecosystem, users are supposed to be able to continue their activities independently, outside RUS[17].

Data downloading via the Copernicus Open Access Hub - Guided User Interface is a viable option for non-expert users and usually does not take much time unless the images are stored in the long-term archive (LTA). In this case, only

---

[12] sentinels.copernicus.eu/web/sentinel/user-guides/sentinel-3-slstr/overview/geophysical-measurements/land-surface-temperature.

[13] inspire.ec.europa.eu/inspire-directive/2.

[14] www.ogc.org/standards.

[15] eea.europa.eu/publications/technical_report_2007_17.

[16] rus-copernicus.eu/portal/.

[17] rus-copernicus.eu/portal/terms-and-conditions.

one archived image can be downloaded every 30 min. As an alternative solution, the LTA hub API[18] can be used. In this case, through appropriate code scripts implemented, for example, in Python, it is possible to download a batch of multiple images at once.

4 Conclusions and Future Works

The EO-UPTAKE regional project acts as a promoter for widespread understanding and adoption of the EO resources freely released by the Copernicus programme. To this end, we deployed a strategy based on an exemplary approach that illustrates how to access, process, and take advantage of these resources.

The document discusses the workflow for calculating the SUHI effect, useful in supporting urban environmental monitoring. The contribution results in a set of guidelines pointed at a wide range of users addressing the challenges and gaps related to the lack of experience in EO data and the GIS sector. We discuss strengths and weaknesses encountered in the scenario development concerning the following aspects: the spatial and temporal factors trade-off, the motivation behind the selection of Copernicus satellite image or a ready-to-use service, the benefits of the Copernicus product integration with different sources of information, and technological performance issues.

Future work foresees the extension of the guidelines based on the user uptake strategy undertaken in the project. We will explore other application scenarios that require the study and use of the Copernicus products to provide a comprehensive overview of the skills required for a non-expert user to benefit from the Copernicus ecosystem. As a final note, we observe that the period selected for the analysis, the summer of the year 2020, was concomitant with the first phase of the COVID-19 pandemic, and the constraints and limitations placed on mobility made traffic and other urban activities lower than in previous years. Further development of the analysis could consider integrating data on mobility, electricity consumption (due to a possible increase in the use of air conditioners in homes) and verify whether and to what extent the urban heat island effect has been different from that recorded in previous years.

Acknowledgments. The work is supported by the European Social Fund, Liguria Region 2014–2020, Axis 3, s.o. 10.5. We thank GISIG, in particular Silvia Gorni and Roderic Molina, for their precious collaboration as project partners.

References

1. Environmental European Agency: CORINE Land Cover Legend (1994). http:// land.copernicus.eu/eagle/files/eagle-related-projects/pt_clc-conversion-to-fao-lccs3_dec2010
2. Copernicus User Uptake (2016). https://op.europa.eu/en/publication-detail/-/publication/62101cd2-fbba-11e5-b713-01aa75ed71a1

---

[18] readthedocs.org/projects/sentinelsat/downloads/pdf/master/.

3. Bonafoni, S.: Downscaling of landsat and MODIS land surface temperature over the heterogeneous urban area of Milan. IEEE J. Select. Topics Appl. Earth Observ. Remote Sens. **9**(5), 2019–2027 (2016)
4. Büttner, G., Feranec, J., Jaffrain, G., Mari, L., Maucha, G., Soukup, T.: The CORINE land cover 2000 project. EARSeL eProc. **3**(3), 331–346 (2004)
5. Cheval, S., et al.: Meteorological and ancillary data resources for climate research in urban areas. Climate **8**(3), 8030037 (2020)
6. Clay, R., Guan, H., Wild, N., Bennett, J., Vinodkumar, Ewenz, C.: Urban Heat Island traverses in the City of Adelaide, South Australia. Urban Clim. **17**, 89–101 (2016)
7. Dash, P., Göttsche, F.M., Olesen, F.S., Fischer, H.: Land surface temperature and emissivity estimation from passive sensor data: theory and practice-current trends. Int. J. Remote Sens. **23**(13), 2563–2594 (2002)
8. Deilami, K., Kamruzzaman, M., Liu, Y.: Urban heat island effect: a systematic review of spatio-temporal factors, data, methods, and mitigation measures. Int. J. Appl. Earth Observ. Geoinf. **67**, 30–42 (2018)
9. Doldrina, C.: Open data and earth observations: the case of opening up access to and use of earth observation data through the global earth observation system of systems. J. Intell. Prop. Info. Tech. Electr. Com. L. **6**, 73 (2015)
10. Donlon, C., et al.: The global monitoring for environment and security (GMES) sentinel-3 mission. Remote Sens. Environ. **120**, 37–57 (2012)
11. Faccini, F., Giardino, M., Paliaga, G., Perotti, L., Brandolini, P.: Urban geomorphology of Genoa old city (Italy). J. Maps 1–14 (2020)
12. Hidalgo García, D., Arco Díaz, J.: Modeling of the Urban Heat Island on local climatic zones of a city using Sentinel 3 images: Urban determining factors. Urban Clim. **37**, 100840 (2021)
13. Huang, B., Wang, J., Song, H., Fu, D., Wong, K.: Generating high spatiotemporal resolution land surface temperature for urban heat island monitoring. IEEE Geosci. Remote Sens. Lett. **10**(5), 1011–1015 (2013)
14. Li, H., et al.: A new method to quantify surface urban heat island intensity. Sci. Total Environ. **624**, 262–272 (2018)
15. Lu, L., Weng, Q., Xiao, D., Guo, H., Li, Q., Hui, W.: Spatiotemporal variation of surface urban heat islands in relation to land cover composition and configuration: a multi-scale case study of Xi'an, China. Remote Sens. **12**(17), 12172713 (2020)
16. Nichol, J.E., Fung, W.Y., se Lam, K., Wong, M.S.: Urban heat island diagnosis using ASTER satellite images and 'in situ' air temperature. Atmosph. Res. **94**(2), 276–284 (2009)
17. Oke, T.R.: The energetic basis of the urban heat island. Q. J. R. Meteorol. Soc. **108**(455), 1–24 (1982)
18. Quarati, A., De Martino, M.: Open government data usage: a brief overview. In: Proceedings of the 23rd International Database Applications & Engineering Symposium (IDEAS 2019), Athens, Greece, June 10–12, 2019. pp. 28:1–28:8. ACM (2019)
19. Quarati, A., De Martino, M.: Geospatial open data usage and metadata quality. ISPRS Int. J. Geo-Inf. **10**, 10010030 (2021)
20. Quarati, A., Raffaghelli, J.E.: Do researchers use open research data? Exploring the relationships between usage trends and metadata quality across scientific disciplines from the Figshare case. J. Inf. Sci. (2020)
21. Quarati, A.: Open government data: usage trends and metadata quality. J. Inf. Sci. (2021, to appear)

22. Ravanelli, R., et al.: Monitoring the impact of land cover change on surface urban heat island through google earth engine: proposal of a global methodology, first applications and problems. Remote Sens. **10**(9), 10091488 (2018)
23. Schwarz, N., Schlink, U., Franck, U., Grossmann, K.: Relationship of land surface and air temperatures and its implications for quantifying urban heat island indicators–an application for the city of Leipzig (Germany). Ecol. Indic. **18**, 693–704 (2012)
24. Shumilo, L., Kussul, N., Shelestov, A., Korsunska, Y., Yailymov, B.: Sentinel-3 urban heat island monitoring and analysis for kyiv based on vector data. In: 2019 10th International Conference on Dependable Systems, Services and Technologies (DESSERT). pp. 131–135. IEEE (2019)
25. Sobrino, J.A., Irakulis, I.: A methodology for comparing the surface urban heat island in selected urban agglomerations around the world from Sentinel-3 SLSTR data. Remote Sens. **12**(12), 2052 (2020)
26. Stathopoulou, M., Cartalis, C.: Downscaling AVHRR land surface temperatures for improved surface urban heat island intensity estimation. Remote Sens. Environ. **113**(12), 2592–2605 (2009)
27. Tran, H., Uchihama, D., Ochi, S., Yasuoka, Y.: Assessment with satellite data of the urban heat island effects in Asian mega cities. Int. J. Appl. Earth Observ. Geoinf. **8**(1), 34–48 (2006)
28. Voogt, J., Oke, T.: Thermal remote sensing of urban climates. Remote Sen. Environ. **86**(3), 370–384 (2003)
29. Zhao, X., Yang, S., Shen, S., Hai, Y., Fang, Y.: Analyzing the relationship between urban heat island and land use/cover changes in Beijing using remote sensing images. In: Gao, W., Jackson, T.J. (eds.) Remote Sens. Model. Ecosys. Sustain. VI, vol. 7454, pp. 320–329. International Society for Optics and Photonics, SPIE (2009)
30. Zhou, D., et al.: Satellite remote sensing of surface urban heat islands: progress, challenges, and perspectives. Remote Sens. **11**(1), 48 (2019)

Vulnerability of State-Provided Electronic Identification: The Case of ROCA in Estonia

Astrid Valtna-Dvořák[1], Silvia Lips[1], Valentyna Tsap[1(✉)], Rain Ottis[2],
Jaan Priisalu[2], and Dirk Draheim[1]

[1] Information Systems Group, Tallinn University of Technology, Estonia,
Akadeemia tee 15a, 12618 Tallinn, Estonia
{silvia.lips,valentyna.tsap,dirk.draheim}@taltech.ee
[2] Centre for Digital Forensics and Cyber Security, Tallinn University of Technology,
Estonia, Akadeemia tee 15a, 12618 Tallinn, Estonia
{rain.ottis,jaan.priisalu}@taltech.ee

Abstract. The purpose of this research is to provide a detailed description of the 2017 ROCA (Return of the Coppersmith's Attack) case in Estonia and to explore what implications this large-scale security risk poses on a fully rolled-out state-provided eID scheme. The analysis focuses on three areas, i.e., (i) the states political tasks and responsibilities, (ii) the role of the ICT industry in the eID provision process; and, (iii) the opportunities and obligations for the end users, including the state itself as the primary end user of the eID. We have conducted a thematic analysis of 32 semi-structured interviews of 41 Estonian high-level experts closely involved in solving the 2017 ROCA vulnerability case in Estonia. These interviews provide a deep insight into the crisis management process as well as into the characteristics of the Estonian eID area. Based on the insights from the Estonian case, we suggest a paradigm shift of eID management that recognises eID as the citizens right and its provision as the state's obligation.

Keywords: Return of the Coppersmith's Attack vulnerability ·
ROCA · eID management

1 Introduction

Electronic identification (eID) is becoming more and more relevant globally. Many societies, business entities and governments are building or redesigning their operational processes upon the functionalities of digital identification, authentication, and the use of digital signatures. This leads to the more specific research problem at hand: the usage of eID necessarily causes wider sociotechnical effects [5,6,10].

© Springer Nature Switzerland AG 2021
A. Kö et al. (Eds.): EGOVIS 2021, LNCS 12926, pp. 73–85, 2021.
https://doi.org/10.1007/978-3-030-86611-2_6

On August 30, 2017, Estonia was notified about the ROCA (Return of the Coppersmith's Attack) cryptography vulnerability on the chips used in the Estonian ID-cards. According to the research group that discovered the vulnerability, the RSA (Rivest-Shamir-Adleman) cryptographic key pair generation in chips contained a critical flaw [15], which allowed private keys to be derived from the public keys, potentially allowing for a malicious misuse of any of the affected ID-cards [7]. The ROCA vulnerability affected an estimated minimum of 1 billion chips around the world in a variety of computing devices and on plastic cards (driving licences, passports, access cards etc.). In Estonia, 750,000 ID-card have been affected. The Estonian case was exceptional due to the significance of the ID-card for the Estonian public administration and business environment.

The aim of this paper is to analyse the implications of the 2017 ROCA case on Estonian state-provided eID. The analysis focuses on three areas: the state's political tasks and responsibilities; the role if the ICT industry in the eID provision process; and thirdly, the opportunities and obligations for the end users, including the state itself as the primary end user of the eID. The paper answers to the following research question: what implications does the 2017 ROCA case in Estonia present on the eID mechanism provided by the state?

We use the model for institutional design for complex technological systems by Koppenjan and Groenewegen [9] to gain deeper understanding of the Estonian e-government systems and e-government ecosystem. The research findings presented below reveal a dependency on eID from the state's perspective and a prevalent demand for eID by the end users (*"Nobody wants to go back to paper."*). We suggest a paradigm shift in eID management that recognises eID as the citizens' right and its provision as the state's obligation.

The paper proceeds as follows. In Sect. 2, we provide an insight into the research design and methods. In Sect. 3, we give an overview of the Estonian eID ecosystem, a more detailed description of the ROCA case, and an overview of the theoretical background. In Sect. 4, we present the results of the thematic analysis of the interviews. In Sect. 5, we analyse the research findings and finish with conclusions in Sect. 6.

2   Research Design and Method

The Tallinn University of Technology, Centre for Digital Forensics and Cyber Security, carried out an in-depth study [3] about the lessons learned from the 2017 ROCA case in February–April 2018. The study was commissioned by the Estonian Information System Authority (ISA) and consisted of 32 semi-structured interviews with 41 individuals. The circle of interviewees included all experts that were the closest involved with the resolution of the ROCA case in Estonia and represented the majority of the public and private sector stakeholders in the Estonian eID area. The main purpose of the study was to identify lessons learned from the ROCA case and formulate a list of policy recommendations for practical application. The study focused on eID management and crisis management aspects of the 2017 ROCA case in Estonia.

The paper at hand is a continuation of this earlier work, an in-depth analysis of the above-mentioned interviews, concentrating on the wider socio-technical implications of the ROCA case on state-provided means of digital identification. The primary research method is thematic analysis of these 32 semi-structured interviews [2]. The interviews addressed each interviewees' role in the eID management and crisis handling process, their knowledge and perspective of the handling of the ROCA vulnerability, thus offering a rich and multi-angled description of the Estonian eID ecosystem at the time of the 2017 ROCA case. The complete data set was used and fully analysed in this research. An inductive, data-driven approach was chosen for conducting the thematic analysis. The themes and codes were formed semantically, resulting from their surface level meaning. The coding phase produced 1049 coding references and 63 codes that represented the full data set. Three themes were chosen to compile the results of the thematic analysis: "State and Policies", "Market and the EU (European Union)"; and "End User".

The first phase of the interview analysis was done independently of scientific literature on eID and related fields. An overview of scientific literature was added to the final conclusions of the research results to better contextualise the author's findings in the relevant academic literature. The thematic analysis was conducted using NVIVO qualitative data analysis software.

3   Background

3.1   The Estonian eID Ecosystem

The Estonian eID ecosystem is based on a PKI (public key infrastructure), which is managed in close cooperation with different public and private authorities [11]. Main involved parties from the public sector: the Information System Authority (ISA)[1] (responsible for the functioning of the eID and the whole PKI system), the Police and Border Guard Board (PBGB) (responsible for identification of persons and identity management)[2], the ICT and Development Center (SMIT) (develops, procures and manages ICT systems related to the identity management and identity documents field)[3] and – from the policy making perspective – several ministries and governmental bodies such as the Ministry of the Interior, the Ministry of Economic Affairs and Communications, the Ministry of Foreign Affairs and the Government Office. From the private sector, the most significant players in the ecosystem are: SK ID Solutions AS (provides certificates for the eID documents and trust services), IDEMIA (eID tokens manufacturer) and Hansab AS (personalization service provider). In 2017, when the ROCA case happened, the eID tokens were provided by Gemalto AG and personalized by Trüb Baltic AS.

---

[1] https://www.ria.ee/en.html.
[2] https://www.riigiteataja.ee/akt/128062017043.
[3] https://www.smit.ee/#siseministeeriumi-infotehnoloogia-ja-arenduskeskus.

The eID ecosystem brings together six different tokens carrying eID functionality: ID-card, residence permit card, digital identity card, e-residency digital identity card, mobile-ID and diplomatic identity card [12]. All these tokens enable authentication in different electronic environments, giving eIDAS compliant digital signatures and encryption of the documents (encryption cannot be used with mobile-ID). The ROCA vulnerability affected five out of these six tokens, as mobile-ID has a different technological setup.

The usage of eID in Estonia is relatively high, about 2/3 of the eID holders use the functionalities (authentication, signing or encryption) regularly [13]. This is also illustrated by the fact that since 2017 digital authentication and digital signing are considered as part of the state-critical infrastructure by the Estonian Emergeny Act[4].

3.2   About the Security Vulnerability

In August 2017, ISA was informed about a potential security vulnerability (CVE-2017-15361) in Infineon chips that were used in Estonian eID cards. The vulnerability was discovered by Slovak and Czech scientists during their research regarding RSA key generation [15]. No Estonian ID-card keys were compromised at that time, but it was clear that immediate action by the state is necessary [16]. Approximately two thirds of the Estonian ID-cards, those issued after October 2014, needed renewal of the certificates as soon as possible [7]. Further research revealed that 100% of the secret keys were recoverable with varying level of computational complexity [18]. Due to the large number of the digital certificates affected and their broad use in both state and private sector services, revoking the cards would have meant extensive impact on the accessibility of public services – such step would have disrupted the use of e-health systems, the digital services of Tax and Customs Board, financial transactions etc. Work at and between government agencies would also have been disrupted. The impact on the private sector is harder to assess, but the eID connects the Estonian residents and e-residents to over 3000 services[5].

As reaction to the ROCA incident, a solution based on elliptic curve cryptography (ECC) was chosen to avoid using the affected RSA library on the ID-cards. The solution was implemented by a software update which then enabled the certificate renewal procedure either remotely by the end users or in the PBGB service points [13]. Ability to update software and additional cryptographic algorithms were recommended by a technical report ordered before acquisition of eID cards [17].

3.3   Theoretical Background

We consider the model for institutional design for complex technological systems by Koppenjan and Groenewegen (2005) [9] as vastly relevant for describing

---

[4] https://www.riigiteataja.ee/en/eli/516052020003/consolide.
[5] https://www.ria.ee/en/state-information-system/electronic-identity-eid.html.

e-government systems and ecosystems [1]. We use this model to depict the Estonian eID management scheme. The four-layer model portrays the current eID management model in Estonia and helps to understand how the socio-technical effect deriving from the use of eID has occurred. Looking at institutional design also helps to better understand the eID provision and management processes.

The Koppenjan and Groenewegen model incorporates three different design processes. The technological design, the institutional design, and the process design. The model further distinguishes four layers of analysis to better grasp the functioning of complex technological systems. Each layer describes different kinds of institutions "with regard to the kind of things they address, the way they work and evolve, and the extent to which they can be influenced", thus allowing to grasp the larger context in which the institutional arrangements form [9].

4   Research Results

This section provides an overview of the thematic analysis results by three main themes identified - "State and Policies", "Market and the EU" and "End User". The research findings present the narrative and key statements contained in the 32 semi-structured interviews.

4.1   Theme "State and Policies"

The "State and Policies" theme analyses the various aspects concerning policies and security of the ROCA case. The main conclusion in this theme is that the primary responsibility for the state is to guarantee the security of the eID. This responsibility can be elaborated into the following tasks: a) continuous political steering and oversight; b) determining the roles and responsibilities of all stakeholders involved in the eID area; c) provision of security and durability of the eID service; d) reviewing operational management models and crisis management guidelines in respect to eID management.

Among the key understandings that arose from the ROCA case is the acknowledgement of the state's dependency on the eID service. At the onset of the ROCA case, the Estonian state did not have either an accurate risk assessment nor an overview of its vast dependency on the eID, compare with [20].

Primarily, the theme illustrates how the concept of digital identity has changed in Estonia. Digital identity is seen as a multi-use electronic authentication and signature tool in various digital environments, widely used to access numerous services on-line by individual users, businesses and state actors. The broad use of the eID seamlessly interlinks the Estonian business environment, public services and the residents. The potential threat to the eID service presented by the ROCA case led to the understanding in which extent the Estonian state has become dependent on its eID. The Estonian public administration, the country's digital ecosystem, and even human lives (in certain circumstances), depend on the secure and uninterrupted functioning of the Estonian eID.

A most substantial conclusion from the research material is the need for acknowledging the importance of the eID for the Estonian digital ecosystem and taking full political responsibility deriving from that. Through its dependency on the eID and the long-term political guarantee it has given to its citizens and residents, the state is obliged to guarantee the continuity of the digital identity document and all the related infrastructure elements.

4.2 Theme "Market and the EU"

The "Market and the EU" theme analyses the roles of market, the state's external partners, and international legal regulation. The ROCA case reveals challenges in the interaction between the state and the EU in terms of regulation and procedure. As a most significant finding emerging from this theme, the ROCA case brought forward the relation of the European Cybersecurity Act[6], the international security frameworks SOG-IS (Senior Officials Group Information Systems Security)[7] and the European cybersecurity certification framework with Estonian domestic eID scheme. At large, these frameworks can support as well as hinder the eID area and eID security provision. The ROCA case demonstrated that the European cybersecurity certification framework poses a market barrier for new trust services in the EU and that it is inefficient in providing security and trust among the EU member states.

The purpose of the EU Cybersecurity Certification Framework[8] (under the Cybersecurity Act) is to establish and maintain trust and security for cybersecurity products, services, and processes. This is to allow end users and service providers to determine the level of security assurance of products, services and processes in procurements. During the ROCA case, the certification mechanism was seen as overly time consuming. When a new product needs the certification to be granted in order to replace an outdated or insecure product, the long-lasting certification process in fact reduces security. It is yet to be seen whether recent updates of this framework currently drafted by ENISA[9] provide an answer to this criticism.

Moreover, the analysis indicates that the Estonian state has a remarkable responsibility in terms of digital identity verification and trustworthiness. Considering conventional identity documents such as national passports and ID-cards, the responsibility to ensure the security and authenticity lies entirely on the state issuing these documents. In the digital realm, the EU has the oversight as stipulated in the eIDAS regulation. The interviews suggest that eIDAS over-regulates the field and actually interferes with the state's autonomy in issuing their eID documents. Reasons behind these claims derive from the ROCA case when Estonia experienced a risk that eID technologies would malfunction, i.e.,

---

[6] https://eur-lex.europa.eu/eli/reg/2019/881/oj.
[7] https://www.sogis.eu/.
[8] https://www.enisa.europa.eu/topics/standards/certification.
[9] https://www.enisa.europa.eu/publications/cybersecurity-certification-eucc-candida te-scheme/.

the Estonian state was responsible for the potential losses and the immense effect on the day-to-day functioning of the society; and not the producer of the technology, certification provider or the EU as the regulator. It was stated that the central certification authority can only issue a stamp of trustworthiness, but it has no means to enforce the guarantee that the certified product remains secure and uncorrupted. It can only be the document issuing state who can guarantee the trustworthiness of its eID and take measures in case its eID is misused.

The eIDAS regulation harmonises the European trust services market (including the eID area), defines and sets the standards for the trust Services, and also establishes the inter-state notification duty and procedures. In the 2017 ROCA case, both notification mechanisms, i.e., the pan-European and the technology-producer-related, proved to be ineffective as they failed at spreading the information regarding the ROCA vulnerability on the chips used on the Estonian ID-card. The primary reason for this failure was because no security incident occurred but the discovery of the ROCA vulnerability remained at the level of a risk or a threat. The two formal notifications made by Austria in June and Estonia in September 2017, remained largely unnoticed by other EU countries that were also affected (Spain, Slovakia and Poland). Thus, the Estonian Information System Authority makes a potent claim for the EU member states to compare the interpretation and the emerging practice of Article 19 of the eIDAS regulation[10].

The private sector business interests collided with the state's responsibility to guarantee service quality, security, and uninterrupted availability. The interviews suggest that the information regarding the ROCA vulnerability was likely kept broadly undisclosed intentionally for security concerns and to protect the chip and the ID-card producers' business interests, which resulted in setting the entire Estonian digital ecosystem at a heightened risk. For the Estonian state with its digital ecosystem built upon eID, the knowledge of the ROCA vulnerability was of fundamental importance; as stated in an interview: "Two formal means of notifying let us down. Partly because they are built for a crisis, not risks, partly because Estonia is just such a small client."

The ROCA case displayed that public-private partnerships are inevitable in the Estonian eID supply chain. While the state wins from purchasing its software solutions and related products from private sector providers, there is a trade-off: the state is influenced by the business interests of private sector companies and has to give up a some control and confidentiality by consuming the private sector services and products. According to our analysis, some experts find it desirable to acquire more control over the Estonian eID supply chain by developing certain capabilities within the state structures.

In contrast with the international market, the domestic public-private cooperation within the Estonian e-ecosystem is portrayed as constructive and helpful in the research material. As the 2017 ROCA case emerged, a number of public and private sector stakeholders together with individual ICT experts voluntarily

---

[10] https://www.ria.ee/en/news/estonia-offers-recommendations-light-eid-vulnerabilit y.html.

offered the state their help – without mentioning contracts, payments, or other business interests. The ROCA case demonstrated that the people engaged in the crisis management shared common values towards their work and the state, irrespective of whether they represented a private or public sector stakeholder. The attitude and prevalent work ethics within the organisations was equally important as the institutional hierarchy and formally established workflows. This aspect was important for successfully solving the ROCA case in Estonia and was described as the "the Estonian cooperation model" in the interviews.

4.3   Theme "End User"

The "End User" theme brings out the obligations and opportunities of the state and the individual while using the eID ecosystem. While the obligations on both perspectives centre around the provision of security and maintenance, the opportunities of eID range from enabling business models and communication channels to enhancing democratic participation by enabling Internet voting.

In this theme, the Estonian state is recognised as the primary end user of the eID. The daily functioning of its institutions and the provision of public services is built on the usage of eID and the information exchange infrastructure X-Road [19]. The ROCA case prompted the Estonian state to acknowledge that via the broad-scale and built-in usage of the eID, some state services primarily exist in the electronic version. These public services are thus fully dependent on the country's digital ecosystem and its key enabling elements (the eID and the X-Road), attesting to the importance of the eID for the Estonian state.

Moreover, by enabling Internet voting, the eID enhances participation in elections in Estonia and directly influences the country's democratic processes. The ROCA case occurred less than two months ahead of local elections in October 2017 in Estonia. The usage of the ID-card remained high throughout the ROCA case and the 2017 local elections presented the highest i-voter turnout in Estonian history[11], which means that trust in the e-state remained high despite the ROCA case.

5   Discussion

This section aims at answering the main research question of this study: what implications does the ROCA case present on state-provided eID?

When viewed in alignment with the market and international regulation, the ROCA case reveals that the state appears in a versatile role as a provider of eID, positioned on a borderline where public and private spheres meet; where national sovereignty and international regulation become intertwined. The state's interaction with other actors on the ICT market and finding the balance between domestic and inter-state legal regulation become increasingly important. The ROCA case reveals challenges in the interaction between the state and the EU in terms of regulation and procedure.

---

[11] https://www.valimised.ee/en/archive/statistics-about-internet-voting-estonia.

First and foremost, relating to the aspects of state and policies and the end user, the 2017 ROCA case demonstrated the dependency of a digitally transformed society on the eID. The Estonian state was recognised as the primary beneficiary of the eID. There are public services in Estonia which cannot work without the use of eID. Considering the large number of ID-cards affected by the ROCA vulnerability and the end users' high dependence on the Estonian eID, the ROCA case was considered a highly sensitive and large-scale security issue for the Estonian state. The success in handling that security threat by the Estonian authorities is viewed as a result of effective and agile management, which relied heavily on public-private partnership, openness (transparent public communication), advanced technologies of the country, and continuous review of its performance [13].

Secondly, the ROCA case laid out a number of necessary improvements in the political sphere, in crisis management and in eID management. Before the ROCA case, the eID management in Estonia seems to have been rather experimental and on-demand [4]. As consequence of the ROCA case, eID management is now recognised as an area that needs to be thoroughly planned, developed and secured. Other studies come to similar conclusions. The study [3] points out a series of anticipated improvements in the Estonian eID area, mainly in the political oversight and crisis management functions. In [13], Lips et al. list the positive effects of the ROCA case on the overall eID management in Estonia: improved crisis management readiness, heightened awareness of eID security. Also, [13] emphasizes the importance of public-private sector cooperation. According to the ISA, the ROCA case triggered continuity planning and risk management for public and private entities alike[12]. Moreover, two comprehensive strategy documents – the White Book on Identity Management and Identity Documents 1.0 [11] and the Digital Agenda 2020 for Estonia have been compiled taking into account the lessons learned from the ROCA case.

Finally, the research results indicate a change within the Estonian society since the eID was introduced in 2001. The usage of the eID bears a series of socio-technical effects. First, the Estonian digital identity represents the extension of the conventional identity document into the digital realm. The Estonian legislation equalises the digital identity with a traditional identity document (as well as the handwritten signature with the digital signature). A person has only one digital identity, even though the person may have more than one eID token[13]. As a second socio-technical effect, the population increasingly expects that eID is available to all end users and that the eID service is uninterrupted and secure. This is reinforced by the a clearly expressed political direction and an extensive state's guarantee for the reliability of the eID. End users from both the public and the private sector do not want to (and often cannot) turn back to the paper-versions of transactions. During the ROCA case, the trust in the eID remained high and Estonian residents expected the flaw to be fixed with

---

[12] https://www.ria.ee/en/news/estonia-offers-recommendations-light-eid-vulnerability.html.

[13] https://www.ria.ee/en/state-information-system/electronic-identity-eid.html.

shortest possible delay. The Estonian citizens perceive having a digital identity as their right, as the eID enables the citizens to extend their activity and carry out transactions in the digital realm. A further socio-technical effect is related to the plethora of public and private sector services connected to the use of the eID and the information exchange infrastructure X-Road. The ROCA case demonstrates that providing and maintaining the eID is not only the legal obligation of the Estonian state, but the eID represents a focal element of the digital ecosystem which, together with the Estonian X-Road, has become a key enabler, a connector of businesses, citizens and the state in reciprocal manner. The research material depicts that the concept of identity has changed in Estonia due to widespread use of the eID. Moreover, the way and the extent in which the Estonian society has rearranged itself as a result of the widespread use of the eID, gives proof of a significant socio-technical effect. In Estonia, the digital identity itself is fundamentally simple and is not separated from physical identity documents. Estonia has chosen this is a path over 20 years ago. Yet, today, its relevance for businesses and individuals is paramount. The eID is a cornerstone of the Estonian digital transformation and related concepts such as the e-residency.

Based on evidence so far, we suggest that the 2017 ROCA case illustrates a process that has unrolled in Estonia through two decades, allowing us to witness a paradigm shift. The digital identity which equals to a person's physical identity, has become a right for the citizen and its provision the obligation for the state. Through the set of norms and attitudes described as the "Estonian cooperation model", the story of Estonia's digital transformation becomes helpful in understanding the emergence of this socio-technical change. In [8], Kattel and Mergel give an extensive explanation to this phenomenon. In their perspective, Estonia demonstrates an informal, agile, and extremely close-knit network of high-profile politicians and their private sector IT advisers that continually seek mutual advice and guidance. This network has emerged as a historic evolvement of the Estonian ICT sector starting from early nineties, along with efforts in rebuilding the public administration. According to Kattel and Mergel, reliance on this public-private network is one of the fundamental governance principles upon which the whole Estonian digital transformation is built.

Furthermore, the "Estonian cooperation model" can be viewed through Koppenjan and Groenewegen's model for institutional design; more precisely through the different layers of institutions and their (inter)action. Table 1 presents the different layers of institutions and their (inter)action in the context of Estonia. The first layer "Actors and Games" concerning the *"actors/agents and their interactions aimed at creating and influencing (infrastructural) provisions, services, outcomes"* [9] represents the independent interests of those actors present in the Estonian ICT sector network. The second layer "Formal and informal institutional arrangements" which represents *"gentleman agreements, covenants, contracts, alliances, joint-ventures, merges, etc."* [9] displays how the policies driving Estonia's digital transformation evolved hand-in-hand with the pursuit of business interests of the banking and telecom companies in Estonia [8].

Table 1. Institutional design of the Estonian eID ecosystem

Layer	Estonian eID ecosystem
Layer 4: Informal institutional environment	People trust government and public sector institutions responsible for eID ecosystem and provision of e-services [14,20]. Work attitude and incentives to contribute
Layer 3: Formal institutional environment	Estonian eID ecosystem relies from European Union side on the European Parliament and of the Council regulation on eID and trust services for electronic transactions in the internal market (eIDAS). On a national level two main legal acts are regulating eID ecosystem: Electronic Identification and Trust Services for Electronic Transactions Act and Identity Documents Act
Layer 2: Formal and informal institutional agreements	Underlying principles on technical specifications, ownership, roles. Important element of compulsory roll-out, numerical value for representing the digital identity; the Estonian citizens perceive having a digital identity as their right. Identity documents strategy proposed by public and private sector experts. Regular meetings for public and private sector representatives organized by ISA. PBGB and IDEMIA S.A.S. have concluded a contract for the production of eID cards. Public and private institutions develop the eID area in close cooperation and set strategical goals together [13]
Layer 1: Actors and games	Public (ministries, ISA, PBGB, SMIT etc.) and private (SK ID Solutions AS, IDEMIA, Hansab etc.) sector authorities. Indirectly involved stakeholders: banks, telecom companies on the Estonian market that contribute to and benefit the most from the use of eID

Following, the third layer "Formal institutional environment" which depicts the *"formal rules, laws and regulations, constitutions (formal institutions)"* [9] shows how these early developments of the Estonian state's ICT area likely gave a reason and direction for developing the respective legislation in Estonia. The fourth and final layer "Informal institutional environment of socio-technical systems", contains *"norms, values, orientation, codes (in-formal institutions, culture)"* [9].

The unanimous approach towards resolving the ROCA case (the "Estonian cooperation model") shows how the contracts and underlying principles set up in the first and second layer are translated into the organisational culture and informal contact making in the fourth layer; and partially even allowed to bypass the normative framework presented in the third layer. This indicates that the state's ICT sector is strongly driven by those fundamental principles which evolved together with the modern Estonian state since the 1990's; and which now translate into actions at the surface and are visible in individual actor's behaviour, as displayed by the 2017 ROCA case. Understanding the evolution of Estonia's digital transformation allows us to draw a parallel with the way the Estonian eID management has evolved and how a multitude of incremental advancements over two decades have led the Estonian society. Both the Estonian digital transformation and the Estonian eID management model can be explained very well through Koppenjan and Groenewegen as follows: *"It is difficult to change institutions consciously since, to a large extent, they have been created along informal and incremental processes: they are the manifestation of unique, historical learning experiences of parties that have interacted over a longer period of time in a specific context and have developed rules on that basis."* [9].

6   Conclusion

The 2017 ROCA case demonstrated the dependency of a digitally transformed society on eID. Considering the large number of ID-cards affected by the ROCA vulnerability and the end users' high dependence on the Estonian eID, the ROCA case was considered a highly sensitive and large-scale security issue for the Estonian state. The ROCA case serves as a ground for continuity planning and risk management for public and private entities alike. The eID is a cornerstone of the Estonian digital transformation and further concepts, such as e-residency, are built on the usage of the eID. In terms of market and international cooperation, the ROCA case reveals challenges in the interaction between the state and the EU in terms of regulation and procedure.

The 2017 ROCA case illustrates a process that has unrolled in Estonia through two decades, allowing us to witness a paradigm shift. The digital identity has become a right for the citizen and its provision the obligation for the state. The Koppenjan and Groenewegen model of complex institutional design offers a four-layer model of institutional design, which helped us to contextualise the Estonian eID management and its emerged change.

This study can provide valuable input for the other countries while developing their eID systems as the latest developments on the international scale in the COVID-19 pandemic situation force the countries to rely more and more on the digital solutions in the service delivery. It is not possible to avoid completely the technical faults and security vulnerabilities similar to ROCA. However, based on the in-depth analysis of the particular case and mapping the lessons learned, it is possible to improve the existing environment and processes to cope with this kind of events in the future.

References

1. Bharosa, N., Lips, S., Draheim, D.: Making e-government work: learning from the Netherlands and Estonia. In: Hofmann, S., et al. (eds.) ePart 2020. LNCS, vol. 12220, pp. 41–53. Springer, Cham (2020). https://doi.org/10.1007/978-3-030-58141-1_4
2. Braun, V., Clarke, V.: Using thematic analysis in psychology. Qual. Res. Psychol. **3**(2), 77–101 (2006)
3. Buldas, A., et al..: Id-kaardi kaasuse õppetunnid. Tallinn University of Technology, School of Information Technolgy, Technical Report (2018)

4. Compton, M., Hart, P.: Great policy successes. Oxford University Press, Oxford (2019)
5. van Dijck, J., Jacobs, B.: Electronic identity services as sociotechnical and political-economic constructs. New Media Soc. **22**(5), 896–914 (2020)
6. Hedström, K., Wihlborg, E., Gustafsson, M.S., Söderström, F.: Constructing identities-professional use of eID in public organisations. Transf. Govt: People Process Policy **9**(2), 143–158 (2015)
7. Information System Authority: Estonia offers recommendations in the light of eID vulnerability (2018). https://www.ria.ee/en/news/estonia-offers-recommendations-light-eid-vulnerability.html
8. Kattel, R., Mergel, I.: Estonia's digital transformation: mission mystique and the hiding hand. In: Compton, M., Hart, P. (eds.) Great Policy Successes, pp. 143–160. Oxford University Press, Oxford (2019)
9. Koppenjan, J., Groenewegen, J.: Institutional design for complex technological systems. Int. J. Technol. Policy Manag. **5**(3), 240–257 (2005)
10. Latour, B.: Technology is society made durable. Sociol. Rev. **38**(1), 103–131 (1990)
11. Lips, S., Aas, K., Pappel, I., Draheim, D.: Designing an effective long-term identity management strategy for a mature e-state. In: Kő, A., Francesconi, E., Anderst-Kotsis, G., Tjoa, A., Khalil, I. (eds.) EGOVIS 2019. LNCS, vol. 11709, pp. 221–234. Springer, Cham (2019). https://doi.org/10.1007/978-3-030-27523-5_16
12. Lips, S., Bharosa, N., Draheim, D.: eIDAS implementation challenges: the case of Estonia and the Netherlands. In: Chugunov, A., Khodachek, I., Misnikov, Y., Trutnev, D. (eds.) EGOSE 2020. CCIS, vol. 1349, pp. 75–89. Springer, Cham (2020). https://doi.org/10.1007/978-3-030-67238-6_6
13. Lips, S., Pappel, I., Tsap, V., Draheim, D.: Key factors in coping with large-scale security vulnerabilities in the eID field. In: Kő, A., Francesconi, E. (eds.): EGOVIS 2018. LNCS, vol. 11032 , pp. 60–70. Springer, Cham (2018). https://doi.org/10.1007/978-3-319-98349-3_5
14. Muldme, A., Pappel, I., Lauk, M., Draheim, D.: A survey on customer satisfaction in national electronic id user support. In: Proceedings of ICEDEG 2018 - the 5th International Conference on eDemocracy & eGovernment. pp. 31–37. IEEE (2018)
15. Nemec, M., Sys, M., Svenda, P., Klinec, D., Matyas, V.: The return of Coppersmith's attack: practical factorization of widely used RSA moduli. In: Proceeding of the 2017 ACM SIGSAC Conference on Computer and Communications Security, pp. 1631–1648 (2017)
16. Parsovs, A.: Solving the Estonian ID card crisis: the legal issues. In: Proceeding of ISCRAM'2020 - the 17th International Conference on Information Systems for Crisis Response and Management, pp. 459–471 (2020)
17. Pedak, M.: ID-1 formaadis dokumentide funktsionaalsuse uuring. Tech. rep., e-Governance Academy (2013)
18. Produit, B.: Optimization of the ROCA (CVE-2017-15361) Attack. Master's thesis, University of Tartu, Institute of Computer Science, Estonia (2019)
19. Saputro, R., Pappel, I., Vainsalu, H., Lips, S., Draheim, D.: Prerequisites for the adoption of the X-Road interoperability and data exchange framework: a comparative study. In: Proceeding of ICEDEG'2020 - the 7th International Conference on eDemocracy & eGovernment, pp. 216–222. IEEE (2020)
20. Tsap, V., Lips, S., Draheim, D.: Analyzing eID public acceptance and user preferences for current authentication Options in Estonia. In: Kő, A., Francesconi, E., Kotsis, G., Tjoa, A.M., Khalil, I. (eds.) EGOVIS 2020. LNCS, vol. 12394, pp. 159–173. Springer, Cham (2020). https://doi.org/10.1007/978-3-030-58957-8_12

Identity Management and Legal Issues

Transparency by Default: GDPR Patterns for Agile Development

Baraa Zieni[1]([⊠]), Dayana Spagnuelo[2][iD], and Reiko Heckel[1]

[1] University of Leicester, University Rd, Leicester, UK
{bz60,rh122}@leicester.ac.uk
[2] Vrije Universiteit Amsterdam, Amsterdam, The Netherlands
d.spagnuelo@vu.nl

Abstract. Users have the right to know how their software works, what data it collects about them and how this data is used. This is a legal requirement under General Data Protection Regulation (GDPR) and fosters users' trust in the system. Transparency, when used correctly, is a tool to achieve this. The adoption of agile approaches, focused on coding and rapidly evolving functionality in situations where requirements are unclear or fast changing, poses new problems for the systematic elicitation and implementation of transparency requirements which are driven by, but lag behind, the functionality. We propose requirements patterns addressing GDPR's principle of transparency *by default*, *i.e.*, through a systematic and structured approach based on the artefacts of agile development. We present a case study using a SCRUM process to demonstrate the effectiveness and usability of the patterns.

Keywords: Transparency · GDPR · Agile development · Requirements patterns · Trust

1 Introduction

In 2018, new data protection rules were put in place that changed the notion of transparency in supporting user-centred approaches [25]. Transparency is one of the main principles in the GDPR[1], not only in terms of the contents of the information provided to data subjects, but also its quality and understandability. Data controllers must implement transparency in their data processes, and by doing so they help in enhancing people's trust [20].

Today, many software projects rely on agile methods like SCRUM to rapidly deliver high quality software. Unlike more traditional methods, agile approaches

---

[1] *EU General Data Protection Regulation (GDPR)*: Regulation (EU) 2016/679 of the European Parliament and of the Council of 27 April 2016 on the protection of natural persons with regard to the processing of personal data and on the free movement of such data, and repealing *Directive 95/46/EC* (General Data Protection Regulation), OJ 2016 L 119/1.

© Springer Nature Switzerland AG 2021
A. Kö et al. (Eds.): EGOVIS 2021, LNCS 12926, pp. 89–102, 2021.
https://doi.org/10.1007/978-3-030-86611-2_7

embrace change through frequent iterations of development and feedback, focusing on production code and using tests as specifications [29]. Detailed requirements engineering is mostly avoided as it entails substantial documentation [4]. A criticism of this approach is that requirements are inadequately addressed [29], recommending systematic practices such as identifying non-functional requirements [3]. If requirements are left implicit, this drives developers to implement them prematurely by "filling in the gaps". Hence, agile development with its focus on speed can cause a lack of consideration for the user [2]. We argue instead for a systematic approach to transparency requirements.

Transparency means to provide users with adequate information for informed choices whether to trust a system, when and how to use it to achieve their goals [5]. While trust can be addressed systematically [22], with methods including software patterns [6] and factor analysis [14], methods for engineering transparency requirements in software have not been studied in this context. In fact, transparency requirements are often underestimated during software development. This can be due to stakeholders' lack of understanding of the trust-transparency relation and worrying that users with a detailed understanding of how their data is processed may be less willing to provide it or consent to its use [23], leaving users to trust blindly in how systems handle their data [19].

We address this problem by proposing transparency patterns for requirements engineering in agile processes, designed to support analysts in applying best practices. We evaluate our proposal by a case study in a healthcare company to examine the patterns' capabilities and limitations. The evaluation answers the questions: *How has GDPR been addressed by the daily practices of agile development? How do patterns work within an agile process?* and *How do they ensure users are informed about their data concerns?* The remaining of this paper is structured as follows. Section 2 presents related work on agile development and transparency. We describe our Transparency patterns and the methodology used to create them in Sect. 3. Section 4 covers the evaluation and Sect. 5 discusses the results, concludes the paper and presents the future work.

2   Background and Related Works

In data protection law, business and governance, transparency is a user-centred principle as it refers to openness and disclosure of information to the user [25]. Transparency is seen as a meta-requirement as well as a quality in use [8]. It works at a meta level compared to functional requirements, enabling the user to know "how requirements can be fulfilled" [8]. A transparent system must provide information contextually relevant to the users' concerns actions and personal data [21]. When it is, it has been shown to elicit a high level of trust, and enhance the stakeholder-system relationship [7,10,21]. Based on this literature, transparency can be described as the appropriate amount of information that users require for better decision making and to enhance their trust.

From another perspective, in software engineering the concept of transparency can be interpreted as making the development processes of the software visible to the stakeholders, for example, through frequent cycles of development and feedback in agile processes [26]. Such process transparency is distinct from the transparency of the end product. In this paper, we refer to the latter, transparency of the software system in the context of GDPR and agile development.

Little research has been carried out for better understanding the GDPR's practical implications in requirements engineering and software architectures. Some authors have examined transparency and its dependencies with other system goals. For instance, discussing transparency as a non-functional requirement in the context of software engineering as well as organisations: transparency knowledge is presented a graph consisting of 33 soft goals using Softgoal Interdependence SIGs [1]. Transparency has been defined as the possibility of information, intentions, behaviours to be accessed through a process of disclosure [27]. Likewise, it is considered an important concept that can support users in the decision making process. Kim *et al.* [9] states that consumers' trust, security, privacy, and perceived risk have a high influence on their purchasing decisions with websites. Trust therefore is now becoming a more crucial issue especially when it comes to stakeholders making decisions with the software.

In this research, we adopt the view that transparency leads to more informed decisions and to user trust. Therefore, we argue it is important to empower the end user, by giving them control over their data. This requires both knowledge of their rights and being informed of how their data is used in the system. This information, to be more relevant, understandable and actionable, needs to be displayed in relation to the user goals and intentions with the system. We advocate that this transparency can be engineered systematically during the development process.

While most of the papers focus on privacy requirements of GDPR (*i.e.*, [13]). The closest work presenting such systematic approach to transparency during development time is presented by Meis *et al.* [12]. Their research has mainly examined the flow of the personal data in a system in order to generate the static requirements of privacy that are related to personal information and its corresponding transparency requirements. Those requirements are static in the sense that they help the user understanding what data the system hold on them, but not necessarily about changes that may happen to this data, or how to execute their rights with respect to the data. In our research we develop a set of static and dynamic patterns that generate transparency requirements about user data. These patterns help to inform the user about their data rights under GDPR, who has access to their data, how it has been stored, *et cetera*. For instance, the user can be informed when data is collected, edited or accessed, as well as they are given the control on who accesses their data. Further to that, we focus on the application of the patterns in agile practices of development to help the requirements analyst and developers to generate and implement the resulting requirements.

3   Methodology and Patterns

To generate the transparency patterns we follow a *design science* methodology proposed for Information Systems [18]. This methodology is based on six steps:

1. problem identification; 2. definition of objectives; 3. design and development; 4. demonstration; 5. evaluation; and 6. communication.

We briefly describe our approach to steps two to five. The first step is done through the review of the literature we present in Sect. 2, which identifies and justifies the problem we address. While the last refers to communicating the software artefact developed (*i.e.*, our patterns), we do so throughout this paper.

Definition of Objectives. The regulation and literature advocate that users must have clarity on the data the system holds, the underlying mechanisms, data storage and access controls [15]. We define the objectives of our patterns in reference to these demands. We underline the pieces that led to such objectives.

The GDPR takes a user-centred approach. It regulates not only on what constitutes lawful processing of personal data, but on a series of rights that ensure data subjects (the end-users, or people whose data is collected and processed) are informed about such processing, and empowered to control it. In this work we focus on the right to transparent information, which states that the data controller (the system collecting and processing personal data) is responsible for presenting the data subjects with information that is transparent concise and clear[2]. This right is laid down by the regulation in reference to other Articles (such as Article 13 and 14, and 15 to 22) which define the content of the information to be presented to data subjects, including: the categories of data being processed[3], the purposes for processing it[4], and communication regarding their rights, such as rectification or erasure of personal data[5].

Existing literature reviews the demands of GDPR in view of systems development, often beyond the actual regulation and including information security into the list of concerns relevant to data subjects. For instance, they recommend that information should be shared with the data subjects regarding where data is stored, how data is protected and who has access to it [25], as well as information about the choices on limiting the processing of their data [13].

Design and Development. The patterns are developed following a well-accepted methodology [28]. Requirements patterns generate specific types of requirements. We opt for them as they can be used during early stages of software developments and provide benefits such as reusability, consistent vocabulary and enhanced communication [11]. Additionally, patterns can be used to solve the issue of incomplete requirements [17]. Patterns are normally defined and classified in domain types. In our work, these domains are based on the system aspects (*i.e.*, data, operations) that systems are required to be transparent about. This paper only discusses Data Driven Patterns (DDP) [see full description of the patterns and their domains][6].

---

[2] *Ibid.*, Art. 12(1).

[3] *Ibid.*, Art. 15(1)(a).

[4] *Ibid.*, Art. 13(1)(c) and Art. 14(1)(c).

[5] *Ibid.*, Art. 19.

[6] https://github.com/Bara60/Supplementary-info-Transparency.git.

The patterns abstract requirements and systematically guide the analyst to address them early in the development. How to best present such information falls outside the scope of this work. For this topic, we refer to the literature on qualifiers of transparency [24] and user-friendly presentation of privacy-related information [16,20]. The patterns only help to decouple the presentation choices when passing information to the user by separating the contents from the design options (*i.e.*, whether users receive information promptly, or need to seek for it). This is done so that patterns can be applied by different teams of experts.

Demonstration. We applied our patterns in a case study with Spirit Health-care, an organisation with a small technology branch who handles sensitive and individually identifiable medical data across several applications including remote patient monitoring, and education booking and management. Spirit Healthcare is one of 50 fastest growing companies in the UK. They are of manageable size and use SCRUM in their software development. The patterns are applied by their requirements analysts[7] and developers.

Evaluation. To evaluate the resulting artefact, we used a qualitative approach through semi-structured interviews, focus groups and questionnaires. The evaluation is conducted with the development team, and patterns run on an entire application where the domain experts and developers are the spokesperson for end users. We use thematic coding to analyse their responses.

3.1   Transparency Patterns

The patterns are described through templates that contain basic details (pattern number, last update, domain, and author); *applicability* information defining the cases in which to use the pattern; *contents* that need to be covered by the requirement; guidance on how to derive the contents; the *template* specifying how to write the requirement; and an *example*. Due to space constraints we show only essential parts of the template (*emphasised* in the text). Table 1 presents details on the *contents* and how to derive them.

Our patterns are data driven and include static and dynamic types. Static patterns describe information related to the data schema in a type-level (*i.e.*, data classes, attributes, and associations). While dynamic patterns cover the actual instance of data, *e.g.*, what data is currently stored about users and when it is being used. In Tables 2, 3, and 4 we present a summary of the Data Protection Transparency Pattern (static), the Data Subject Rights Pattern (dynamic, static), and Data Pattern (dynamic) respectively. A fourth pattern, the static version of the Data Pattern, is proposed but omitted due to space limitations.

---

[7] Even though the task of eliciting and analysing requirements can be assigned to different roles depending on the specific development process, in our context the distinction between such roles is not relevant. For example, in agile processes the product owner is responsible for requirements elicitation, but the scrum master and scrum team are involved in requirements analysis.

Table 1. Pattern contents and how the requirements analyst can define them.

Summary	Description
Data type	The system's data schema (classes, attributes, associations); also referred to as categories of data by the regulation (Art. 15(1)(b))
Data instance	The actual contents of the data concerning the data subjects (*e.g.,* their specific *names,* or *addresses*)
Data interest	Any detail deemed relevant to data subjects including but not limited to personal data; can include an area of personal data (*e.g., shipping* data combines *name* and *address*), or other concerns (*e.g., choices on restricting data process* [13])
Data storage	The conditions in which data is stored (*e.g.,* how data protected, if in an encrypted format, anonymous or pseudonymised, their retention period, location of storage [25], and others)
Data access	The recipients of data, either natural persons, or third party organisations (Art. 13(1)(e) and Art. 14(1)(e))
Data subject's rights	The rights described by the GDPR (Art. 15 to 22), such as the right to access, to rectification, to erasure, to data portability, and others
Data gathered	The source of the data (when not obtained from the data subject) and where the data has been gathered, inferred, or aggregated (Art. 14)
Conditions	Logical statements composed of combinations of data operations with the actors performing them, of the form «actor» «data operation» «data type», *e.g.,* "system admin updated address" where *system admin* is the actor, *updated* the data operation, and *address* the data type. These conditions are defined by the requirements analyst and are checked during run-time

Table 2. Data Protection Transparency Pattern (with an example of its application).

Summary	Definition
Applicability	Use Pattern to generate transparency requirements for the specified data types of the data falling under data protection legislation the system holds about the end user. This pattern illustrates the data accessibility and storage
Contents	Data interest. Data types. Data storage. Data access
Template for *«data type»*	If «Data Type» is a «Data Interest»: The system must communicate to the user that it holds data of the type «Data Type» which has been «Data access» & «Data storage»
Example	
Template for *Address data*	The system must communicate to the user that it holds data of the type "address" which has been "accessed by system admin." This data is encrypted and will be stored until your account deletion

Table 3. Data Subject Rights Pattern (with an example of its application).

Summary	Definition
Applicability	Use this pattern to provide information about what data system holds about the user and their rights on that data under GDPR
Contents	Data interest. Data types. Data subject's rights
Information Template for «*data type*»	If «data type» is a «data interest» The system must communicate to the user that it holds data of «data type» and «data subject's rights» can be performed by data subject
Feature Template for «*data type*»	If «data type» is a «data interest»: In case *Condition* The system must implement action of «data subject's rights» on this data hold of «data type» that can be performed by data subject
Example	
Information Template for *Address data*	The system must communicate to the user that it holds data of the type of *Address* and actions of *access*, *erasure*, and *data portability* can be performed by the user (data subject)
Feature Template for *Address data*	The system must implement an action of *access* on this data hold of *Address* that can be performed by data subject

Table 4. Dynamic Data Pattern (with examples of its application).

Summary	Definition
Applicability	Use the pattern for the specified data instance that the system holds about the end user. This pattern gives information, during run-time, about what are the system actions being performed and by which actors
Contents	Data instance. Data Interest. Data type. Data gathered. Condition
Transparency of Instance of «*Data Type*» because «*condition*»	If «data type» is a «data interest»: In case «condition», the system must communicate to the user «the «Data Type» (data instance) & «data gathered» by «actor» | «condition»»
Example	
Transparency of Instance of *"Address"* because *"system admin updated address"*	In case "system admin updated address", the system must communicate to the user "system admin updated address"
Transparency of Instance of *"Address"* because *"system admin updated address"*.	In case "system admin updated address", the system must communicate to the user "University of Leicester, University road, UK LX1RH" «gathered» by system admin

A complete list of the patterns can be seen in the supporting materials (See Footnote 6), this list also contains patterns developed for other domains not covered in this paper.

3.2 Applying the Patterns

To apply the patterns, the first step is to *identify data interests* based on user goals, laws and regulation. The requirements analyst uses this process to define data interests over the whole system for consistent results. Data interests are a reference to data that are defined under the same concern or information that matters to the user (*e.g.*, shipping data). This process gives flexibility to identify any data group that relates to the user, not limited to personal data. Users' data concerns often depend on their goals, *e.g.*, "I want to see my shipping address before confirming payments". The analyst in this case creates a data interest called "shipping data" to represent this concern. For each data interest, the analyst can then derive the other concepts in Table 1.

Next, the analyst lists the user goals (given by user stories in agile development) that are (to be) implemented in the system. These goals are mapped to one or more of the pattern categories (Data, GDPR). Goals can refer to functionality already in the system, or to be added in the next iteration. Then, for each data interest, they identify the corresponding patterns and generate the requirements by following the pattern template. The last step is to finalise the transparency requirements document by applying a consistency check for removing duplicates and conflicted requirements, and aggregating requirements that can be combined. In particular, the analyst checks for unintended information disclosures or conflicts with security or privacy requirements. For example, information about data servers could cause a security breach.

4 Evaluation

The evaluation used qualitative approaches such as semi-structured interviews, focus groups, pre- and post-questionnaires. Participants included *domain experts* (DE1, DE2) with long clinical experience in the NHS, *senior developers*, and *developers* (D1..D4) from Spirit Health. Four pre-questionnaires were used to gauge the current agile development and GDPR practices in the digital team prior to the case study. Post-questionnaires captured how introduction of patterns impacted those practices and helped keeping users informed about their data.

The digital team manages their development life cycle by organising user stories into Product Backlog Items (PBIs) broken down into development tasks. The PBIs are arranged into biweekly sprints with free selection of PBIs by developers. PBIs are written primarily by the domain expert and senior developer and discussed biweekly in backlog reviews. Daily stand ups manage task progression, and communication with the business is through the product owner (domain expert) or the senior developer (also scrum master).

To analyse the data from questionnaires and semi-structured interviews we coded responses and clustered them to report results and find any similarities. An initial set of themes was extended in the coding processes, some derived from research questions (see Sect. 1) on how patterns impact on *time and effort of development*, and how *data and GDPR's transparency* are integrated into the process by the use of patterns. One theme was discovered while analysing responses: *informing the user*. The themes are discussed next.

Time and Effort. All participants agreed that agile requirements engineering practices reduce their workload. Moreover, participants D1, D2, D3 agreed and D4 neither agree nor disagree that they speed up the work in the project. After applying the patterns to their user stories, the developers mentioned that the workload remains the same, if not increased. D3 mentioned this is "due to a more complete description of the tasks". Moreover, D3 mentioned that applying patterns will also speed up the work, in contrast with D4 who said that the work would not speed up "but it would improve the quality of the system".

Data and GDPR Transparency. The experts stated how important it is to report to the user what data is being collected. D3 reported that using the patterns helps to consider the relevant data interests and referred to an issue in their system: "We often collect data without telling the users what it is being used for, so it was good to consider why at each point in the application we are collecting given things. Makes you rethink the validity in collecting certain things, such as user personality ethnic details were removed from the system as we had no real reason to collect it". Having to systematically think of the data interests made developers and domain experts review the purpose for collection and processing data. As a consequence, where this purpose was no longer valid, they were able to apply data minimisation[8] (one of the pillar principles in the GDPR). The developers stated that the data interests help in grouping related data, then added "Data interests are a great extension on the concept of data tables – you can group many tables under a data interest".

Figure 1 presents an excerpt of an original user story and its requirements outputs after applying our GDPR transparency patterns. This illustrates how patterns systematically bridge gaps in the user story, *e.g.*, that *data is stored 2 years after account deletion* was not mentioned in the original user story. During a group session one developer pointed out the importance of informing the users about their data and access rights, D3 also mentioned "if people know their rights, they are more likely to fight for them".

---

[8] GDPR, Art. 5(1)(c).

User Story: Edit personal details.

Test Case 1: When an email address is entered or changed an email requesting confirmation should be sent to the email address. The email should not be deemed valid until the link in the email has been clicked.

Test Case 2: When a user logs into the system, if their email address has been changed and has not been validated it should be stated that the email address has not been validated in the personal details and the user should be prompted at each login attempt to validate their email address. The username will remain as the previous email address before changes were made. A link should also be presented resending the email validation email.

Test Case 3: When any information is entered or edited in the personal details the old and new value should be audited in an audit table and timestamped along with the user who made the change.

Dynamic Data- requirement result:
If email address is updated by admin the system must communicate to the user, the currently in use email address which is being used by the user and other admins – informing them that the email could have been changed.

Data Protection-requirement result:
The system must communicate that it holds data of the type of personal details which has access by the admin team and selected members of other user types stored even after the account has been deleted due to auditing for at least 2 years.

Data Subject Rights- requirement result:
The system must communicate to the user that any changes made to their data are audited and details of the changer recorded.

Fig. 1. Original user story and its test cases, the GDPR resulting requirements.

Domain experts also stated that the patterns help building users' trust and enable them to make informed decisions. DE2 noted that it will help the user to decide if they want to use the software or not. Trust is equated with "a user feels very confident about the system" (quote from DE1, but also voiced by DE2). To achieve user confidence, the system needs to give "feedback [...] after carrying out commands" (DE1) and inform the users of their data (DE2).

Informing the User. D1 said "informing the user about the data being collected and the process being performed should be a requirement itself." D4 mentioned an example from their project experience on where and what they inform the user about: "We have a specific text on first login to our system (CliniTouch Vie) that the patient must agree to in order to use the system". It is clear that the team has considered transparency on a case-by-case basis, rather than systematically across the application. Previous practices have regarded transparency on a *need-to-know* rather than a *right-to-know* basis and not consistently applied it throughout the applications.

The developers have stated that the patterns help to sustain the user focus (the perspective fostered by the GDPR). D4 stated that applying the patterns aids in informing the user about their data and other system aspects as it "raises the thought and discussion between stakeholders, which then if carried out will certainly help the user in their use of the system." They highlighted that patterns aid them to reflect on the data protection issues. One of the developers stated that a *user centred view* on transparency related mostly to the information disclosed directly by users. However, a big part of personal data is gathered indirectly via behavioural, statistical and usage data. This is often not identified as a data concern and the user is rarely informed about it. This data can be passively collected: "When the system collects information not directly from the user but could be critical – when attempted login – when successful etc.". For instance, IP addresses, information about time spent on the website, or any other behavioural data could affect the user or even be used to identify them. The data interests provide a way to discover all relevant data types and inform the user about them, whether they are collected directly or indirectly, as required by the rights described under GDPR Art. 13 and 14.

5   Discussion and Concluding Remarks

The patterns have been shown to systematically generate transparency requirements according to the GDPR. This transparency is extended to indirect collection of data where informing the user is often overlooked. This, in turn, increases the developers' ability to structure actionable requirements in their applications. The patterns take in high level user stories, data interests and processes and generate transparency requirements on who has access to the data and the existing data processes. The patterns bring the users' perception to the implementation *by default* and drive the user focus (in line with the GDPR) to the point of writing code. Integrating transparency across the software process, the patterns are designed to fit agile practices and management tools. The dynamic aspect of patterns, using the concept of conditions, proves useful to build transparency contextually and in relation to user goals.

Transparency is a pillar concept in the GDPR, but our work's relevance is not limited to the European Union. There are international implementations of the GPDR that place similar emphasis on transparency, for instance the Data Protection Act in the United Kingdom[9], and the LGPD in Brazil[10]. Other prominent data protection regulations also touch upon the concept: the CCPA in California, USA[11] calls it the "right to know"; and the APPI in Japan[12] mentions the provision of information in its Articles 15 and 18, for instance. Although, a note of caution should be taken when discussing compliance with those regulations. Our patterns approach transparency from early development phases, but we do not claim they alone are sufficient for compliance with those regulations' requests. The GDPR, for instance, requires data controllers to provide the contact of the controller's Data Protection Officer. This request also composes transparency,

---

[9] https://www.legislation.gov.uk/ukpga/2018/12/contents/enacted.
[10] http://www.planalto.gov.br/ccivil_03/_Ato2015-2018/2018/Lei/L13709compilado.htm.
[11] https://oag.ca.gov/privacy/ccpa.
[12] https://www.ppc.go.jp/en/legal/.

but is not covered by our patterns, as it does not directly refer to personal data (our goal).

How personal data is handled in secondary processes (*e.g.*, collecting behavioural data) was all but completely ignored in the initial elicitation process carried out on the Spirit Health application. This information is not accessible through other standard elicitation methods due to not being directly related to the system's functionality, and is thus ignored. The patterns expose lack of transparency, particularly in secondary processes. The patterns generate details on what users must know about system aspects and data processing. This aids the requirements analysts' and developers' decision on what information to show. We believe this process should be formalised into a standard, so that it can be leveraged by other companies as well.

The case study with the Spirit Healthcare demonstrates that patterns fit well with agile practices. Current limitations in agile are that requirements are not well defined and the users' perspective is not fully included, because of a focus on rapid iteration. The patterns contribute to addressing these issues by extending the agile process. Teams can continue to work in a familiar structure whilst more deeply rooting the users' considerations into the process.

The main limitation of our approach is that the completeness and consistency of the generated requirements highly depends on identifying the related data interests as one of the developers mentioned in the evaluation: "I can see the same things being repeated and to be able to standardise them across the application would be great". Therefore, it is important that the requirements analyst has sufficient domain and application knowledge. Another limitation is that transparency can overwhelm the user. Specifying different types of users (with different data interests) can help, and this option needs to be clear in the condition section. However, developers have not explored presentation choices in this evaluation.

Concluding Remarks. The results from the evaluation showed that the patterns are effective in bringing the end-users' perception into the development process. This happens by informing users what data the system collects about them, how this data is used, and by whom it is accessed, according to GDPR requests. This information is provided in relation to the user goals. The patterns prompt the developers and requirements analyst to consider the data aspects that the user must know about. Furthermore, implementing the resulting transparency requirements has advanced other data protection concepts, such as exposing information which is not directly accessible to the user, thus ignored by standard elicitation methods, and the one of improving data minimisation through systematically reflecting on the purpose for data collection. This has been done systematically and based on the artefacts of agile development.

Future work for this research could investigate how to standardise the patterns using ISO standards. This could be used in a transparency certification awarded to companies that adhere to the defined practices by the standard.

Acknowledgement. The research is supported by University of Leicester. We also would like to thank Dr Mahmood Hosseini for the valuable input and Spirit Healthcare team for their collaboration, experience.

References

1. Cappelli, C., Leite, J.: Software transparency. Bus. Inf. Syst. Eng. **2**, 127–139 (2010). https://doi.org/10.1007/s12599-010-0102-z
2. Drury, M., Conboy, K., Power, K.: Obstacles to decision making in agile software development teams. J. Syst. Softw. **85**(6), 1239–1254 (2012)
3. Eberlein, A., Leite, J.: Agile requirements definition: a view from requirements engineering. In: Proceedings of the International Workshop on Time-Constrained Requirements Engineering, pp. 4–8 (2002)
4. Erickson, J., Lyytinen, K., Siau, K.: Agile modeling, agile software development, and extreme programming: the state of research. J. Database Manag. (JDM) **16**(4), 88–100 (2005)
5. Herrnfeld, H.H.: Article 67 data protection by design and by default. In: European Public Prosecutor's Office, pp. 513–514. Nomos Verlagsgesellschaft mbH & Co. KG (2020)
6. Hoffmann, A., Söllner, M., Hoffmann, H., Leimeister, J.M.: Towards trust-based software requirement patterns. In: 2nd IEEE International Workshop on Requirements Patterns, pp. 7–11. IEEE (2012)
7. Hosseini, M., Shahri, A., Phalp, K., Ali, R.: Foundations for transparency requirements engineering. In: Daneva, M., Pastor, O. (eds.) REFSQ 2016. LNCS, vol. 9619, pp. 225–231. Springer, Cham (2016). https://doi.org/10.1007/978-3-319-30282-9_15
8. Hosseini, M., Shahri, A., Phalp, K., Ali, R.: A modelling language for transparency requirements in business information systems. In: Nurcan, S., Soffer, P., Bajec, M., Eder, J. (eds.) CAiSE 2016. LNCS, vol. 9694, pp. 239–254. Springer, Cham (2016). https://doi.org/10.1007/978-3-319-39696-5_15
9. Kim, D.J., Ferrin, D.L., Rao, H.R.: A trust-based consumer decision-making model in electronic commerce: the role of trust, perceived risk, and their antecedents. Decis. Support Syst. **44**(2), 544–564 (2008)
10. Kizilcec, R.F.: How much information? Effects of transparency on trust in an algorithmic interface. In: Proceedings of the 2016 CHI Conference on Human Factors in Computing Systems, pp. 2390–2395 (2016)
11. Loizides, F., Winckler, M., Chatterjee, U., Abdelnour-Nocera, J., Parmaxi, A.: Human Computer Interaction and Emerging Technologies: Workshop Proceedings from the INTERACT 2019 Workshops. Cardiff University Press (2020)
12. Meis, R., Heisel, M.: Computer-aided identification and validation of privacy requirements. Information **7**(2), 28 (2016)
13. Meis, R., Wirtz, R., Heisel, M.: A taxonomy of requirements for the privacy goal transparency. In: Fischer-Hübner, S., Lambrinoudakis, C., Lopez, J. (eds.) TrustBus 2015. LNCS, vol. 9264, pp. 195–209. Springer, Cham (2015). https://doi.org/10.1007/978-3-319-22906-5_15
14. Moyano, F., Fernandez-Gago, C., Lopez, J.: Building trust and reputation in: a development framework for trust models implementation. In: Jøsang, A., Samarati, P., Petrocchi, M. (eds.) STM 2012. LNCS, vol. 7783, pp. 113–128. Springer, Heidelberg (2013). https://doi.org/10.1007/978-3-642-38004-4_8

15. Murmann, P., Fischer-Hübner, S.: Tools for achieving usable ex post transparency: a survey. IEEE Access **5**, 22965–22991 (2017)
16. Murmann, P., Karegar, F.: From design requirements to effective privacy notifications: empowering users of online services to make informed decisions. Int. J. Hum.-Comput. Interact. 1–26 (2021)
17. Palomares Bonache, C.: Definition and use of software requirement patterns in requirements engineering activities. In: Proceedings of REFSQ 2011 Workshops, REFSQ 2011 Empirical Track, and REFSQ 2014 Doctoral Symposium, pp. 60–66 (2014)
18. Peffers, K., Tuunanen, T., Rothenberger, M.A., Chatterjee, S.: A design science research methodology for information systems research. J. Manag. Inf. Syst. **24**(3), 45–77 (2007)
19. GSMA Mobile Privacy: Consumer research insights and considerations for policymakers (2014)
20. Rossi, A., Lenzini, G.: Transparency by design in data-informed research: a collection of information design patterns. Comput. Law Secur. Rev. **37**, 105402 (2020)
21. Schwab, K., Marcus, A., Oyola, J., Hoffman, W., Luzi, M.: Personal data: the emergence of a new asset class. In: An Initiative of the World Economic Forum (2011)
22. Söllner, M., Hoffmann, A., Hoffmann, H., Leimeister, J.M.: How to use behavioral research insights on trust for HCI system design. In: CHI 2012 Extended Abstracts on Human Factors in Computing Systems, pp. 1703–1708. ACM (2012)
23. Verizon Enterprise Solutions: Verizon 2014 data breach investigations report. verizon.com (2016)
24. Spagnuelo, D., Bartolini, C., Lenzini, G.: Qualifying and measuring transparency: a medical data system case study. Comput. Secur. **91**, 101717 (2020)
25. Spagnuelo, D., Ferreira, A., Lenzini, G.: Transparency enhancing tools and the GDPR: do they match? In: Mori, P., Furnell, S., Camp, O. (eds.) ICISSP 2019. CCIS, vol. 1221, pp. 162–185. Springer, Cham (2020). https://doi.org/10.1007/978-3-030-49443-8_8
26. Tu, Y.-C., Tempero, E., Thomborson, C.: An experiment on the impact of transparency on the effectiveness of requirements documents. Empir. Softw. Eng. **21**(3), 1035–1066 (2015). https://doi.org/10.1007/s10664-015-9374-8
27. Turilli, M., Floridi, L.: The ethics of information transparency. Ethics Inf. Technol. **11**(2), 105–112 (2009). https://doi.org/10.1007/s10676-009-9187-9
28. Withall, S.: Software Requirement Patterns. Pearson Education (2007)
29. Zhu, K.: Information transparency in electronic marketplaces: why data transparency may hinder the adoption of B2B exchanges. Electron. Mark. **12**(2), 92–99 (2002)

Anonymization Between Minimization and Erasure: The Perspectives of French and Italian Data Protection Authorities

Emanuela Podda$^{(\boxtimes)}$ (iD) and Francesco Vigna (iD)

Alma Mater Studiorum, CIRSFID - Alma AI, Università Di Bologna, Bologna, Italy
{emanuela.podda,francesco.vigna}@studio.unibo.it

Abstract. Two years after the General Data Protection Regulation (GDPR) went into effect, data anonymization remains one of the main issues linked to fragmentation in the Member States' anonymization policies, in which regard stakeholders would like additional guidelines.

In keeping with this premise, this article aims to analyze and compare trends in the implementation and enforcement of anonymization policies put in place by data protection authorities in two countries: France and Italy.

This analysis makes it possible to trace the evolution of these policies and highlight their critical importance in applying the data minimization principle and in enforcing the right to erasure under Art. 17 GDPR.

Keywords: Anonymization · Risk-based approach · Data protection · Data minimization · Right to erasure

1 Introduction

The anonymization of personal data, stemming from the statistical context, was originally used by the National Statistical Institutes to ensure a sustainable trade-off between data utility and data protection. With the advent of big data it has been extensively applied to *real data*, posing remarkable challenges and tensions in terms of data protection and privacy.

To overcome and relieve this tension, the General Data Protection Regulation (GDPR) seems to be relying on the right of data subjects to be informed about the way data is processed and on the risk-based approach.

Anonymization generally protects data and takes data outside of the scope of data protection and privacy: information rights ensure that data subjects have control over their own data, and risk assessment obliges data controllers to evaluate the level of the risk inherent in the data processing.

The level of anonymity should consequently be tailored to the needs agreed to during the information-giving process, as a person's identity can be revealed by way of either.

– direct identifiers, such as names, postcodes, or pictures; or

A. Kö et al. (Eds.): EGOVIS 2021, LNCS 12926, pp. 103–114, 2021.
https://doi.org/10.1007/978-3-030-86611-2_8

– indirect identifiers, which do not in themselves identify anyone but *can* do so in combination with other information available about them, examples of such indirect identifiers being information about someone's workplace, occupation, salary, or age.

For this reason anonymization, together with pseudonymization, represents the main data processing tool the law provides for protecting data and personal identity.

For an official definition of anonymization in the legal data-protection framework in force in Europe, the only source we can turn to is Opinion 05/2014 on Anonymization Techniques[1], issued by Working Party 29, in which anonymization is defined as *"the process by which data are made anonymous"*. So defined, anonymization means that the data in question must be stripped of identifying elements, enough so that the data subject can no longer be identified, which in turn means that in order for the data to count as anonymous, anonymisation must be irreversible under all conditions.

From a mere legal point of view, the friction point lies in what is considered an acceptable level of reidentification risk: the legislator acknowledges the problem of reverse-engineering the anonymization process and circumventing data protection tools—a problem that will continue to persist as long as the available technology and technological development keep advancing.

Indeed Recital 26 of the GDPR stresses that *"[t]he principles of data protection should apply to any information concerning an identified or identifiable natural person.* [...]"[2].

The whole structure of this Recital strengthens the approach contained in the WP29 Opinion on Anonymization Techniques, where the main focus is not on anonymization *per se* but rather on its outcome. Indeed, in this opinion Working Party 29 stresses the need to test the anonymization techniques against three main risks:

– singling out
– linkability
– inference.

---

[1] See https://ec.europa.eu/info/law/law-topic/data-protection/communication-two-years-applic ation-general-data-protection-regulation_en. The Communication is also accompanied by a Staff Working Document detailing the main issues relating to fragmentation in the Member States' policies and providing guidance for the follow-up. See https://eur-lex.europa.eu/legal-content/EN/TXT/PDF/?uri=CELEX:52020SC0115&from=EN.

[2] The article continues as follows: *"To determine whether a natural person is identifiable, account should be taken of all the means reasonably likely to be used, such as singling out, either by the controller or by another person to identify the natural person directly or indirectly. To ascertain whether means are reasonably likely to be used to identify the natural person, account should be taken of all objective factors, such as the costs of and the amount of time required for identification, taking into consideration the available technology at the time of the processing and technological developments. The principles of data protection should therefore not apply to anonymous information, namely information which does not relate to an identified or identifiable natural person or to personal data rendered anonymous in such a manner that the data subject is not or no longer identifiable. This Regulation does not therefore concern the processing of such anonymous information, including for statistical or research purposes".*

Consistent with this background is the advice provided by WP29: the optimal solution for crafting an anonymization process needs to be decided on a case-by-case basis, as it should be aimed at reducing the risk of deanonymization.

The literature on this topic is vast but can be broken down into two main buckets: on one hand is research focused on empirical cases of deanonymization[3]; on the other the research asks whether compliance requires a zero-risk approach or whether a residual-risk approach will do[4]. Therefore, it seems that the discussion on anonymization mainly revolves around the question of risk (zero vs. acceptable risk), without offering any theoretical approach on which to implement and provide solutions for overcoming this impasse.

---

[3] In 1990, it was demonstrated that the governor of Massachusetts could be reidentified from deidentified medical data by cross-referencing the deidentified information with publicly available census data used to identify patients. See Sweeney, L.: Policy and Law: Identifiability of de-identified data, in http://latanyasweeney.org/work/identifiability.html. In 2006, the online service provider AOL shared deidentified search data as part of a research initiative, and researchers were able to link search queries to the individuals behind them. See https://en.wikipedia.org/wiki/AOL_search_data_leak. In 2009, Netflix released an anonymized movie rating dataset as part of a contest, and researchers successfully reidentified the users. See Narayanan, A., Shmatikov, V.: Robust De-anonymization of Large Sparse Datasets in https://www.cs.utexas.edu/~shmat/shmat_oak08netflix.pdf. In 2013, another study, conducted on anonymized cell phone data, showed that: *"four spatio-temporal points are enough to uniquely identify 95% of the individuals"*. See de Montjoye, Y., et al.: Unique in the Crowd: The privacy bounds of human mobility, Scientific Reports volume 3, Article number: 1376 (2013), https://www.nature.com/articles/srep01376. In 2017, researchers released a study stating that *"web-browsing histories can be linked to social media profiles using only publicly available data"*. See Su, J., et al.: De-anonymizing Web Browsing Data with Social Networks, in Proceedings of the 26th International Conference on World Wide WebApril 2017 Pages 1261–1269, in https://doi.org/10.1145/3038912.3052714. Recently, studies have shown that deidentified data was in fact reidentifiable, and researchers at UCL in Belgium and Imperial College London found that *"99.98% of Americans would be correctly re-identified in any dataset using 15 demographic attributes"*. See Rocher, L., Hendrickx, J. M., de Montjoye, Y.: Estimating the success of re-identifications in incomplete datasets using generative models, in Nature Communications, Volume 10, 3069, 2019, https://ui.adsabs.harvard.edu/abs/2019NatCo..10.3069R/abstract. The amount of personal information leaked keeps growing, as the exposition of personal data through breaches keeps increasing.

[4] Spindler, G., Schmechel, P.: Personal Data and Encryption in the European General Data Protection Regulation. Journal of Intellectual Property Information, Technology & Electronic Communication, 163 (2016); Kuner, C., et al.: Risk management in data protection. International Data Privacy Law, 2015, Vol. 5, No. 2.; Veale, M., Binns, R., Ausloos, J.: When data protection by design and data subject rights clash. International Data Privacy Law, 2018, Vol. 8, No. 2; 7. Gellert, R.: We Have Always Managed Risks in Data Protection Law: Understanding the Similarities and Differences between the Rights-Based and the Risk-Based Approaches to Data Protection. European Data Protection Law Review, 481 (2016); Gellert, R.: Understanding the notion of risk in the General Data Protection Regulation. Computer Law & Security Review 34 (2018) 279–288; Finck, M., Pallas, F.: They who must not be identified—distinguishing personal from non-personal data under the GDPR. International Data Privacy Law,2020, Vol. 10, No. 1.

Moreover, these polarized perspectives and approaches have certainly come to the notice of investors and stockholders. Indeed, when the European Commission, pursuant to Art. 97 GDPR[5], released its first report on the first two years of GDPR application[6], it listed anonymization among several areas for future improvement. The Commission's report highlights a certain fragmentation in the policy landscape across Member States and data protection authorities, while stakeholders are asking for additional guidelines from the European Data Protection Board (EDPB)[7]. It turns out that there is a great need for theoretical solutions by which to implement anonymization in complying with the principle of data minimization (*ex-ante processing*) and the principle of storage limitation (*ex-post processing*), and even in enforcing Art. 17 GDPR (the right to erasure, or right to be forgotten).

One of the main guidelines provided by the EDPB can be recalled in Opinion 04/2019, addressing the effectiveness of anonymization/deletion in light of these principles. The EDPB specified that whenever personal data is no longer needed after it is first processed, *it must by default be deleted or anonymized*. In keeping with this premise, the EDPB specified that any retention should be objectively justifiable and demonstrable by the data controller in an accountable way, thereby bearing out the view that anonymization of personal data is an *alternative to deletion*, provided that all the relevant contextual elements are taken into account and the likelihood and severity of the risk, including the risk of reidentification, is regularly assessed.

In both cases (deletion and anonymization) the controller is obligated to limit the retention period to what is strictly necessary.

A survey of all the different approaches followed by data protection authorities (DPAs) will reveal that some of them gain paramount importance because they seem to set the trend in clearing up these gray areas of interpretation and practice.

---

[5] Art. 97 GDPR requires the Commission to review the regulation, issuing an initial report two years after its entry into force and every four years thereafter.

[6] Communication from the Commission to the European Parliament and the Council - two years of application of the General Data Protection Regulation, 24 June 2020, Justice and Consumers, COM(2020) 264 final; SWD(2020) 115 final & Staff Working Document accompanying the Communication - two years of application of the General Data Protection Regulation. See https://ec.europa.eu/info/law/law-topic/data-protection/communication-two-years-application-general-data-protection-regulation_en.

[7] The Commission has also issued a study titled "Assessment of the Member States' Rules on Health Data in the Light of GDPR" (Specific Contract No SC 2019 70 02 in the context of the Single Framework Contract Chafea/2018/Health/03), in which anonymization is recognized as an important issue among Member States. See https://ec.europa.eu/health/sites/health/files/ehe alth/docs/ms_rules_health-data_en.pdf.

This paper therefore intends to analyze and compare the approaches taken by two of the DPAs that are leading the way when it comes to policy implementation, data reuse, open data approach, and enforcement: the French and Italian DPAs[8].

2 The Approach of the French Data Protection Authority: The Commission Nationale de l'Informatique et des Libertés

The French Data Protection Authority—the Commission Nationale de l'Informatique et des Libertés (or CNIL)—defines personal data as *any anonymous data that can be double-checked to identify a specific individual*. Under this definition, certainly stricter than the one contained in Art. 4 GDPR, the CNIL is expressively stating that personal data can be deemed personal even after it has been anonymized.

The CNIL highlights that the process of *anonymizing process personal data should make it impossible to identify individuals within data sets*, and that this must therefore be an *irreversible process*. It follows that *when anonymization is effective, the data are no longer considered personal and the GDPR is no longer applicable*. However, the CNIL recommends that *raw datasets* containing personal data which have been anonymized *should never be deemed anonymous*, requiring a case-by-case evaluation in keeping with the WP29 opinion.

If we look at the trendline in the case-by-case approach adopted by the CNIL, we will find that since the WP29 Opinion on Anonymization Techniques was released, the approach was making possible to store personal data (after the time limit, consistently with the purpose of collection) for statistical purposes, once *effectively* anonymized—thereby confirming the storage exception allowed for statistical purposes under the GDPR.

However, apart from the statistical exception, the approach adopted by the CNIL was also based on detecting the risk of deanonymization, specifying that a dataset is *effectively* anonymous if, prior to dissemination, it meets the following criteria:

– It does not contain individual data.
– It is not possible to correlate the data with any other dataset.
– It is not possible to infer any new information about individuals.

If, and only if, all three criteria are simultaneously satisfied can the dataset be considered *anonymous*, meaning that if even only one criterion is not satisfied, the CNIL will

---

[8] In December 2020, the European Data Portal issued an annual benchmark study on developments in open data, listing France among the trendsetters and Italy among the fast-trackers. See https://www.europeandataportal.eu/sites/default/files/edp_landscaping_insight_report_n6_2020.pdf.Moreover, Italy and France are listed among the top ten Countries with the highest fines in GDPR enforcement. See https://www.enforcementtracker.com/ In details, see also: Daigle, B., & Khan, M.: The EU General Data Protection Regulation: An Analysis of Enforcement Trends by EU Data Protection Authorities. Journal of International Commerce and Economics. May 2020. https://www.usitc.gov/joumals.

have to carry out a specific impact assessment on the risk of reidentification, demonstrating that the dissemination of the anonymized dataset has no impact on the data subjects' private lives or freedoms[9].

The trend that can be observed in the CNIL's practice in the wake of WP29 Opinion 05/2014 shows a remarkable number of authorizations for anonymization processing requested by firms, suggesting that firms want to avoid taking the deanonymization risk, and would much rather take the safer and more convenient route of falling back on the CNIL to test anonymization techniques[10].

Given the risk of deanonymization, and especially the indirect risk due to data export, the CNIL, in authorizing anonymization processing, reiterates that only anonymous data can be exported outside an *approved environment* (especially when it comes to health and research data, for which the rules are certainly stricter), confirming that personal data export is prohibited.

Only *anonymous* data can be exported, only once internal validation is obtained, followed by a systematic and preliminary audit to attest to the effective anonymity of the requested export, thus imposing a double check on the dataset and confirming that in the risk of deanonymization lies the difference between anonymized and anonymous data. The first risk test is designed to ascertain whether data have undergone an anonymization process, while only the second test ascertains that the risk of deanonymization equals zero[11]. On more than one occasion, the CNIL has stressed that the criteria and procedures should be regularly reviewed in light of changing anonymization and reidentification techniques.

This trend confirms what is started in the CNIL's guidance on anonymization[12], namely, that anonymization processing is not required under the GDPR but is a way the GDPR is implemented under certain conditions.

Along the same lines, personal data need to be treated in secure environments (*bulle sécurisée*) and be stored and processed as long as is necessary for the purposes of collection, after which the data needs to be destroyed.

Moreover, a specific role in the implementation of anonymization is provided for by *Loi 2004–801 du 6 août 2004*, on the protection of individuals in relation to personal data

---

[9] Among the first cases brought before the CNIL immediately after the publication of the WP29 Opinion on Anonymization Techniques was *Délibération N° 2015–425 du 3 décembre 2015 autorisant l'association réseau périnatal de l'Ile-de-France Sud à mettre en œuvre un traitement automatisé de données à caractère personnel dénommé « Hygie TIU » ayant pour finalité le suivi des transferts in utero en Ile-de-France.*

[10] Among the most recent examples, see *Délibération n° 2020–055 du 14 mai 2020; Délibération n° 2019–124 du 10 octobre 2019; Délibération n° 2019–112 du 5 septembre 2019; Délibération n° 2019–122 du 3 octobre 2019; Délibération n° 2019–110 du 05 septembre 2019*; etc.

[11] An extensive definition can be found in *Délibération N° 2015–425 du 3 décembre 2015.*

[12] *CNIL, L'anonymisation de données personnelles, 19 mai 2020*, cfr. https://www.cnil.fr/fr/lan onymisation-de-donnees-personnelles.

processing[13], amending *Loi n° 78–17 du 6 janvier 1978 relative à l'informatique, aux fichiers et aux libertés* (Law 78–17 of January 6, 1978, relating to computers, records, and freedoms).

The 2004 law, anticipating the new framework proposed by the European Commission in its first draft of the Data Governance Act[14], states that the CNIL may certify and publish general repositories or methods for certifying anonymization through the services of approved or accredited third parties.

What initially emerges from the foregoing analysis is that the French DPA took a more stringent attitude towards anonymization, relying on specific and multiple tests and controls for detecting and ensuring that the risk of deanonymization is down to zero.

3 The Approach of the Italian Data Protection Authority (Garante per la Protezione dei Dati Personali)

The Italian Data Protection Authority—Garante per la Protezione dei Dati Personali (GPDP)—has never provided its own interpretation of the concept of anonymization, at least not explicitly: There are to date no opinions or guidelines the GPDP has issued specifically explaining anonymization as a concept. However, the GPDP has dealt with the issue of anonymization several times, in general and special provisions alike.

Instead, the GPDP usually refers to the interpretation given by the Article 29 Working Party (WP29), or, sometimes, even to documents issued by the Information Commissioner Officer (ICO) or by the Commission Nationale de l'Informatique et des Libertés (CNIL)[15].

The problem of how the anonymization concept is to be interpreted has been widely discussed in the literature. Insightful contributions focus on the risk approach for evaluating the robustness of the anonymization technique[16].

But what is the position of the GPDP on evaluating the risk of anonymization techniques? An investigation of the acts issued by the GPDP shows that the Italian authority does not adopt the same approach in all situations. Which is to say that on some occasions the GPDP states that anonymization needs to be irreversible, while on others it

---

[13] This law was introduced to transpose Directive 95/46/EC of the European Parliament and of the Council of 24 October 1995 on the Protection of Individuals with regard to the Processing of Personal Data and the Free Movement of such Data. It was designed to adapt the law governing computer records to technological advances and contemporary realities, and to do so consistently with the basic principles set forth in law of January 6, 1978. It was in turn amended by *Loi 2018–493 du 20 juin 2018 relative à la protection des données personnelles*, by which the GDPR was transposed into national law.

[14] The 2004 law does so specifically by introducing the concepts of *data altruism* and *secure data-processing environments* and providing for data altruism services in complying with additional technical, administrative, or organisational requirements, including through an authorisation or certification regime. Here, anonymization is framed as a dynamic process using risk analysis, supported by intermediaries and certified actors, and introducing safe environments for data processing.

[15] See, for example, GPDP, doc. web 2014 – 3134436.

[16] In this regard, see note 4 above.

takes account of the risk of reidentification, and on others still it does not indicate at all what approach is to be followed.

For example, in dealing with a number of situations, the GPDP has ordered data controllers to ensure that personal data is *"deleted or made definitively anonymous"*[17], apparently not allowing any residual risk of identifying the data subject. In another provision, using an even stronger *formula*, the GPDP states that personal data—once the retention period has lapsed—must be *"automatically deleted or permanently and irreversibly anonymised"*[18].

Differently, in other measures the GPDP has explicitly recalled the identification risk assessment under Recital 26 GDPR.

For instance, in a document titled "Deontological Data Processing Rules for Statistical or Scientific Research" the authority states that a data subject is deemed identifiable where, "by the use of reasonable means, it is possible to establish a significantly probable association" between a statistical unit and the data identifying the same data subject[19]. The same guidelines also provide some examples of "reasonable means", such as economic resources and time; they also suggest risk-assessment criteria, recommending that data controllers consider how confidential the data at stake is and that they adopt a reasonableness approach in making the assessment[20].

In that same vein, there are several occasions on which the GPDP seems to be aware that the anonymization process cannot be taken as a fixed outcome but is rather something that could change depending on context.

Thus, for example, in regard to the "preliminary check" on data processing carried out for profiling purposes, the GPDP recalls the WP29 opinion on anonymization techniques, stating that reaching a "high degree" of anonymization is a matter of reasonableness. Specifically, the GPDP requires data controllers to take into account all the means that could be reasonably used to identify a data subject, while also, at the same time, evaluating the "likelihood of re-identification"[21] inherent in the data processing.

Finally, there are also situations where the GPDP does not specify whether the approach to be followed should be the irreversible kind or a reasonable-risk assessment, a case in point being where the GPDP merely states that data is to be "deleted or made anonymous"[22], without explicitly taking a stance on the residual risk that the data subject might be reidentified[23].

From a different perspective, the GPDP's acts could be interpreted in light of the purpose ascribed to the anonymization process, meaning that this process may understood as designed to implement either.

---

[17] GPDP, doc web 2020 – 9356568, p. 12.

[18] GPDP, doc web 2018 – 8998319, p. 3; see also GPDP doc web 2018 – 8997404, p. 4.

[19] GPDP, doc web 2018 – 9069637, p. 7; see also, along the same lines, GPDP, doc web 2020 – 9069677.

[20] GPDP doc web 2015 – 4015426; GPDP, doc web 2015 – 3881392.

[21] GPDP doc web 2015 – 4698620, p. 6; see also GPDP, doc web 2020 – 9520567, doc web 2015 – 3843693, doc web 2020 – 9356568 for similar reasoning.

[22] GPDP, doc web 2016 – 4943801, p. 5.

[23] See also GPDP, doc web 2019 – 9124510; GPDP, doc web 2018 – 9068972.

1) the minimization principle or
2) the storage-limitation and the purpose-limitation principles.

These principles have a different role in the data processing: while the first represents the main basis for implementing the security measures, the second acquires importance once the scope of the data collection has been achieved.

In what concerns anonymization as a minimization measure, we might point to an opinion the GPDP issued relating to the Italian contact-tracing app for the COVID-19 outbreak: referring to the EDPB guidelines on scientific research and contact-tracing apps in the COVID-19 context[24], the GPDP reminded the Italian Presidency of Ministers that under the minimization principle, it is necessary to collect "only the data that is strictly necessary to detect possible infections, while using reliable anonymization and pseudonymization techniques"[25].

Along the same lines, the GPDP, in an opinion about a decree scheme put out by the Italian Labour Minister, seems to endorse the draft decree in part because it provides for the use of "anonymous or aggregated data by the Minister [...] in keeping the data minimization principle (Art. 5(1)(c) of the Regulation)"[26].

Less recently, but still significantly, in a 2017 provision relating to a particular data processing operation under GPDP scrutiny, the data protection authority stated that the final purposes could be pursued "consistently with the data minimization principle [...] without processing the personal data of the clientele [...], but only processing anonymized data and/or data for which consent has been obtained"[27].

On the other hand, the Italian DPA requires data controllers to implement the anonymization process as a tool for complying with the principles of purpose and storage limitation; this means that the GPDP allows data controllers to further process personal data without deleting it if data is anonymized[28].

On this approach, the GPDP treats anonymization as equivalent to cancellation. In these cases, an irreversible outcome is usually (but not always) explicitly required by the GPDP[29].

What emerges from this analysis by way of an initial assessment is that the Italian DPA takes a tailored attitude to anonymization, which can become more or less strict depending on the specific situation and even on the data processing context.

Usually, in situations where anonymization is carried out as an alternative to data cancellation, and therefore the scope of data processing is achieved, the GPDP seems to require an irreversible, zero-risk approach. Even if, this last one - as a practical matter, as previously mentioned – cannot be considered to be achieved.

---

[24] EDPB Guidelines 3/2020 and 4/2020.

[25] GPDP, doc web 2020 – 9328050, p. 3.

[26] GPDP, doc web 2019 – 9122428, p. 5.

[27] GPDP, doc web 2017 – 6844421, p. 3.

[28] GPDP, doc web 2020 – 9356568, doc web 2018 – 8998319, doc web 2018 – 8997404, doc web 2015 – 4698620, doc web 2015 – 4015426, doc web 2015 – 3881392.

[29] For cases where irreversibility is not explicitly required even though anonymization is equated with erasure, see GPDP, doc web 2016 – 4943801, doc web 2015 – 4698620.

On the contrary, when the GPDP treats anonymization as an implement measure of the minimization principle (or as a measure for protecting data subjects' rights and freedoms) another approach is requested. Specifically, since the data processing is still ongoing, assessing the re-identification risk is preferable.

4   A Comparative Conclusion

The two approaches followed by the two DPAs certainly bear out the considerations previously made: that there is a great need for theoretical solutions by which to implement anonymization as a tool for complying with the principle of data minimization (*ex-ante processing*) and the principle of storage limitation (*ex-post processing*), and even for enforcing Art. 17 GDPR (right to erasure, or right to be forgotten). Moreover, these approaches show that, overall, anonymization is an essential requirement for data reuse in the digital economy. As such anonymization appears to be called for as an operation to be executed on the datasets which pose a steep challenge on law enforcement.

Looking at the evolution of anonymization in the legal framework and at its follow-up as determined by the previously analyzed trends in the practice of the two DPAs, the WP29 seems to view anonymization as a tool aimed at the *desirable/preferable* zero-risk outcome.

However, over time—at first with the GDPR and national law, and subsequently with the DPAs—anonymization seems to be a tool in constant evolution: the desirable outcome envisioned by the WP29 therefore seems to be becoming utopian.

This certainly cannot mean that its function should be neglected[30], as it remains an essential standard for processing personal data, even if in the risk-management literature it is widely accepted that risk can never be brought to zero[31].

In view of these premises, the question could be whether the GDPR risk-based approach should be considered an exception to the traditional conception of risk (given that the data subject's rights and freedoms are at stake), and so whether a requirement of a zero-risk level should be introduced aimed at protecting fundamental rights and freedoms[32].

Zero risk seems particularly difficult to implement, mainly for two reasons: (1) the concept of risk is by its nature scalable; and (2) a zero-risk level would be impossible to enforce. This last reason is particularly meaningful in the data protection domain, considering how dynamic the context is, especially when innovative technologies are involved.

On the contrary, attention should be focused on the acceptable risk of reidentification, that is, the question should be: When is a risk level low enough to be considered compliant with the data protection legislation? And how to ensure that level?

---

[30] See, extensively, Biega, A., & Finck, M., Reviving Purpose Limitation and Data Minimisation in Per-sonalisation, Profiling and Decision-Making Systems, Max Planck Institute for Innova-tion and Competition Research Paper No. 21–04.

[31] See, extensively, Gellert, R.: We Have Always Managed Risks in Data Protection Law: Understanding the Similarities and Differences between the Rights-Based and the Risk-Based Approaches to Data Protection. European Data Protection Law Review, 481 (2016).

[32] Gellert, R.: Understanding the notion of risk in the General Data Protection Regulation. Computer Law & Security Review 34 (2018) 279–288.

In this regard, there is an essential role to be played by instruments such as codes of conduct and certification mechanisms (pursuant to Arts. 40–42 GDPR). Even if the GDPR specifies that these solutions can be adopted on a voluntary basis, they could include specific procedures to be followed by data controllers entrusted with compliance. That they can serve as reliable tools of compliance is a view also supported by the mandatory preapproval that needs to be obtained from the national DPA in charge or from the EDBP.

Therefore, on this approach, a twofold objective could be pursued. On the one hand, DPAs could endorse specific ways of applying the GDPR provisions that have no easy interpretation (e.g., the management of the reidentification risk). On the other hand, these instruments would help data controllers in achieving and demonstrating compliance in situations and contexts of particular complexity, ultimately making it possible to standardize the procedures for assessing the risk of reidentification.

Of course, it cannot be left unsaid that, being adopted on a voluntary basis, enforcement could be problematic, even if it can certainly be listed among the *best practices*, setting a responsible trend in mitigating the risks associated with data processing.

In any case, the analysis of the DPAs' provisions also shows that the residual reidentification risk is managed in different ways depending on the purpose of anonymization and its context. In fact, anonymization seems to have different aims[33], since it could be a measure/safeguard for reducing risk, but it could also be construed as further data processing, and it could even be an operation explicitly required by a DPA.

It can even be argued that the optimum level of reidentification risk is ultimately best assessed by looking at the *context* of anonymization. On that basis it would be possible to determine whether anonymization is required by the DPA as an alternative to the cancellation of data, whether the anonymized dataset will be used for purposes different from the original aim of data collection, or whether anonymization is used as measure by which to ensure compliance with the minimization principle.

In conclusion, it appears to the authors of this study that since anonymization in itself constitutes data processing, whenever controllers intend to anonymize personal data, they should do a risk assessment and, if need be, a data protection impact assessment (DPIA).

To this end, in view of the aim of anonymization, particular attention needs to be paid where the output data resulting from the anonymization process are further processed outside the original data context. Indeed, if anonymization is carried out as a data security measure or for data minimization purposes, and then as a measure for decreasing the general data processing level, the risk of reidentification could reasonably be considered lower. On the contrary, if anonymization is used to further process personal data—thereby exiting the original data context and falling outside the scope of the GDPR—the risk of reidentification could be higher.

Overall, a rigorous approach is still desirable in all situations where anonymization allows data controllers to process personal data fully outside the scope of the GDPR and for unrecognized purposes that could jeopardize data subjects' rights and freedoms.

---

[33] S. Stalla-Bourdillon, A. Knight, Anonymous Data v. Personal Data – a False Debate: an EU Perspective on Anonymization, Pseudonimization and Personal Data.

References

1. Barocas, S., Nissembaum, H.: Big data's end run around anonymity and consent. In: Lane, J., et al. (eds.) Privacy, Big Data and the Public Good, Frameworks for Engagement, Cambridge University Press, Cambridge (2014)
2. Biega, A., Finck, M.: Reviving purpose limitation and data minimisation in personalisation, profiling and decision-making systems. Max Planck Institute for Innovation and Competition Research Paper No. 21-04
3. Daigle, B., Khan, M.: The EU general data protection regulation: an analysis of enforcement trends by eu data protection authorities. J. Int. Commer. Econ. May 2020. https://www.usitc.gov/journals
4. de Montjoye, Y., et al.: Unique in the crowd: the privacy bounds of human mobility. Sci. Rep. **3**, 1376 (2013). https://www.nature.com/articles/srep01376
5. El Emam, K., Alvarez, C.: A critical appraisal of the Article 29 working party opinion 05/2014 on data anonymization techniques. Int. Data Priv. Law **5**(1), 73–87 (2015)
6. Finck, M., Pallas, F.: They who must not be identified—distinguishing personal from non-personal data under the GDPR. Int. Data Priv. Law **10**(1), 11–36 (2020)
7. Gellert, R.: We have always managed risks in data protection law: understanding the similarities and differences between the rights-based and the risk-based approaches to data protection. Eur. Data Prot. Law Rev. **481** (2016)
8. Gellert, R.: Understanding the notion of risk in the general data protection regulation. Comput. Law Secur. Rev. **34**, 279–288 (2018)
9. Kuner, C., et al.: Risk management in data protection. Int. Data Priv. Law **5**(2), 95–98 (2015)
10. Narayanan, A., Shmatikov, V.: Robust De-anonymization of Large Sparse Datasets in https://www.cs.utexas.edu/~shmat/shmat_oak08netflix.pdf
11. Rocher, L., Hendrickx, J.M., de Montjoye, Y.: Estimating the success of re-identifications in incomplete datasets using generative models. Nat. Commun. **10**, 3069 (2019). https://ui.adsabs.harvard.edu/abs/2019NatCo.10.3069R/abstract
12. Spindler, G., Schmechel, P.: Personal data and encryption in the European general data protection regulation. J. Intellect. Prop. Inf. Technol. Electr. Commun. **163** (2016)
13. Stalla-Bourdillon, S., Knight, A.: Anonymous data v. personal data – a false debate: an EU perspective on anonymization, pseudonimization and personal data. Wiscon. Int. Law J. **34**(284), 284–322 (2017)
14. Su, J., et al.: De-anonymizing web browsing data with social networks. In: Proceedings of the 26th International Conference on World Wide Web April 2017, pp. 1261–1269 (2017). https://doi.org/10.1145/3038912.3052714
15. Sweeney, L.: Policy and law: identifiability of de-identified data. http://latanyasweeney.org/work/identifiability.html
16. Veale, M., Binns, R., Ausloos, J.: When data protection by design and data subject rights clash. Int. Data Priv. Law **8**(2), 105–123 (2018)

A Legal Framework for Digital Transformation: A Proposal Based on a Comparative Case Study

Rozha K. Ahmed[1]([✉]) [iD], Khder H. Muhammed[2], Awat O. Qadir[2],
Soran I. Arif[2], Silvia Lips[1] [iD], Katrin Nyman-Metcalf[3] [iD], Ingrid Pappel[1] [iD],
and Dirk Draheim[1] [iD]

[1] Information Systems Group, Tallinn University of Technology, Tallinn, Estonia
{rozha.ahmed,silvia.lips,ingrid.pappel,dirk.draheim}@taltech.ee
[2] Judicial Council of Kurdistan Region of Iraq, Sulaimaniyah, Iraq
{khidr.muhammed,awat.qadir,soran.ibrahim}@sulicourt.com
[3] Department of Law, Tallinn University of Technology, Tallinn, Estonia
katrin.nyman-metcalf@taltech.ee

Abstract. Digital transformation is crucial for governments to provide better and more efficient services to the citizens. A legal framework is a necessary component of each e-government ecosystem to ensure proper delivery of e-services. This research proposes a legal framework for e-government in the Kurdistan Region of Iraq (KRI). The research started with the KRI's e-Court system project as the first pilot project towards the systematic introduction of e-government in general. The research is based on a qualitative comparative case study of the KRI and Estonia, which is known to have a particularly mature set of e-government regulations. Data have been collected from legal databases, existing literature, and other available legal documentations from both countries. This study aims to provide a foundation for the Kurdistan Regional Government (KRG) to conclude plans for digital expansion and implementation of e-government in the KRI. Beyond that, the authors hope that this study extends the existing body of knowledge and literature in a way that is useful for e-government practitioners in other projects and researchers alike.

Keywords: ICT laws · e-services · e-government · e-Court · e-File · Legal framework · Kurdistan region · Iraq · Estonia

1 Introduction

Governments can provide better and more efficient services to citizens by digital means through the implementation of e-government. However, the decision to move toward digital transformation and e-government implementation requires in-depth analysis and strategy, in particular, to guarantee a clear road map to digital inclusion. Caring for legal issues is crucial to ensure that the necessary

© Springer Nature Switzerland AG 2021
A. Kö et al. (Eds.): EGOVIS 2021, LNCS 12926, pp. 115–128, 2021.
https://doi.org/10.1007/978-3-030-86611-2_9

regulatory framework exists to enable digital transformation while protecting citizens' rights [10,11].

Initiatives of digital transformation have taken place in the Kurdistan Region of Iraq (KRI) since 2014 through the implementation of a Court Information System. This project aimed to digitize court processes to increase efficiency and deliver better justice services to the citizen. The system has been introduced in the Sulaimaniyah Appellate Court at the Sulaimaniyah City as the first step. Next, it is planned to expand the solution to all other courts in the KRI.

This e-Court system has improved court efficiency concerning court internal daily operations, enhanced court cases' security, extended access to the judiciary, and increased transparency in the court processes [3]. On the other hand, the project has faced many challenges; among them, the lack of a digital signature and the absence of supporting laws are considered significant issues [2]. Hence, the authors considered legal issues that support the smooth operation of an entirely paperless e-Court system and to ensure the validity of the process. Furthermore, as there is a clear willingness in the KRI to move toward a comprehensive government transformation with the implementation of e-government and prepare for future missions, this research also considers the relevant laws for e-government implementation.

This research investigates Estonia and the KRI cases from a legal perspective by analyzing existing literature, reviewing available laws and legal documents related to digital transformation. The Estonian case has been selected because the country already has a mature legal framework that supports e-government, and Estonia has implemented a successful e-Court system. The KRI is taking the first steps towards e-government by implementing its e-Court system. Therefore, the comparison of two different practices helps to identify the existing gaps in the KRI case.

As an outcome of this study, the authors propose a legal framework for digital transformation in the KRI through a set of laws essential to regulate technology usage concerning e-Court systems and e-government implementation. The research aims at extending the body of knowledge for academics, practitioners, decision-makers, judiciaries, and regulators. The results will serve the Kurdistan Regional Government (KRG) to prepare digital inclusion concerning legal issues.

In Sect. 2, we present the research questions and methodology. In Sect. 3, we provide a general description of the e-court systems of both Estonia and the KRI. In Sect. 4, we present overview about digital transformation in Estonia and the KRI. In Sect. 5, we present relevant legislation for both e-Court system as domain-specific and e-government as general laws in Estonia and the KRI. In Sect. 6, we present the proposed legal framework for the KRI. We finish with a conclusion in Sect. 7.

2   Research Methodology

Providing government services in electronic format requires an infrastructure that is fully dependent on the use of technological tools, and laws play a crucial role in determining the legal and valid usage of these all technological components together. Hence, it is necessary to clarify a proper understanding of introducing the necessary new laws and what amendments need to be done to existing ones.

Therefore, this paper answers the following research questions:

- What are the necessary laws for implementing an e-Court system in the KRI as a specific part of the e-government realm?
- What are the necessary laws for the implementation of e-government in the KRI?

This research uses a qualitative, analytical comparative case study approach [17]. This strategy analyzes and compares practices in Estonia and the KRI's different contexts and jurisdictions. In both cases, two types of sources will be analyzed: (i) legal databases and other types of necessary rules and (ii) existing literature and other available documentation (i.e., official documents of public organizations). The research started with an in-depth analysis of the legal environment of the Estonian e-government followed by the analysis of the available relevant laws to e-government implementation in the KRI. By comparing the analyses of both cases it is possible to determine whether new laws or other forms of rules are needed or whether existing ones shall be amended – or perhaps, no change is needed other than a different interpretation for the KRI case.

3   Digital Transformation of Courts

3.1   Implementation of the Court Information System in Estonia

Estonia uses a modern court information management system for all its court types, including the first and the second instance, and the Supreme Court[1]. The system is called the e-File and manages all case types and jurisdictions for civil, criminal, and administrative issues. It is composed of different integrated systems such as the Police Information System, the Court Information System, the Prison Information System, and the Criminal Case Management Register through the Public Prosecutor's Office, in addition to availability of public portal for citizens and lawyers to access their cases, see Fig. 1. The system uses an ID card as an authentication method for actors in the system to access all e-services but with different access rights provided depending on the role. Data are securely exchanged between different parties, and claimants can submit their claims online: the system generates a notification for the addressee. The system went live in 2005.

3.2   Implementation of the Court Information System in the KRI

A court information system called an e-Court system is implemented in the Sulaimaniyah Appellate Court in the Sulaimaniyah city as a first pilot project [3],

---

[1] https://www.rik.ee/et/node/489.

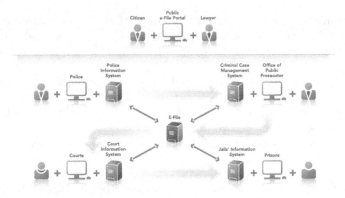

Fig. 1. The Estonian e-File system. (See Footnote 1)

and planned to be extended in other cities of the KRI. The project started in 2014 and launched in 2016, while support and constant improvements of the system last until now. The system manages three types of court proceedings, i.e., court cases from civil and criminal jurisdictions, certificates, and other transactions that are processed similarly to court cases but without disputes between parties.

The system is composed of integrated subsystems that allow smooth communication and secure data exchange between different parties. The collaborative activities are achieved successfully through a central database that allows case management and access by courts, the prosecution office, and police stations. Furthermore, as shown in Fig. 2, outside agencies, lawyers, and case participants (citizens) can access the system through a public portal for case monitoring and status updates.

While the system has increased the efficiency and effectiveness of court processes [3], in contrast, several challenges were identified during the implementation before the system could be extended to other courts. The lack of a digital signature and insufficiency of the legal environment were identified as critical problems [2]. Furthermore, there is a need for an e-government infrastructure, electronic identity (eID) and its management systems to support the KRI e-Court initiative [1].

4   Digital Transformation of Governments

4.1   e-Government

A general common definition of e-government could be the use of technological tools to enhance the government performance, transparency, efficiency, citizen trust, and provision of high-quality services through a single shared infrastructure across the entire private and public governmental sectors, made up of integrated systems with an interoperable data exchange layer [5,6,8,10,16]. On the

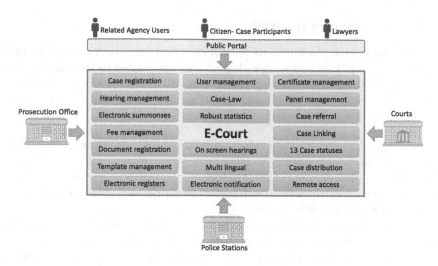

Fig. 2. Kurdistan e-Court system.

other hand, technology usage might expose different risks and challenges compared to the traditional paper-based system, such as security risks, data protection, privacy issues, and others. [9] consider these challenges as significant factors and suggest legislative analysis to mitigate these risks. Therefore, legislation plays a crucial role in regulating the usage of technology and electronic transitions. The working procedures of e-government have to be valid and legally equivalent to the paper world procedures; furthermore, online transactions' legal validity ensures citizen trust towards electronic services [13].

4.2   e-Government in Estonia

In 2001, Estonia started implementing e-government and developed a platform for providing e-services with a secure data exchange layer called X-Road that connects decentralized governmental databases to provide access to the state information systems through a single public portal [4,11,12,14]. X-Road was implemented step by step through different versions once the state was ready from the legal and organizational perspective [6]. Increasing transparency in governance was one of the main goals [5], to achieve a higher quality of service delivery while considering citizen democracy and participation [8], as well as providing a "fully integrated one-stop-shop" for almost 99% of e-services [15] to allow digitalized interaction between citizens and local governments. Estonia has been focusing on digital government ecosystems and investigating technologies that support digital transformation by understanding architectural needs and process re-engineering considering enterprise architecture. Based on experience over decades one most crucial component in Estonian e-governance developments has been digital data exchange [4] as well as digital signing [12] as critical step to move to paperless government.

4.3   e-Government in the KRI

The KRI is located in the northern part of Iraq and from 1992 formed an independent administration; and within this administration, an independent parliament and judicial system have been established. The KRG has planned to move towards digitization and implementation of e-government since 2014 through initiating the following projects:

- Mapping public services: the project aims to map all the government services provided directly or indirectly to citizens to improve service delivery with less bureaucracy. The outcome of this project will identify the number of services, creating a one-stop-shop for providing information and guidelines about the services through a public portal.
- Implementation of eID: this project draws a road map for the implementation of a unique digital identity card through registering the biometric data of all citizens. However, this project will be a long term plan of reform consisting of different phases. In the initial phase of the biometric registration system, data were collected, stored, and validated. The outcome was used to improve government wage earners' salary payment in a scalable and centralized biometric system.
- Building pilot information systems: digital transformation in organizations started by analyzing systems "as is" and re-engineering the current processes. One crucial component of an e-government structure is the availability of integrated information systems to allow digital transactions and electronic data exchange between different sectors. In this regard, the Court Information System is built as a first pilot project. The outcome of this project provides vision for future expansion.

5   Digital Transformation and Relevant Legislation

5.1   The Case of Estonia

It is clear from the literature that Estonia has not created too many laws regarding e-government and there is no centralized legal act regulating the e-government domain. This is a deliberate decision by the relevant decision-makers, as specialized legislation on e-government risks creating a parallel system that the government wants to avoid, in addition, Estonia is a member of the European Union (EU), and EU law applies fully to Estonia (including e-government related regulations such as eIDAS[2] and GDPR[3].

---

[2] EU Parliament and Council regulation (EU) no 910/2014 on electronic identification and trust services for electronic transactions in the internal market and repealing Directive 1999/93/EC.

[3] EU Parliament and Council regulation (EU) no 2016/679 on the protection of natural persons with regard to the processing of personal data and on the free movement of such data, and repealing Directive 95/46/EC (General Data Protection Regulation).

It is also important to distinguish three types of legal acts: laws, which are legal acts issued by the Parliament of Estonia, legal acts adopted by the government, and legal acts issued by different ministers. As in any jurisdiction, laws are the most important, and other legislation must be in accordance with the law. For e-government, many rules are found in other instruments than laws. Regarding domain-specific laws, several specific acts to the court system regulating the e-Court system and digital information exchange in the court procedures as presented in Fig. 3.

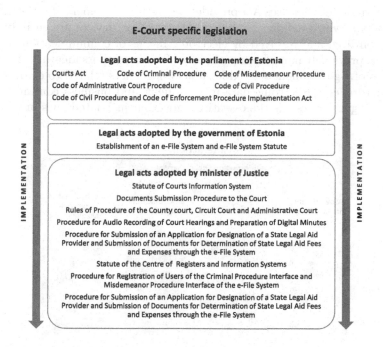

Fig. 3. Estonian e-Court specific legislation.

The Courts Act establishes a court information system. The system aims to organize the work of courts, collect statistics, collect and systematize decisions, and make them available to courts and the public[4]. The Code of Criminal Procedure[5], the Code of Misdemeanour Procedure[6], the Code of Administrative Court Procedure[7], and the Code of Civil Procedure[8] enable processing of digital documents and evidence in the specific procedure in the information system.

---

[4] https://www.riigiteataja.ee/en/eli/519122019009/consolide.
[5] https://www.riigiteataja.ee/en/eli/507012020008/consolide.
[6] https://www.riigiteataja.ee/en/eli/515012020005/consolide.
[7] https://www.riigiteataja.ee/en/eli/512122019007/consolide.
[8] https://www.riigiteataja.ee/en/eli/512122019004/consolide.

The Code of Civil Procedure and the Code of Enforcement Procedure Implementation Act[9] sets the information system requirements.

One of the most relevant provisions is establishing an e-File system and e-File system statute that enables digital data storage, management, access, and security requirements[10]. Other legal acts named in Fig. 3, issued by the Minister of Justice, specify different data-related procedures and relations and communication between other information systems.

Moving on to the general laws, there are significant laws that allow the smooth electronic transaction and data transfer in e-government in Estonia. Information Society Services Act provides the basic requirements for the information society service providers [11]. Information society services are entirely transmitted, conveyed and received by electronic means of communication. In addition to the previously named comprehensive act, the authors identified four main categories of e-government related legal acts: legal acts related to e-government infrastructure, eID, electronic data management, and business continuity management. Figure 4 presents the essential e-government related laws in Estonia.

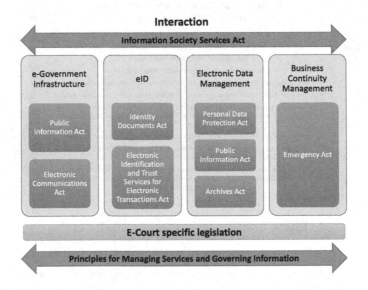

Fig. 4. Estonian e-Government related laws.

- Public Information Act aims to ensure that every person has access to public information. It is also the basis for establishing and administering databases and their supervision[12]. This Act is in force since 2001 and provides a basic

---

[9] https://www.riigiteataja.ee/en/eli/511042019002/consolide.

[10] https://www.riigiteataja.ee/akt/109032018005.

[11] https://www.riigiteataja.ee/en/eli/515012019001/consolide.

[12] https://www.riigiteataja.ee/en/eli/529032019012/consolide.

regulatory framework for e-government infrastructure and electronic data management. Consequently, the following three Government regulations are derived from the Public Information Act.

- Information Systems Data Exchange Layer: this regulation is in force since 2016 and contains requirements for the data exchange layer of information systems (also called X Road), its usage, and management[13].
- Information Systems Security Measures: this regulation is created for managing the security of different public sector information systems and is in force since 2008[14].
- State Information System Management: this regulation creates the main principles of state information system management and in force since 2008[15].

- Electronic Communications Act is in force since 2005 and establishes the necessary conditions for developing electronic communications and promotes electronic services[16].
- Identity Documents Act states the requirements for all identity documents (including digital documents, eIDs) issued by the Republic of Estonia and in force since 2000[17].
- Electronic Identification and Trust Services for Electronic Transactions Act regulates electronic identification and trust services for electronic transactions. More specifically, the Act contains requirements for the trust service provider and its supervision. It is in force since 2016[18].
- Personal Data Protection Act states the main data protection principles of natural persons, and in force since 2018[19].
- Archives Act is relevant for the management, organization, and preservation of archival records (including digital records). It is in force since 2012 (See Footnote 6).
- Emergency Act ensures the continuity of primary services during emergencies. According to this Act, digital identification and digital signing are vital services. The Act is in force since 2017[20].

All these e-governance related acts complement each other and influence e-Court specific legislative acts. It should be noticed that these acts do not deal only with digital or e-government related matters but also cover, for example, protection of or access to paper-based data, archiving of traditional forms of data, and so on. They, however, contain the necessary provisions for e-government and the e-Court.

---

[13] https://www.riigiteataja.ee/akt/127092016004.
[14] https://www.riigiteataja.ee/akt/13125331.
[15] https://www.riigiteataja.ee/akt/106082019018.
[16] https://www.riigiteataja.ee/en/eli/513012020007/consolide.
[17] https://www.riigiteataja.ee/en/eli/504022020003/consolide.
[18] https://www.riigiteataja.ee/en/eli/511012019010/consolide.
[19] https://www.riigiteataja.ee/en/eli/523012019001/consolide.
[20] https://www.riigiteataja.ee/en/eli/511122019004/consolide.

5.2   The Case of the KRI

The KRI generally follows the Iraqi legal system, and some laws of the Iraqi government are used in the KRI. However, the KRI has an independent judicial system, government, and parliament, so there is a set of laws issued by the Kurdistan Parliament. The legal pyramid is the traditional one, consisting of the constitution, which forms the basis of laws. Laws which are passed by the parliament about a particular subject. The next stage consists of regulations that are detailed by the Council of Ministers or a specific ministry. Finally, instructions, policies, and orders are issued by a specific ministry or institution based on a specific law to regulate a particular issue relevant to that sector.

Considering the relevant laws for an e-Court system, no law exists to support and regulate the electronic court system's operation. Hence, the current implemented court information system in the Sulaimaniyah Appellate Court is designed to operate with old existing laws that govern the physical world. However, the system is very flexible and can adapt to new changes easily. Furthermore, from analysis, It is found that the primary laws that are used in courts for solving court cases are very old laws meant to govern the paper world and do not support technological advancements and usage of e-Court systems. Examples of these laws include the Criminal Procedure Law, the Civil Procedure Law, the Civil Law, the Penal Code, the Labour Law, the Personal Status Law, the Evidence Law, the Civil Status Law, the Care of Minors Law, the Juvenile Welfare Law, and the Penal Code for the Internal Security Forces[21].

Moving on to the general laws for e-government, only one ICT relevant law exists that is used and issued in the KRI, as described in the following:

– Law of Banning the Misuse of Communication Devices describes the era of technology and how communication mediums such as phone devices, electronic mail, social media, and related issues can be appropriately used, and what punishment will be the consequence for the wrong usage and crimes committed through them, it is in force since 2008 (See Footnote 21)[22].

6   Findings

Creating a legal framework needs careful analysis and study of laws in any country that wants to start the digital transformation. It is also advisable that over-regulation should be avoided. New laws might not be needed for every matter, but existing laws can be amended if required to fit the smooth transformation of the government towards digitization, providing legal validity of electronic data and transactions.

As the e-Court system is one kind of information system that is considered a component of the whole e-government infrastructure, hence, the relevant laws that support the operation of e-government apply to specific domains like e-Courts as well. All general laws established at the higher level are generic, and

---

[21] http://iraqld.hjc.iq.
[22] https://www.parliament.krd/english/.

each specific domain will use them. The KRI does not have a constitution, while new laws can be issued, and amendments in the existing laws can be made through the Kurdistan Parliament that was established in 1992 (See Footnote 19).

6.1   Domain-Specific Laws

Concerning an e-Court system, authors found that, in general, courts operate through two categories of laws: procedural laws to organize court operations and substantive laws that detail how to solve disputes in courts. The e-Court system is more related to procedural laws, particularly the Criminal Procedure Law and the Civil Procedure Law, as well as the Evidence Law. It needs to be analyzed what amendments needed to be made in these three laws to support the case management procedures from claim submission, electronic hearings, video conferencing, electronic notifications to final case disposal in the e-Court system.

6.2   General e-Government Laws

Regarding the legal framework of e-government for the KRI, after the Estonian case is analyzed, it can be concluded that dealing with the legal aspect can be made by identifying essential key enablers for the digital transformation. The results present main key enablers along with necessary legal acts to ensure expected quality and liability of the e-service delivery in the following points:

Electronic Identity Document. eID is one of the main enablers in the digital environment. It is crucial to uniquely identify every citizen through an electronic identity to ensure the citizen's ability to sign digitally in electronic transactions. Hence, a new law is needed to regulate electronic identification and trust services and give such legal validity to the digital signatures that are equivalent to the manual signature while furthermore establishing rights and obligations related to the use of the signature [7].

Interoperability. One of the critical enablers of e-government is interoperability between interconnected registers and information systems and a set of technological tools. Data exchange and electronic transactions are the core factors to be considered and access to the public information shared through the e-government environment. For that purpose, the following findings can be applied to the case of the KRI.

– New legislation that includes an Electronic Transactions Law. Although such specific law does not exist in Estonia and it is not advisable for countries with more advanced e-government systems to have it, as amendments to existing law are often sufficient. For the KRI, authors feel that a law needs to be issued, regulating how institutions should organize their business processes according to the advancement of technology. This can be done by issuing a very general law to validate electronic transactions while giving authority to the Council of Ministers and the relevant ministers to create instructions and regulations to regulate each particular ministry without referring to the issuance of separate specific main laws.

- Relevant laws for banks and electronic payments are needed. Transforming government digitally involves business sectors and banks. Giving validity to electronic payment is essential along with regulating banks in the digital environment.
- Amendments can be made to the Access to Information Right Law. The Kurdistan Parliament already issued this law in 2013 (See Footnote 19). It governs the rules for obtaining public information in the physical world, enhancing transparency in the government. However, it can be amended to suit electronic information and control access to government databases and systems.
- New law for archiving electronic data and documents needed to define rules for preservation, access, and protection of archival records.

Cybersecurity. The availability of public services digitally, information systems, interconnected databases, networking, and electronic transactions, creates, shares and exchanges a massive amount of data. Hence, security concerns such as privacy, individual data protection, confidentiality, trust, service continuity, cyber attacks, data integrity, identity protection, and authentication will become increasingly important issues. Legal measures allow defining reaction mechanisms to these cybersecurity aspects by adopting a "harmonized set of laws" that can guarantee the proper usage of ICT [15]. From this viewpoint, it can be seen that the followings changes are needed in the case of the KRI:

- Amendments in the Law of Banning the Misuse of Communication Devices, to guarantee the proper usage of ICT tools in particular within the e-government infrastructure. Currently, the law defines only limited devices.
- A Personal Data Protection Law needs to be adopted to ensure proper protection of individual data and user privacy in the e-world.
- Adoption of a new law for cybercrime may be considered. The law should define service providers' rights and obligations, cyber incidents, privacy, and liability of the systems.

Figure 5 presents the proposed legal framework for both the e-Court system and e-government for the KRI.

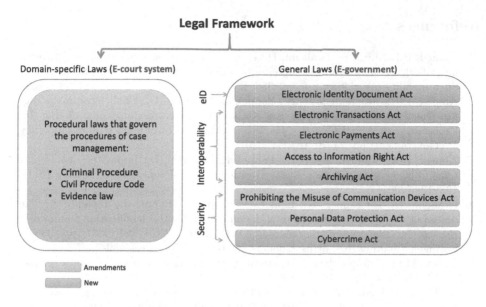

Fig. 5. Legal framework proposal for the Kurdistan Region.

7 Conclusion

Legislation plays a significant role in the digital transformation process. The existence of a regulatory framework ensures the validity of the electronic format's business processes and supports technological tools' right usage. It increases citizens' trust and helps the government to deliver better services in accordance with the law. The results of this study presented a proposal of a legal framework that can be established for specific domain laws such as an e-Court system and general laws relevant to the e-government in light of a comparative analysis with Estonia's case. The Estonian case can be used to evaluate the legal readiness to implement different e-governance initiatives in the KRI.

Some limitations of this research include limited availability of legal databases in the English language in the KRI case.

The future research direction would be towards conducting more in-depth analysis and validation of the proposed legal framework based on the KRI legal environment by a team of selected legal experts and making needed changes in the laws content as well as preparing regulation drafts for the successful implementation of e-government in the KRI.

Acknowledgment. Special thanks to Safeen Ghafour, Senior Reform Advisor to the Deputy Prime Minister of the KRG, for supporting this research by providing updated data and documentation on e-government initiatives in the KRI. We are also grateful to Aleksander Reitsakas for his steady support of this research. Additionally, we are thankful to Hiwa Afandi, the head of KRG Department of Information Technology for his valuable comments and support of this research.

References

1. Ahmed, R.K., Lips, S., Draheim, D.: eSignature in eCourt Systems. In: Proceedings of 2020 Fourth World Conference on Smart Trends in Systems, Security and Sustainability (WorldS4), pp. 352–356. IEEE (2020)
2. Ahmed, R.K., Muhammed, K.H., Pappel, I., Draheim, D.: Challenges in the digital transformation of courts: a case study from the Kurdistan region of Iraq. In: Proceedings of ICEDEG 2020—The 7th International Conference on eDemocracy & eGovernment, pp. 74–79. IEEE (2020)
3. Ahmed, R.K., Muhammed, K.H., Pappel, I., Draheim, D.: Impact of e-court systems implementation: a case study. Transform. Gov. People Process Policy **15**(1), 108–128 (2021)
4. Draheim, D., Koosapoeg, K., Lauk, M., Pappel, I., Pappel, I., Tepandi, J.: The design of the estonian governmental document exchange classification framework. In: Kő, A., Francesconi, E. (eds.) EGOVIS 2016. LNCS, vol. 9831, pp. 33–47. Springer, Cham (2016). https://doi.org/10.1007/978-3-319-44159-7_3
5. Goede, M.: E-Estonia: the e-government cases of Estonia, Singapore, and Curaçao. Arch. Bus. Res. **7**(2), 216–227 (2019)
6. Kalja, A., Reitsakas, A., Saard, N.: eGovernment in Estonia: best practices. In: Portland International Conference on Management of Engineering and Technology 2005, pp. 500–506 (2005)
7. Kim, H.: Globalization and regulatory change: the interplay of laws and technologies in E-commerce in Southeast Asia. Comput. Law Secur. Rev. **35**(5), 105315 (2019)
8. Kitsing, M.: An evaluation of E-government in Estonia. In: Internet, Politics and Policy 2010: An Impact Assessment Conference at Oxford University (2010)
9. Layne, K., Lee, J.: Developing fully functional E-government: a four stage model. Gov. Inf. Q. **15**(18), 122–136 (2001)
10. Nyman-Metcalf, K.: e-Governance: a new reality for legislative drafting? Int. J. Legis. Draft. Law Reform **6**, 39 (2017)
11. Nyman-Metcalf, K.: How to build e-governance in a digital society: the case of Estonia. Revista Catalana de Dret Public **58**, 1–12 (2019)
12. Pappel, I., Pappel, I., Tepandi, J., Draheim, D.: Systematic digital signing in Estonian e-government processes. In: Hameurlain, A., Küng, J., Wagner, R., Dang, T.K., Thoai, N. (eds.) Transactions on Large-Scale Data- and Knowledge-Centered Systems XXXVI. LNCS, vol. 10720, pp. 31–51. Springer, Heidelberg (2017). https://doi.org/10.1007/978-3-662-56266-6_2
13. Rikk, R., Roosna, S.: e-Estonia: e-Governance in Practice. eGA (2016)
14. Tsap, V., Pappel, I., Draheim, D.: Key success factors in introducing national e-identification systems. In: Dang, T.K., Wagner, R., Küng, J., Thoai, N., Takizawa, M., Neuhold, E.J. (eds.) FDSE 2017. LNCS, vol. 10646, pp. 455–471. Springer, Cham (2017). https://doi.org/10.1007/978-3-319-70004-5_33
15. United Nations: The United Nations e-government survey 2018. Technical report, United Nations, Department of Economic and Social Affairs (2018)
16. Wirtz, B.W., Daiser, P.: A meta-analysis of empirical e-government research and its future research implications. Int. Rev. Adm. Sci. **84**(1), 144–163 (2018)
17. Yin, R.K.: Applications of Case Study Research. Sage, Los Angeles (2011)

Artificial Intelligence and Machine Learning in E-Government Context

Classification and Association Rules in Brazilian Supreme Court Judgments on Pre-trial Detention

Thiago Raulino Dal Pont[1] , Isabela Cristina Sabo[2] ,
Pablo Ernesto Vigneaux Wilton[3] , Victor Araújo de Menezes[2] , Rafael Copetti[2] ,
Luciano Zambrota[2] , Pablo Procópio Martins[3] , Edjandir Corrêa Costa[3] ,
Edimeia Liliani Schnitzler[3] , Paloma Maria Santos[3] ,
Rodrigo Rafael Cunha[3(✉)] , Gerson Bovi Kaster[3] , and Aires José Rover[2,3]

[1] Department of Automation and Systems, Federal University of Santa Catarina, UFSC,
Florianópolis, Brazil
[2] Department of Law, Federal University of Santa Catarina, UFSC, Florianópolis, Brazil
[3] Department of Knowledge Engineering and Management, Federal University of Santa
Catarina, UFSC, Florianópolis, Brazil

Abstract. Brazil has a large prison population, which places it as the third country in the world with the most incarceration rate. In addition, the criminal caseload is increasing in Brazilian Judiciary, which is encouraging AI usage to advance in e-Justice. Within this context, the paper presents a case study with a dataset composed of 2,200 judgments from the Supreme Federal Court (STF) about pre-trial detention. These are cases in which a provisional prisoner requests for freedom through habeas corpus. We applied Machine Learning (ML) and Natural Language Processing (NLP) techniques to predict whether STF will release or not the provisional prisoner (text classification), and also to find a reliable association between the judgment outcome and the prisoners' crime and/or the judge responsible for the case (association rules). We obtained satisfactory results in both tasks. Classification results show that, among the models used, Convolutional Neural Network (CNN) is the best, with 95% accuracy and 0.91 F1-Score. Association results indicate that, among the rules generated, there is a high probability of drug law crimes leading to a dismissed habeas corpus (which means the maintenance of pre-trial detention). We concluded that STF has not interfered in first degree decisions about pre-trial detention and that is necessary to discuss the drug criminalization in Brazil. The main contribution of the paper is to provide models that can support judges and pre-trial detainees.

Keywords: E-justice · Criminal law · Pre-trial detention · Text classification · Association rules · Machine learning

E-Government UFSC Research Group - egov.ufsc@gmail.com.

© Springer Nature Switzerland AG 2021
A. Kö et al. (Eds.): EGOVIS 2021, LNCS 12926, pp. 131–142, 2021.
https://doi.org/10.1007/978-3-030-86611-2_10

1 Introduction

Brazil has a large prison population. According to the National Penitentiary Department, there were more than 750 thousand people in detention in the country in 2019 [1]. This situation places Brazil as the third country in the world with the most incarceration rate [2].

There are two groups of prison population: permanent and provisional. The difference between them is that the provisional ones have not yet been definitively judged. Provisional prisoners should await the judgment with their freedom restricted because they represent imminent danger or may interfere with the process. This situation should be an exception and represent a smaller percentage of the prison population. However, the number of pre-trial detainees in Brazil is high. In 2019, there were 222,558 provisional prisoners, which corresponds to 29% of the total prisoners in the country [1].

Furthermore, 2.4 million new criminal cases entered the Brazilian Judiciary in 2019, of which 121.4 thousand (4.3%) were in the Superior Courts [3]. To minimize the problem of increasing caseload (which includes criminal cases about pre-trial detention), Brazilian Judiciary has been trying to advance in e-Justice with regulations encouraging the use of Artificial Intelligence (AI) in its domain [4, 5].

For this purpose, this paper presents a case study with the Brazilian Supreme Federal Court (STF) judgments on pre-trial detention and the use of AI to generate models that can support judges and provisional prisoners. Our research questions are: 1. Can we accurately predict whether STF will release or not the prisoner in an habeas corpus judgment on pre-trial detention? 2. Can we find a reliable association between the judgment outcome and the prisoners' crime and/or the Judge-Rapporteur? To answer them, we resort to two Machine Learning (ML) tasks: classification and association rules.

The paper is organized as follows: In Sect. 2, we present some concepts on pre-trial detention in Brazilian Law and ML tasks. In Sect. 3, we expose some other works about predictions with Superior Courts' judgments. In Sect. 4, we describe the case study methodology, including the dataset construction and the techniques applied. In Sects. 5 and 6, we show and discuss the results. Finally, there are concluding remarks and new perspectives of study in Sect. 7.

2 Background

2.1 Pre-trial Detention and Habeas Corpus in Brazilian Law

According to the Brazilian Criminal Procedure Code [6], pre-trial detention is a kind of precautionary arrest and aims to provide security and effectiveness to criminal prosecution, preventing that accused and/or third parties can hamper the regular progress of the process. It can be decreed from the investigation stage until the end of the criminal proceedings.

Brazilian Constitution [7] states that no one shall be arrested unless in "flagrante delicto" or by a written and justified order of a competent judicial authority, save in the cases of military transgression or specific military crime, as defined in law.

It is, therefore, a precautionary instrument, lasting as long as the reasons that gave rise to it. Pre-trial detention may be decreed as a guarantee of public order, economic order, for the convenience of criminal instruction or to ensure the application of criminal law, when there is evidence of the crime and sufficient evidence of authorship and danger generated by the state of freedom of the accused [6].

The habeas corpus is a constitutional action which aims to protect the individual against any restraining measure from the public power to his/her right of freedom. It is preventive (aims to cease imminent violence or coercion) or repressive (when a concrete prejudice occurs) [7]. It is an instrument frequently used to prevent the maintenance of preventive detention in criminal actions in the STF.

2.2 Machine Learning Tasks: Classification and Association Rules

AI aims to understand intelligence for the construction of intelligent entities. AI can be divided into six fields: Knowledge representation; Natural Language Processing (NLP); Automated Reasoning; ML; Computer vision; Robotics [8].

ML, one of the fields of AI, is concerned with the development of systems capable of learning from data. Géron [9] classifies the learning process in four major categories:

- supervised learning: the training dataset has the solution or the labels;
- unsupervised learning: the training dataset doesn't have the solution, that is, it is unlabeled;
- semi supervised learning: part of the training dataset is labeled;
- reinforcement learning: the system learns as it receives rewards.

Classification is the main ML task of supervised learning category. It estimates a finite set of discrete labels, so the algorithms predict a class for unlabeled data. Metrics are used to assess the level of correctness of the result of the task [10]. The most used metrics to evaluate classification results are:

- accuracy: number of correct predictions divided by total of predictions made;
- precision: number of true positive divided by the sum of true positive and false positive;
- recall: true positive divided by the sum of true positive and false negative;
- F1-Score: harmonic mean of precision and recall: 2 × precision × recall/(precision + recall).

Association rules is one of the ML tasks of unsupervised learning category. It is used to find interesting associations in large sets of data items [11]. Algorithms can be used to implement association rules and metrics as support and confidence to measure the quality of the rules [12]:

- support: ratio of transactions containing the set of items of the association rule;
- confidence: the ratio of correct results of the association rule, considering the set of items of the support.

3   Related Works

At the United States Supreme Court, experiments predicted cases outcome using the votes of several judges who have integrated it, in which a decision is confirmed or changed in a higher instance. They also used attributes such as the year of the case, the legal matter discussed and the location of the lower court. The approach with Decision Trees and Random Forest (ensemble method) classifiers achieved an 70.2% accuracy on the case outcome and 71.9% on the judge vote predictions [13, 14].

At the European Court of Human Rights, an experiment predicted if a Member State act might be a violation or non-violation of human rights, based on the cases and premises of civil and political rights included in the European Convention on Human Rights. The approach with Linear Support Vector Machines (SVM) classifier had 79% of accuracy [15].

Another experiment at the Supreme Court of France with Linear SVM classifier reported results of 96% F1-Score in predicting a case ruling, 90% F1-Score in predicting the law area of a case, and 75.9% F1-Score in estimating the decade to which the case belongs. They used cases and decisions from the 1880s to 2010 as input [16].

At the Supreme Court of the Philippines, to reduce court litigation and problems with pending cases, experiments predicted the case outcome in the criminal context. They used public processes as input and obtained 59% of accuracy with Random Forest classifiers [17].

In Brazil, the "VICTOR" project at the STF aims to automatically linking cases that constitutes general repercussion (GR). The GR is a procedural instrument that acts as a "filter", allowing the Court to select the appeals that it will analyze according to the criteria of legal, political, social or economic relevance. The solution based on deep learning had an accuracy of 90.35% in a preliminary evaluation with Convolution Neural Networks (CNN) [18].

Advancing the state of the art, our work brings not only classification but also association rules with attributes extracted from the judgments texts.

4   Methodology

The research is a case study since it investigates a contemporary problem with real data [19]. To achieve this, we constructed a dataset and applied ML and NLP techniques to generate models which embraced two tasks: classification and association. We used Orange 3 [20] in most of our classification and association experiments. As a complement, we applied Python Programming language with ML libraries in one of the classification models [21].

4.1   Dataset: Collection and Attribute Extraction

Our dataset is composed of around 2,200 judgments (collective judicial decision) from STF between June 2004 and February 2020. They are limited to the subject of pre-trial detention, where a provisional prisoner requests for freedom through habeas corpus. Once this type of data is public in Brazil, we collected the legal cases from STF's web platform [22] as Portable Document Format (PDF). However, we ignored documents composed only of scanned images, i.e., without any selectable text. Due to the structure of the documents, a more refined work would be necessary in order not to lose the formatting and consequently lose data. Thus, it was easier to extract the contents of the PDF files to raw text files. Using open-source tools such as the Python programming language [23] and open-source libraries for PDF and text processing [24], we extracted the text from the PDF documents to raw text files, which we used as part of our dataset in our experiments for classification (2,015) and association rules (1,776).

The dataset was analyzed by an interdisciplinary research group, which extracted 3 attributes from each judgment: a) final outcome; b) crime category; and c) Judge-Rapporteur. One group manually extracted attributes "a" and "b" while the other one automatically extracted "c" using NLP techniques like named-entity recognition and regular expressions since the rapporteur's name is usually in the same place in all documents.

a) Final outcome: Knowing that there are many ways to represent the same outcome in the decision text, for this attribute we came in terms on the assumption of a "released" or "not released" binary outcome. When house arrest was granted, the classification was "not released" because it did not imply the incarceration of such a person. Thus, "released" means that the punishment is not carried out in a penitentiary. The ratio for final outcome in the dataset is: not released (75.73%) and released (24.27%).

b) Crime category: Considering the various forms of text that represents the crimes, we created a framework with 10 categories based in the Brazilian criminal laws, done by a manual extraction of all the legal terms that could indicate the crimes and a computational processing to generate a dataset with the terms categorized. For example: we found 93 terms related to drug-related crimes, including different ways to express the same law and article; different articles for a similar legal concept and even orthographic errors for the writing of a crime, resulting in the category "drug law crime". This category included individual drug traffic, criminal association for drug traffic and international drug traffic, all crimes found in the same act. The ratio of each crime category in the dataset was: drug law crime (30.85%), crime against property (17.43%), crime against person (17.10%), criminal organization (10%), crime against the government (7.36%), crime against public safety (5,06%), firearms law (4.14%), money laundering (3.26%), sexual crimes (3.13%), crimes provided in special laws (1.67%).

c) Judge-Rapporteur: During the judgement, one judge function as a Rapporteur designated to analyze the case and send its vote to the others, that must follow the vote or refrain to do so. This is a relevant factor because the Rapporteur is the one who is going to expose the legal matters regarding the case in a report to the other judges. We noticed that some of them are more bound to have their votes followed-up by their counterparts. The ratio of reported cases for each Rapporteur in the dataset and their corresponding initials were: MA (48.42%), GM (10.25%), CL (7.10%), RL (6.98%), DT (6.76%), RW (4.96%), LF (4.62%), TZ (3.43%), CM (2.64%), AB (1.57%), RB (1.29%), EF (0.73%), JB (0.51%), EG (0.28%), CV (0.11%), CP (0.11%), AM (0.06%), HES (0.06%), IG (0.06%), OG (0.06%).

4.2 Text Preprocessing

Text processing relates to the set of NLP techniques applied on raw texts so they can be used in a cleaner format as inputs for ML tasks [25]. We applied the text processing techniques as follows:

a) Noise Filtering: after extracting raw text from PDF documents, we need to remove the noise characters, where we keep only alphanumeric characters.
b) Normalization: To uniformly process the words, we convert the whole text to lowercase [26].
c) Tokenization: To interpret the structure of words we have to detect their starting and ending points to form tokens (pieces of text). We use regular expressions to detect sequences of letters and numbers [26].
d) Stemming: Words can be contracted to the root form or stem so we can reduce the variations of words [27]. In this work, we used the Porter Stemmer to the Portuguese language.
e) Filtering: In the text, there will be very common words, also called stopwords, which do not help to better capture the meanings of the text. These words include prepositions and articles. We removed those words from the corpus [28].
f) N-Grams: Words can have different meanings according to their surrounding words [29]. Thus, we consider, as a single unit, the sequences of two (bi-grams), three (tri-grams) or more, that consistently appear together [27] In this work, we used one-grams and bi-grams.

After the pre-processing steps, text representation techniques transform the corpus from a textual to a numerical format.

4.3 Text Representation

ML techniques often require the data to be represented as vectors, that is, as sequences of numbers. Thus, we needed to transform each textual document to a sequence of numbers and a simple technique is the Bag of Words (BOW) model, where each number represents the Term Frequency (TF) of a word or N-gram in the document. This text representation technique achieves good results in Text Mining applications [30–32], but it loses the notion of sequences in the text [33]. In this work, we used the BOW model as input to classical ML techniques using Orange 3.

When using deep learning techniques, we may need a more robust representation. In recent years, new techniques for representation based on neural networks have been proposed, which efficiently represent the text considering its syntactic and semantic structures [29, 34, 35]. In our experiments with deep learning techniques, we used the pre-trained representation for the GloVe [36] technique trained using Brazilian legal texts from Supreme, Superior and State Courts [37].

4.4 Classification Models

In the classification task, we want to predict the result of the legal case having only the legal text as input and the result as output labels. We used two kinds of ML models for classification: classical and deep learning. Classical ML refers to the techniques that have few parameters in the training step while deep learning refers to the techniques represented as deep neural networks that have thousands, millions or billions of parameters. Deep learning techniques improve as they have more data to learn, while classical techniques improve until it reaches a plateau [38].

We employed available approaches of classical ML in Orange 3: linear, tree based, neural based, instance based. In terms of linear models, we used SVM, Naïve Bayes and Logistic Regression. As tree-based methods, we applied Decision Tree, Random Forest and AdaBoost. In terms of neural based, we used Multi-Layer Perceptron. And as instance based, we had K-Nearest Neighbors (KNN) [33]. In terms of deep learning, we applied the Convolutional Neural Network (CNN) [39], using word embeddings representation, as mentioned, and Keras framework with the Python programming language [21].

To evaluate our classification models, we divided our dataset into two groups, train and test, with cross-validation for classical ML techniques and random sampling for CNN. We applied the train set in the learning step of our models and used the test set in the evaluation step to make predictions. We checked the performance using accuracy and F1-Score metrics (explained in Sect. 2.2).

4.5 Association Rules Model

In the association task, we want to find correlations between the extracted attributes from our dataset (Final outcome, Crime category and Judge-Rapporteur). To do so, we applied the FP-Growth algorithm through Orange 3 to create association rules with the attributes as input. FP-Growth generates a tree from frequent patterns by scanning the whole dataset following the support threshold. Then the rules are formed by constructing a conditional tree, which saves the costly dataset scans in the subsequent mining processes [40, 41]. The rule is expressed in the form of an implication, e.g. A → B.

To evaluate our association rules, Orange 3 allows us to manipulate the support and confidence metrics (explained in Sect. 2.2), as well as filter the rules with the desirable attributes in the consequent and antecedent.

5 Classification Results and Discussion

As a response to question 1, we set up a classification pipeline with 2.015 documents and the attribute/label "final outcome", to predict whether the prisoner will be released or not. We followed the steps in the methodology, that is, pre-processing, representation, classification models training with train set and evaluation with test set. After evaluating our models with the test set, we calculated the accuracy and F1-Score as shown in Fig. 1.

In terms of accuracy, our models achieved good results, since all techniques had accuracy values higher than 70%. And the best accuracy comes from the deep learning technique, CNN, that achieved a high accuracy of 95%.

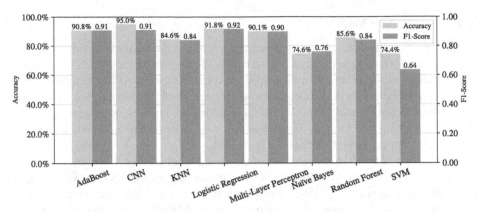

Fig. 1. Accuracy and F1-score for predictions in test set.

On the other hand, F1-Score also leveraged good results for most techniques except SVM. We also have to note that the best technique is no longer CNN but Logistic Regression. Furthermore, we note that we need both metrics to better perceive the performance of our models. When we have a label, such as "not released", comprising almost 75% of the dataset, and we also have a model that assigns that label to all documents, we will have a higher accuracy. Thus, we need F1-Score which will balance the performance across the existing labels in the dataset.

Considering both metrics, we can point CNN as the best model, followed by Logistic Regression, AdaBoost, Multi-Layer Perceptron, Random Forest, KNN, Naïve Bayes and SVM.

6 Association Results and Discussion

As a response to question 2, we generated association rules with transactions from 1.776 judgments and the three attributes extracted. We organized the results into two groups: a) rules with minimum support 5%, minimum confidence 70% and "not released" as the consequent (Table 1); and b) rules with minimum support 1%, minimum confidence 90% and "not released" as the consequent (Table 2). According to Orange 3 tutorials [42], for large datasets it is normal to set a lower minimal support (e.g. between 2%–0.01%), so one must increase confidence.

We did not find rules with "released" as the consequent within reasonable confidence. It means that there is no strong correlation between this outcome and any crimes and/or any Judge-Rapporteur in the dataset.

This first group (Table 1) represents the rules that have a balance between support and confidence. We can infer from this group that the habeas corpus on pre-trial detention in drug law crime and criminal organization, also in crimes against person and property, will probably have the judgment as "not released". In other words, the prisoner who commits these crimes will be kept in pre-trial detention.

Another inference is that certain judges as rapporteurs (MA, CL and RL) suggest the probability of the outcome being "not released". Also, the presence of the Judge-Rapporteur MA minister with crimes against property and person, and drug law crime,

Table 1. Group of association rules "a".

Supp	Conf	Antecedent		Consequent
0.055	0.860	Criminal organization	→	Not released
0.058	0.831	Judge-Rapporteur RL	→	Not released
0.398	0.822	Judge-Rapporteur MA	→	Not released
0.073	0.822	Judge-Rapporteur MA, Crime against property	→	Not released
0.076	0.813	Judge-Rapporteur MA, Crime against person	→	Not released
0.057	0.810	Judge-Rapporteur CL	→	Not released
0.178	0.806	Crime against person	→	Not released
0.164	0.804	Judge-Rapporteur MA, Drug law crime	→	Not released
0.141	0.749	Crime against property	→	Not released
0.292	0.729	Drug law crime	→	Not released

indicates the probability of the outcome "not released". However, we emphasize that the judgment is composed of the votes of all the Judges, and the vote of Judge-Rapporteur MA may not be "not released".

Considering both metrics, we can point that the strongest association rules are "Drug law crime → Not released" and "Judge-Rapporteur MA → Not released".

Table 2. Group of association rules "b".

Supp	Conf	Antecedent		Consequent
0.016	1.000	Judge-Rapporteur MA, Firearms law crime	→	Not released
0.011	1.000	Judge-Rapporteur MA, Drug law crime, Firearms law crime	→	Not released
0.017	0.968	Drug law crime, Firearms law crime	→	Not released
0.013	0.958	Judge-Rapporteur RL, Crime against person	→	Not released
0.012	0.955	Drug law crime	→	Not released
0.019	0.944	Judge-Rapporteur MA, Crime against property	→	Not released
0.025	0.936	Firearms law crime	→	Not released
0.033	0.921	Crime against property	→	Not released
0.042	0.914	Judge-Rapporteur MA, Criminal organization	→	Not released
0.016	0.906	Judge-Rapporteur RL, Crime against property	→	Not released

This second group (Table 2) represents the rules with the highest confidence, but not necessarily with high support. We realize that it contains the same or similar rules to the previous group. The main difference between Table 1 and Table 2 is a new crime that appears: firearms law crime. This crime appears associated with the drug law crime, so that both have a high probability of resulting in "not released".

Although the low support, we highlight that the rules "Judge-Rapporteur MA, Firearms law crime → Not released" and "Judge-Rapporteur MA, Drug law crime, Firearms law crime → Not released" obtained 100% confidence.

7 Conclusion and Future Work

The two research questions outlined for this research were answered since, according to the indicated metrics, we obtained satisfactory results both in terms of classification and association rules. We concluded from these experiments that STF has not interfered in first degree decisions about pre-trial detention. Notably, no reasonable metrics were found in association rules with the outcome "released", dispelling the impression of impunity or that certain crimes, such as those against the government, could revoke pre-trial detention.

In terms of application, while the classification results can speed up the judgment, for example, when the period of pre-trial detention has already expired, the association results can identify patterns in judgments and thus reduce biases. Or even point out legal issues for debate, such as the drug criminalization in Brazil, since "drug law crime" is strongly correlated with the outcome "not released".

We emphasize that these experiments had the character of formulating a model based on past judgments and verifying the main variables involved. It was not the scope of this work to discuss automating judicial decisions or hindering access to justice, since the judgment must be the result of a human evaluation. We understand that both results from classification and association rules can be useful as an assist tool and not a replacement for the magistrate, mainly when the object of the case is someone's freedom.

Future prospective studies may address the possible correlations between other attributes, such as the prisoners' location, the other STF judges present at the judgment and their votes.

References

1. Prisoners in Brazil Homepage. https://bityli.com/Bk8Ir. Accessed 10 Sept 2020
2. CONECTAS Homepage. Brazil ranks as the third country with the largest prison population in the world. https://bityli.com/lN18R. Accessed 10 Sept 2020
3. CNJ.: Justiça em Números 2020: ano-base 2019. CNJ, Brasília (2020). https://bityli.com/ORZNy. Accessed 4 Jan 2021
4. CNJ Homepage, Resolution no. 332 of August 21, 2020. https://atos.cnj.jus.br/files/original1 91707202008255f4563b35f8e8.pdf. Accessed 4 Jan 2021
5. CNJ Homepage, Ordinance no. 271 of December 4, 2020. https://atos.cnj.jus.br/files/origin al234208202012155fd949d04d990.pdf. Accessed 4 Jan 2021
6. Brazilian Criminal Procedure Code Homepage. http://www.planalto.gov.br/ccivil_03/dec reto-lei/del3689.htm. Accessed 25 Mar 2021
7. Brazilian Federal Constitution Homepage. http://www.planalto.gov.br/ccivil_03/constitui cao/constituicao.htm. Accessed 25 Mar 2021
8. Russell, S.J., Norvig, P., Davis, E.: Artificial Intelligence: A Modern Approach, 3rd edn. Prentice Hall, New Jersey (2013)

9. Géron, A.: Hands-on machine learning with Scikit-Learn, Keras, and TensorFlow: Concepts, Tools, And Techniques to Build Intelligent Systems, 2nd edn. O'Reilly Media, Inc., Sebastopol (2019)
10. Bobadilla, J., Ortega, F., Hernando, A., Gutiérrez, A.: Recommender systems survey. Knowl.-Based Syst. **46**, 109–132 (2013). https://doi.org/10.1016/j.knosys.2013.03.012,lastaccessed 2021/04/02
11. Cios, K.J., Pedrycz, W., Swiniarski, R.W., Kurgan, L.A. (orgs.).: Data Mining: A Knowledge Discovery Approach. Springer, New York (2007). https://doi.org/10.1007/978-0-387-36795-8
12. Brin, S., Motwani, R., Silverstein, C.: Beyond market baskets: generalizing association rules to correlations. ACM SIGMOD Rec. **26**(2), 265–276 (1997). https://doi.org/10.1145/253262. 253327
13. Katz, D., Bommarito, M., Blackman, J.:. Predicting the behavior of the Supreme Court of the United States: a general approach. ArXiv, 1407.6333 v1, pp. 1–17. (2014)
14. Katz, D., Bommarito, M., Blackman, J.: A general approach for predicting the behavior of the Supreme Court of the United States. PLoS ONE (2017). https://doi.org/10.1371/journal. pone.0174698
15. Aletras, N., Tsarapatsanis, D., Preoţiuc-Pietro, D., Lampos, V.: Predicting judicial decisions of the European Court of human rights: a natural language processing perspective. Peer J. Comput. Sci. **2**(93), 1–19 (2016)
16. Şulea, O., Zampieri, M., Vela, M., Genabith, J.: Predicting the Law area and decisions of French Supreme Court cases. In: Proceedings of Recent Advances in Natural Language Processing, Varna, Bulgaria. 2–8 September 2017, pp. 716–722. INCOMA Ltd Shoumen (2017)
17. Virtucio, M., et al.: Predicting decisions of the philippine supreme court using natural language processing and machine learning. In: IEEE International Conference on Computer Software and Applications, vol. 42. Tokyo (2018). https://doi.org/10.1109/COMPSAC.2018.10348. Accessed 6 Apr 2021
18. Silva, N., et al.: Document type classification for Brazil's Supreme Court using a convolutional neural network. In: International Conference on Forensic Computer Science and Cyber Law, pp. 7–11. HTCIA (2018)
19. Yin, R.K.: Estudo de Caso: Planejamento e métodos. Bookman (2015)
20. Demšar, J., et al.: Orange: data mining toolbox in python. J. Mach. Learn. Res. **14**(1), 2349–2353 (2013)
21. Keras GitHub Homepage. https://github.com/fchollet/keras. Accessed 10 Mar 2021
22. Brazilian Supreme Federal Court Homepage. http://portal.stf.jus.br. Accessed 10 Apr 2021
23. Van Rossum, G., Drake, F.L.: Python 3 Reference Manual. Create Space, Scotts Valley, CA (2009).
24. Bird, S., Loper, E.: NLTK: the natural language toolkit. In: Proceedings of the ACL Interactive Poster and Demonstration Sessions, pp. 214–217. Association for Computational Linguistics, Barcelona, Spain (2004)
25. García, S., Luengo, J., Herrera, F.: Data Preprocessing in Data Mining. Springer International Publishing, Switzerland (2015)
26. Jurafsky, D., Martin, J.H.: Speech and Language Processing: An Introduction to Natural Language Processing, Computational Linguistics, and Speech Recognition, 3rd edn. Stanford University, Draft (2019)
27. Aggarwal, C.C.: Machine Learning for Text. In: Machine Learning for Text, pp. 1–16. Springer International Publishing, Cham (2018). https://doi.org/10.1007/978-3-319-73531-3
28. Kotu, V., Deshpande, B.: Data Science: Concepts and Practice, 2nd edn. Morgan Kaufmann (Elsevier), Cambridge (2019)

29. Mikolov, T., Chen, K., Corrado, G., Dean, J.: Efficient estimation of word representations in vector space. In: 1st International Conference on Learning Representations, ICLR 2013 - Workshop Track Proceedings, pp. 1–12 (2013)
30. Uijlings, J.R., Van De Sande, K.E., Gevers, T., Smeulders, A.W.: Selective search for object recognition. Int. J. Comput. Vis. **104**(2), 154–171 (2013)
31. Meriño, L.M., et al.: A bag-of-words model for task-load prediction from EEG in complex environments. In: 2013 IEEE International Conference on Acoustics, Speech and Signal Processing, pp. 1227–1231 (2013)
32. Milosevic, N., Dehghantanha, A., Choo, K.K.R.: Machine learning aided android malware classification. Comput. Electr. Eng. **61**, 266–274 (2017)
33. Kowsari, K., Meimandi, K.J., Heidarysafa, M., Mendu, S., Barnes, L., Brown, D.: Text classification algorithms: a survey. Inf. (Switzerland) **10**(4), 150 (2019)
34. Devlin, J., Chang, M.W., Lee, K., Toutanova, K.: BERT: Pre-training of deep bidirectional transformers for language understanding. 4171–4186 (2018)
35. Brown, T.B., et al.: Language models are few-shot learners. (2020)
36. Pennington, J., Socher, R., Manning, C.: Glove: global vectors for word representation. In: Proceedings of the 2014 Conference on Empirical Methods in Natural Language Processing (EMNLP). vol. 19, pp. 1532–1543. Association for Computational Linguistics, Stroudsburg (2014)
37. Dal Pont, T.R., Sabo, I.C., Hübner, J.F., Rover, A.J.: Impact of Text Specificity and Size on Word Embeddings Performance: An Empirical Evaluation in Brazilian Legal Domain. In: Cerri, R., Prati, R.C. (eds.) BRACIS 2020. LNCS (LNAI), vol. 12319, pp. 521–535. Springer, Cham (2020). https://doi.org/10.1007/978-3-030-61377-8_36
38. Sewak, M., Sahay, S.K., Rathore, H.: Comparison of deep learning and the classical machine learning algorithm for the malware detection. In: 2018 19th IEEE/ACIS International Conference on Software Engineering, Artificial Intelligence, Networking and Parallel/Distributed Computing (SNPD), pp. 293–296. IEEE (2018)
39. Kim, Y.: Convolutional neural networks for sentence classification. In: Proceedings of the 2014 Conference on Empirical Methods in Natural Language Processing (EMNLP). vol. 2017, pp. 1746–1751. Association for Computational Linguistics, Stroudsburg (2014)
40. Han, J., Pei, J., Yin, Y.: Mining frequent patterns without candidate generation. ACM SIGMOD Rec. **29**(2), 1–12 (2000)
41. Agarwal, R.C., Aggarwal, C.C., Prasad, V.V.V.: Depth first generation of long patterns. In: Proceedings of the Sixth ACM SIGKDD International Conference on Knowledge Discovery and Data Mining (KDD 2000), vol. 2, pp. 108–118. ACM Press, New York (2000)
42. Orange Data Mining Homepage. https://orangedatamining.com. Accessed 9 Apr 2021

Social Security Reform in Brazil: A Twitter Sentiment Analysis

Rafael D. Ricci, Elaine R. Faria🆔, Rodrigo S. Miani🆔,
and Paulo H. R. Gabriel$^{(\boxtimes)}$🆔

School of Computer Science, Federal University of Uberlândia,
Av. João Naves de Ávila, 2.121, Uberlândia, MG, Brazil
{rafael_d_ricci,elaine,miani,phrg}@ufu.br

Abstract. Brazil's social security reform, approved in 2019, moved several social networks, revealing the high polarity of this theme. In this paper, we perform an automatic investigation of this polarity using sentiment analysis techniques. We collected 980,577 tweets published between January and November of that year and compared four supervised machine learning algorithms: Multinomial Naïve Bayes, Logistic Regression, Support Vector Machines, and Random Forest. Due to the large volume of data collected, we employed a transfer learning approach to train these algorithms. As a result, the four algorithms predominantly classified the tweets as "neutral", that is, these posts do not explicitly expose their users' opinion about the topic. Of the tweets that showed polarity, there was a dominance of posts classified as "positive", i.e., their authors have positive feelings (support, affinity) concerning the Social Security Reform proposal.

Keywords: Sentiment analysis · Twitter · Social security reform

1 Introduction

In recent years, social media platforms such as Facebook, Twitter, Reddit, and several blogs have overgrown. This growth has made the Web become a dynamic forum with constantly changing information, allowing people to effortlessly express and share their thoughts and opinions [8]. Thus, these platforms have become crucial for several applications that require an understanding of public opinion on a concept. Such opinions can improve the quality of their services or products or even allow governments to understand the public's view of different issues [8,12].

Social media became environments to express political opinions [22] or even disseminating false news or information [5]. Twitter posts, for example, have reflected the existing polarization regarding controversial public elections [2,7,14,26,28]. Simultaneously, people use this platform to encourage and even coordinate protests [4,25]. Some researchers also suggest that Twitter's feelings directly reflect opinion polls carried out by official research bodies [22].

© Springer Nature Switzerland AG 2021
A. Kö et al. (Eds.): EGOVIS 2021, LNCS 12926, pp. 143–154, 2021.
https://doi.org/10.1007/978-3-030-86611-2_11

In this context, in 2019, the large volume of publications referring to the "Social Security Reform" stood out in Brazil. It is a constitutional amendment authored by the Executive Branch, which alters the Brazilian social security system, establishing changes in retirement rules, such as increasing the minimum age and workers' contribution time (both in public and private sectors) [21]. The polarization around this theme motivated this work to analyze the feelings expressed by Twitter users about the Social Security Reform.

To carry out this analysis, we collected 980,577 tweets published between January and November 2019. We then applied a sequence of treatments to the collected database and compared four algorithms commonly used in the literature [8,12]: Multinomial Naïve Bayes (MNB), Logistic Regression (LR), Support Vector Machine (SVM), and Random Forest (RF). Due to the large volume of data collected, we employed a transfer learning approach [17] to train these algorithms. In other words, the classification models were trained from two public databases already labeled; then, we applied these models to the collected tweets.

This paper's contributions can be summarized as follows: i) Creation of database composed of tweets from January 2019 to November 2019 about Social Security Reform in Brazil containing 980,577 instances; ii) Creation of a framework to preprocessing data from Tweet, which is publicly available; iii) Analysis of four supervised classification algorithms to sentiment analysis of the tweets, that are trained using the transfer learning techniques; and iv) Analysis of the Social Security Reform sentiment in Brazil by comparing the agreement among the classifiers.

The remainder of this paper is organized as follows. Section 2 presents the related works, considering practical applications focused on politics and transfer learning in data classification of social networks. Section 3 presents a proposal for extracting users' feelings regarding the pension reform theme. Section 4 shows our main results, and Sect. 5 draws this paper's conclusions.

2 Related Work

Investigating the impact of Twitter sentiment analysis on political issues is a prominent research field. In general, such studies can be divided into three groups: i) using sentiment analysis to predict elections; ii) using sentiment analysis to identify the behavior of electors; and iii) using sentiment analysis to identify the behavior of candidates.

Tumasjan et al. [26] conducted one of the first studies to predict elections with Twitter. The authors used over 100,000 tweets published in the weeks leading up to Germany's national parliament's election. They use a text analysis software called LIWC2007 and proposed 12 features to profile political sentiment. The software determines the rate at which certain emotions are present in the text. They found that the number of messages mentioning a party reflects the election result, and Twitter may complement conventional political forecasting methods.

Budiharto and Meiliana [6] used a similar methodology to predict Indonesian Presidential results by analyzing tweets from candidates and tweets from relevant hashtags. The authors used well-known polarity calculation software called

Textblob to classify messages in three positive, neutral, and negative messages. They also used metrics such as likes, followers, and retweets. Their prediction results correspond to the results of four survey institutes in Indonesia.

Regarding the behavior of electors, Caetano et al. [7] studied the homophily among Twitter users during the 2016 U.S. Presidential Election. Their idea is to analyze individuals' tendency to have characteristics and behavior similar to their peers, in this case, the relationship between electors and candidates. They found that users with political engagement are more connected and interact more frequently with other users from the same class. The negative users are also more engaged in using common hashtags, and they are mentioned and retweeted more often among fellows. Kušen and Strembec [14] led a similar study in Austria and analyzed each candidate's engagement style and the evidence of different campaigning types. Yaqub et al. [28] and Bhattacharya et al. [2] performed studies to determine the behavior of candidates. While Yaqub et al. [28] analyzed the discourse of 2016 U.S. Presidential Election candidates, Bhattacharya et al. [2] investigate the public perceptions of the two U.S. presidential candidates' personalities in the 2012 elections.

Although important studies have been developed for sentiment analysis from social networks using machine learning models, an important question is how to address the high demand for large amounts of labeled data. Labeling data instances is time-consuming and requires a domain specialist, which is prohibitive in some contexts. Also, several machine learning algorithms require that the training and test data sets be under the same feature space and the same distribution [27].

Transfer learning is one technique used to overcome these issues in which one extracts knowledge from some auxiliary domains to help boost the learning performance in a target domain [18]. Transfer learning techniques allow that the domains, tasks, and distribution used in the training and testing be different [27]. Text mining is a research area that can benefit from these techniques.

Recently, some works have applied transfer learning techniques to sentiment analysis. The work proposed in [3] transfers knowledge acquired from a class of products to other products. In [11], the question that arose is how to choose a proper source data set for training the target classifier. The authors propose to evaluate four metrics to identify the most appropriate labeled dataset from a source domain to train a classifier. In [10], a novel transfer learning approach to real-time sentiment analysis is proposed.

3   Methodology

The first step of this research consists of defining the search key and collecting posts from the Twitter platform (Sect. 3.1). Before being analyzed by the machine learning algorithms, these posts are submitted to a preprocessing step with specific characteristics, described in Sect. 3.2.

Then, it is necessary to choose the classification algorithms and train them. We followed an approach called transfer learning in the training stage, which has been considered an important research direction in machine learning [15,17]. Thus, we used a dataset already labeled with similar characteristics compared to the collect base (Sect. 3.3). After training and validating the algorithms on the labeled basis (Sect. 3.4), they can be applied to the collected data (Sect. 4). Figure 1 summarizes the steps followed in this work.

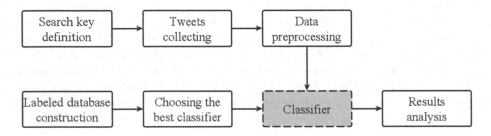

Fig. 1. Diagram of the methodology used in this work

3.1 Data Collection

To collect data from the Twitter platform, we used the *GetOldTweets3* tool [16], written in Python language, which allows extracting tweets from a specific date. As a search key, we adopt only the expression "Reforma da Previdência" (from the Portuguese, "pension system reform"); thus, *GetOldTweets3* returns tweets that contain the entire expression, both in uppercase and lowercase letters, regardless of the presence of accents. Altogether, this search returns 980,577 tweets on this topic between January and November 2019.

Figure 2 represents the number of tweets collected per month. The period with the highest number of posts is between February and July; on the other hand, January (under 30,000) and November (less than 20,000) are the months with the fewest references to the topic. It is essential to highlight that this reform's original text was sent to the Chamber of Deputies on February 20, 2019, and was approved, in the first round, on July 10, 2019; the second-round vote was concluded on August 7 [21]. Therefore, the period between the proposal submission and its approval concentrates the most significant number of tweets. Afterward, the proposal was sent to the Federal Senate and approved in a second-round on October 20 [21]. Note that the number of posts increased in October and significantly reduced the following month (November).

3.2 Data Preprocessing

In this work, the preprocessing task consists of six steps applied incrementally, i.e., we perform each step over the database modified by the previous techniques. The first step is to convert all text to lowercase characters; thus, words written

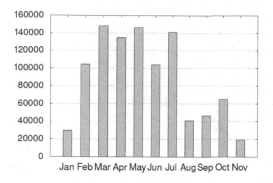

Fig. 2. Number of tweets collect by month.

in a different format can be recognized as being the same. Then, we remove hyperlinks, URLs, and mentions, as these elements have no semantic value for classification. Still, we also decided to remove the hashtags at this stage, as they did not present an easily identifiable pattern. The third step consisted of transforming a phrase into a list of words (tokenization).

The fourth phase of preprocessing is the standardization of abbreviations, so the classifiers do not distinguish two abbreviated words differently. For that, we used a dictionary of terms built from a list with several abbreviations used in the Whatsapp application and made available in [24]. Subsequently, we standardized the emoticons, i.e., symbols used to illustrate or highlight a feeling and whose use can alter the expressed feeling [9]. We employ a similar approach here: build a dictionary based on the work of [1] and [13].

Finally, the sixth preprocessing step consisted of removing stop words, i.e., words without semantic value for the classifiers. We also remove punctuation symbols and the words "reforma" and "previdência", which were present in all collected tweets. Figure 3 illustrates the effect of all these steps. In Fig. 3a, it is notable that the most frequent terms are the Portuguese prepositions "da", "de", "que", "na", in addition to the words "reforma" and "previdência", i.e., terms with no relevance to the classification. On the other hand, in Fig. 3b, the terms "contra" (*against*), "governo" (*government*), "vai" (*will go*), "aprovar" (*to approve*), and "brasil" (*brazil*) receive prominence; also, there is the presence of standardized emoticons (for instance, "emoticon_positivo", or *positive_emoticon*).

After preprocessing, it is possible to start the task of classifying the collected tweets. For this, we converted the post into a structure given as input to the algorithms. In this work, the tweets were converted to bigrams and, then, in a TF–IDF matrix. The TF–IDF (Term Frequency – Inverse Document Frequency) considers the term's relationship in a sentence with the entire textual corpus [20]. Thus, a commonplace term in a corpus is not very relevant since it occurs in many sentences; consequently, this term receives a lower weight to define what the sentence expresses. On the other hand, a term that appears few times has a

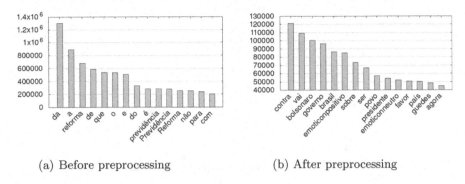

(a) Before preprocessing   (b) After preprocessing

Fig. 3. Most prominent terms before (3a) and after (3b) preprocessing steps.

better descriptive value because it occurs a few times (receiving a more significant weight when present in a sentence).

3.3   Labeled Database

This paper compared four supervised learning algorithms: Multinomial Naïve Bayes (MNB), Logistic Regression (LR), Support Vector Machine (SVM), and Random Forest (RF). These algorithms are frequent in sentiment classification tasks [8, 12], appearing in different related works (Sect. 2). Due to their characteristics, it is necessary to employ a labeled dataset to train and validate these algorithms.

Research in sentiment analysis generally considers a sample of the collected data, performing a manual classification of the same. However, the large volume of tweets collected makes the manual classification process exhaustive since it would be necessary to select a large sample. Besides, this sampling could not be random because it is polarized data, i.e., such selection could skew the training.

For this reason, this paper employed transfer learning concepts; that is, we used a database that was already labeled and had similar characteristics to the base to be analyzed. For this work, we construct this database from two public labeled datasets. The first set comes from the portal *Minerando Dados* [23], a Brazilian website that offers data mining and machine learning courses. It comprises tweets with political and educational terms related to the State of Minas Gerais and labeled as "positive", "negative" or "neutral". In the first two cases, there are no emoticons. Altogether, this set has 3,300 positive, 2,453 neutral, and 2,446 negative tweets; thus, we selected a random sample of 2,450 tweets from the first group to maintain a proportion between classes. Therefore, we consider a total of 7,349 tweets from this dataset.

The second labeled database is entitled "Portuguese Tweets for Sentiment Analysis" and was made available on the *Kaggle* platform, an online community of data scientists who provide data from different domains. This dataset has more than 700 thousand tweets in the Portuguese language already classified and organized in four files. Two of these files consist of tweets labeled as "neutral", one of which comes from communication vehicles and the other from the analysis of hashtags. The third file considered has "positive" and "negative" tweets about political issues. We opted to ignore the fourth file, which does not refer to a specific topic and, therefore, it is not relevant in this work. We decided to consider a random sample from each file due to the volume of posts, totaling 2,450 tweets from each class. Consequently, the training database has a total of 14,699 tweets.

3.4 Classifier Evaluation

Following the transfer learning approach, the four algorithms used in this work (MNB, LR, SVM, and RF) were tested using the labeled dataset (Sect. 3.3), and validated using the 10-fold cross-validation technique. With the results of the cross-validation, it is possible to extract several validation metrics. This paper focused only on accuracy; other metrics were explored (such as precision and recall), but their results were proportional to the accuracy values.

In the training and validation process, we observed that the MNB obtained an accuracy of 86% over the labeled base, while the LR reached 94%, the SVM and the RF both obtained 95%. All algorithms had a relatively high hit rate considering only their accuracy values, with MNB being the lowest value. Confusion matrices were also built for an even more in-depth analysis of the validations, as shown in Table 1. Considering that all classifiers perform well, we employed all of them to classify tweets about the reform.

4 Results and Discussion

With the models created and trained, we focused on classifying the collected tweets (Sect. 3.1), which have already gone through all stages of preprocessing (Sect. 3.2).

We classified 980,577 tweets and computed the quantity of each obtained class. In total, the model based on MNB classified 409,855 (41.80% of the samples) as positive, 358,335 (36.54%) as neutral, and 201,287 (21.66%) as negative. LR classified 20,445 (21.36%) as positive, 724,700 (73.91%) as neutral and 46,425 (4.73%) as negative. SVM classified 222,859 (22.73%) as positive, 704,257 (71.82%) as neutral and 53,461 (5.45%) as negative. Finally, the RF method classified 69,066 tweets (7.04%) as positive, 842,722 (85.94%) as neutral, and 68,789 (7.02%) as negative. Figure 4 shows the number of tweets that each algorithm classified in each of the three classes.

As observed, MNB classified the most significant number of tweets as positive, while in the other methods, there was a predominance of neutrals. It is interesting to note that MNB had the lowest accuracy concerning the training database (Sect. 3.4). Comparing the LR with the SVM, we see very similar results, with both having a higher percentage of positives than negatives. On the other hand, RF had a higher proportion between negatives and positives than the most significant number of neutrals.

Table 1. Confusion matrices.

Real	Predicted			
	Negative	Positive	Neutral	All
Negative	4352	134	410	4896
Neutral	644	3689	570	4903
Positive	1125	217	3558	4900
All	6121	4040	4538	14699

(a) MNB

Real	Predicted			
	Negative	Positive	Neutral	All
Negative	3870	342	684	4896
Neutral	255	4366	282	4903
Positive	619	308	3973	4900
All	4744	5016	4939	14699

(b) LR

Real	Predicted			
	Negative	Positive	Neutral	All
Negative	3983	258	655	4896
Neutral	266	4418	219	4903
Positive	657	265	3978	4900
All	4906	4941	4852	14699

(c) SVM

Real	Predicted			
	Negative	Positive	Neutral	All
Negative	4002	371	523	4896
Neutral	229	4536	138	4903
Positive	835	417	3648	4900
All	5066	5324	4309	14699

(d) RF

It is not possible, in this work, to define which classifier has better performance since these tweets do not have a previous classification. However, when analyzing a random sample of 1,000 tweets, the authors of this paper observed that many of the posts were replications of news headlines, often followed by hashtags expressing the user's opinion. As in the preprocessing, we decided to eliminate hashtags; so, the processed text becomes only the headline itself, i.e.,

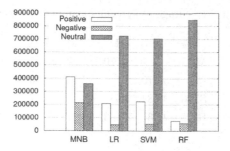

Fig. 4. Number of tweets in each class for each algorithm.

it has a neutral nature. This observation suggests further studies in converting hashtags into conventional text and, thus, adequately expressing the user's sentiment.

Figure 5 shows the sentiment classification along the months for each of the algorithms. RF is the only algorithm that brings an equivalence of negative tweets over positive ones in some months.

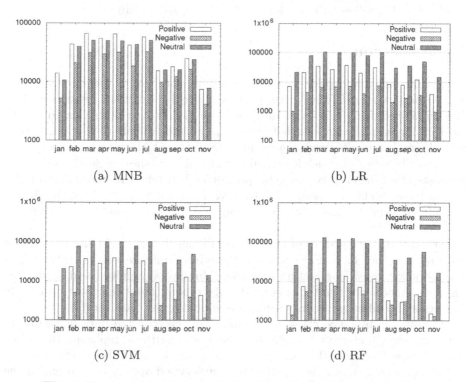

Fig. 5. Number of tweets in each class for each algorithm per month.

Table 2. Percentage of agreement among the methods.

	MNB	LR	SVM	RF
MNB	-	35.79	33.84	22.37
LR	35.79	-	73.52	35.03
SVM	33.84	73.52	-	30.37
RF	22.37	35.03	30.37	-

We also compute the agreement among the classifiers, i.e., when two or more methods detect the same polarity in the same tweet. Table 2 shows the percentage of agreement of each algorithm with all the others. Note that the most significant correlation occurred between the algorithms LR and SVM (higher than 73%). The correspondence was below 40% in the other comparisons, and the most divergent algorithms were between MNB and RF.

The whole framework developed in this work was implemented in the Python 3 language using the *Scikit Learn* library [19]. The full implementation is publicly available in the following repository: http://bit.ly/39MpHhj.

5 Conclusion

This paper aimed to explore data classification algorithms to analyze sentiments about data extracted from Twitter. We choose the Brazilian Pension System Reform as the theme due to the large volume of polarized posts related to this subject. Experiments were carried out to explore and evaluate the performance of four classical and well-known algorithms: MNB, LR, SVM, and RF. We employed a transfer learning approach for training and validated these algorithms. Results suggested that the most considerable portion of Twitter users in Brazil publishes texts without a clear opinion, i.e., they have a neutral position about the theme. Despite these users, most of the posts indicate a favorable judgment about the Reform.

We applied several word processing techniques, but it would also be possible to consider other ones. For example, removing duplicate tweets (retweets) is an important research direction to remove duplicated opinions and adjust the analysis. Another relevant idea is to identify robots (bots) that post automatic messages and influence feelings (and, consequently, the classifiers).

Finally, we intend to classify a sampling of the collected data manually. In this way, we will create a training base for the algorithms, replacing the transfer learning strategy and making a new comparison. It is also possible to use other algorithms and methods, such as unsupervised approaches, to enrich the comparison.

References

1. Araújo, M., Gonçalves, P., Benevenuto, F.: Measuring sentiments in online social networks. In: Proceedings of the 19th Brazilian Symposium on Multimedia and the Web - WebMedia 2013. ACM Press (2013)
2. Bhattacharya, S., Yang, C., Srinivasan, P., Boynton, B.: Perceptions of presidential candidates' personalities in twitter. J. Assoc. Inf. Sci. Technol. **67**(2), 249–267 (2016)
3. Blitzer, J., Dredze, M., Pereira, F.: Biographies, Bollywood, boom-boxes and blenders: domain adaptation for sentiment classification. In: Proceedings of the 45th Annual Meeting of the Association of Computational Linguistics, pp. 440–447. Association for Computational Linguistics, Prague, Czech Republic, June 2007
4. Bosch, T.: Twitter activism and youth in South Africa: the case of #RhodesMustFall. Inf. Commun. Soc. **20**(2), 221–232 (2016)
5. Bovet, A., Makse, H.A.: Influence of fake news in Twitter during the 2016 US presidential election. Nat. Commun. **10**(1), 1–14 (2019)
6. Budiharto, W., Meiliana, M.: Prediction and analysis of Indonesia Presidential election from Twitter using sentiment analysis. J. Big Data **5**(1), 1–10 (2018)
7. Caetano, J.A., Lima, H.S., Santos, M.F., Marques-Neto, H.T.: Using sentiment analysis to define twitter political users' classes and their homophily during the 2016 American presidential election. J. Internet Serv. Appl. **9**(18), 1–15 (2018)
8. Giachanou, A., Crestani, F.: Like it or not: a survey of Twitter sentiment analysis methods. ACM Comput. Surv. **49**(2), 1–41 (2016)
9. Gonçalves, P., Araújo, M., Benevenuto, F., Cha, M.: Comparing and combining sentiment analysis methods. In: Proceedings of the First ACM Conference on Online Social Networks - COSN 2013, pp. 27–38. ACM Press, Boston (2013)
10. Guerra, P.H.C., Veloso, A., Meira, W., Almeida, V.: From bias to opinion: a transfer-learning approach to real-time sentiment analysis. In: Proceedings of the 17th ACM SIGKDD International Conference on Knowledge Discovery and Data Mining - KDD 2011, pp. 150–158. KDD 2011. ACM Press, New York, NY, USA (2011)
11. Guimarães, E., Carvalho, J., Paes, A., Plastino, A.: Transfer learning for Twitter sentiment analysis: choosing an effective source dataset. In: Proceedings of 8th Symposium on Knowledge Discovery, Mining and Learning, pp. 161–168 (2020)
12. Hasan, A., Moin, S., Karim, A., Shamshirband, S.: Machine learning-based sentiment analysis for twitter accounts. Math. Comput. Appl. **23**(1), 11 (2018)
13. Kralj Novak, P., Smailović, J., Sluban, B., Mozetič, I.: Sentiment of emojis. PLoS One **10**(12), e0144296 (2015)
14. Kušen, E., Strembeck, M.: Politics, sentiments, and misinformation: an analysis of the Twitter discussion on the 2016 Austrian Presidential elections. Online Soc. Networks Media **5**, 37–50 (2018)
15. Liu, R., Shi, Y., Ji, C., Jia, M.: A survey of sentiment analysis based on transfer learning. IEEE Access **7**, 85401–85412 (2019)
16. Mottl, D.: GetOldTweets3: Project description. The Python Package Index, November 2019. https://pypi.org/project/GetOldTweets3/
17. Pan, S.J., Yang, Q.: A survey on transfer learning. IEEE Trans. Knowl. Data Eng. **22**(10), 1345–1359 (2010)
18. Pan, W., Zhong, E., Yang, Q.: Transfer learning for text mining. In: Aggarwal, C., Zhai, C. (eds.) Mining Text Data, pp. 223–257. Springer, Boston (2012). https://doi.org/10.1007/978-1-4614-3223-4_7

19. Pedregosa, F., et al.: Scikit-learn: machine learning in Python. J. Mach. Learn. Res. **12**, 2825–2830 (2011)
20. Rajaraman, A., Ullman, J.D.: Data mining. In: Rajaraman, A., Ullman, J.D. (eds.) Mining of Massive Datasets, vol. 1, pp. 1–17. Cambridge University Press, Cambridge (2011)
21. Resende, T.: Senado finaliza nesta quarta reforma da Previdência que pode afetar 72 milhões. Folha de São Paulo, October 2019. https://bit.ly/3qDU40e. (in Portuguese)
22. Rossetto, G.P.N., Carreiro, R., Almada, M.P.: Twitter e comunicação política: limites e possibilidades. Compolítica **3**(2), 189–216 (2013). (in Portuguese)
23. Santana, F.: Análise de Sentimentos Utilizando Dados do Twitter. Minerando Dados (2019). https://minerandodados.com.br
24. Stein, T.: Gírias e abreviações mais usadas do Whatsapp. Dicionário Polular (2019). https://www.dicionariopopular.com/girias-abreviacoes-siglas-mais-usadas-do-whatsapp/. (in Portuguese)
25. Theocharis, Y., Lowe, W., van Deth, J.W., García-Albacete, G.: Using Twitter to mobilize protest action: online mobilization patterns and action repertoires in the Occupy Wall Street, Indignados, and Aganaktismenoi movements. Inf. Commun. Soc. **18**(2), 202–220 (2014)
26. Tumasjan, A., Sprenger, T.O., Sandner, P.G., Welpe, I.M.: Predicting elections with twitter: what 140 characters reveal about political sentiment. In: Cohen, W.W., Gosling, S. (eds.) Proceedings of the Fourth International Conference on Weblogs and Social Media. The AAAI Press (2010)
27. Yang, L., Zhang, J.: Automatic transfer learning for short text mining. EURASIP J. Wirel. Commun. Networking **2017**(1), 1–18 (2017)
28. Yaqub, U., Chun, S.A., Atluri, V., Vaidya, J.: Analysis of political discourse on twitter in the context of the 2016 US presidential elections. Gov. Inf. Q. **34**(4), 613–626 (2017)

Demystifying Tax Evasion Using Variational Graph Autoencoders

Priya Mehta[2], Sandeep Kumar[1], Ravi Kumar[1], and Ch. Sobhan Babu[1($\boxtimes$)]

[1] Indian Institute of Technology Hyderabad, Telangana, India
{sandeep,cs18mtech11028,sobhan}@iith.ac.in
[2] Institute of Insurance and Risk Management, Hyderabad, India
priya@iirmworld.org.in

Abstract. Indirect taxation is a significant source of income for any nation. Tax evasion hinders the progress of a nation. It causes a substantial loss to the revenue of a country. We design a model based on variational graph autoencoders and clustering to identify taxpayers who are evading indirect tax by providing false information in their tax returns. We derive six correlation parameters (features) and three ratio parameters from the data submitted by taxpayers in their returns. We derive four latent features from these nine features using variational graph autoencoder and cluster taxpayers using these four latent features. We identify taxpayers located at the boundary of each cluster by using kernel density estimation, which is further investigated to single out tax evaders. We applied our method to the iron and steel taxpayers data set provided by the Commercial Taxes Department, the government of Telangana, India.

Keywords: Tax evasion · Fraud detection · Goods and services tax · Clustering · Variational graph autoencoders · Kernel density estimation

1 Introduction

Indirect taxation is a significant source of livelihood for any country. An indirect tax (e.g., GST and sales tax) is collected by an intermediary (such as retailer and manufacturer) from the purchaser of goods/services. The intermediary forwards the tax he/she collected to the government by filing tax returns at regular intervals. Indirect taxation is governed by carefully designed rules and regulations to which an intermediary (taxpayer) is expected to adhere. At the outset, indirect tax payment may seem like a liability on the intermediary, but in reality, the intermediary acts as a conduit to the flow of tax from the consumer of the goods/services to the government. These taxes provide much-needed revenue for the growth of the nation. In this article, we work towards handling tax evasion happening in *Goods and Services Tax (GST)*, which is an indirect taxation system followed in India from July 2017 [4].

© Springer Nature Switzerland AG 2021
A. Kö et al. (Eds.): EGOVIS 2021, LNCS 12926, pp. 155–166, 2021.
https://doi.org/10.1007/978-3-030-86611-2_12

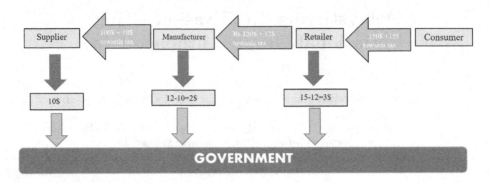

Fig. 1. Tax flow in GST

1.1 Goods and Services Tax

Goods and Services Tax (GST) is a comprehensive, multi-stage, destination-based tax that is levied on every value addition [4]. In GST, the tax is collected incrementally at each stage of the production of the goods/services based on the value addition happened in that stage. This tax is levied at each stage of the supply chain in such a way that the tax paid on purchases (*Input tax* or *Input tax credit*) will be given as a set-off for the tax levied on sales (*Output tax* or *Liability*).

Figure 1 shows how incremental tax is collected at each stage of the supply chain. In this example, the manufacturer purchases goods from the supplier for a value of $100 and pays $10 as tax at a 10% GST rate. The supplier then pays this tax to the government. In the next stage, the retailer purchases processed goods from the manufacturer for a value of $120 by paying a tax of $12. The manufacturer pays ($12 − $10 = $2) to the government, the difference between the tax collected from the retailer and the tax already paid to the supplier. Finally, the consumer buys it from the retailer for a value of $150 with $15 as the tax amount. So the retailer, as in the case with the previous taxpayers in the supply chain, will pay ($15 − $12 = $3) to the government. In essence, for every taxpayer in GST,

$$Tax\,payable = (Output\,tax - Input\,tax) \tag{1}$$

1.2 Tax Evasion

Tax evasion and taxation go hand in hand. Taxpayers deliberately manipulate their monthly tax returns in order to maximize their profits. Tax enforcement officers design new rules and regulations involved in the payment of tax after studying the behavior of known evaders who exploit the loopholes in the existing taxation laws. In this never-ending cat and mouse game, evaders always try to stay one step ahead of the enforcement officers. Hence it is very important for the officials to track down the evasion as quickly as possible and close the loopholes before the techniques used in a particular evasion spreads to the other taxpayers. By doing so, the taxation officers will be able to limit the loss of state revenue due to tax evasion quite substantially.

In general, taxpayers commit tax evasion in the following ways:

1. The taxpayer will collect tax at a higher rate from the customer and remits to the government at a lower rate.
2. The taxpayer does not report all the transactions made by her/him (suppressing the sales).
3. The taxpayer will arrive at a lower taxable turnover by wrongly applying the prescribed calculations.
4. The taxpayer creates fictitious transactions where there is no movement of goods, but only the bills are floated in order to claim Input Tax Credit (ITC) and escape payment of tax. This is called bill trading.

1.3   Our Contribution

Goods and Services Taxation system, which came into effect in India in July 2017, unified the taxation laws in India. Under GST law, the taxpayers are expected to file tax return statements every month by providing the details of sales and purchases that happened in the corresponding month. Taxpayers who observed certain loopholes in the system manipulated their tax return statements to reduce their tax liability. The objective of this work is to identify malicious taxpayers who manipulate their tax return statements to minimize their tax liability. For the same, we clustered the taxpayers over four latent parameters of the taxpayers. These four latent parameters are derived from six correlation parameters and three ratio parameters using variational graph autoencoders. These nine parameters are identified by the tax enforcement officers.

We identified taxpayers located at the boundary of each cluster by using kernel density estimation. These are further investigated to single out tax evaders. This idea can be applied in other nations, where multi-stage indirect taxation is followed.

The rest of the paper is organized as follows. In Sect. 2, we discuss the previous relevant works. In Sect. 3, we describe the data used. In Sect. 4, we give a brief description about autoencoders. In Sect. 5, we give a detailed description of the methodology used in this paper. Results obtained and the validation of the results are discussed in Sect. 6.

2   Related Work

Chandola et al. [3] presented several data mining techniques for anomaly detection. Hussein Issa and Miklos Vasarhelyi [5] described classification-based and clustering-based anomaly detection techniques and their applications. As an illustration, they applied the K-Means algorithm to a refund transaction dataset from a telecommunication company, with the intent of identifying fraudulent refunds. Pamela et al. [2] showed that it is possible to characterize and detect those potential users of false invoices in a given year, depending on the information in their tax payment, their historical performance, and characteristics using different types of data mining techniques. Daniel de Roux et al. [10] presented a novel approach for the detection of potentially fraudulent taxpayers using only unsupervised learning techniques. They demonstrated the ability of their model to identify under-reporting taxpayers on real tax payment declarations, reducing the number of potentially fraudulent taxpayers to audit. Y. Sahin et al. [16] developed classification models based on Artificial Neural Networks (ANN) and Logistic Regression (LR) and applied them to credit card fraud detection problem. In [12], Fei Tian et al. proposed a method, which first learns a non-linear embedding and then runs a K-means algorithm on the embedding to obtain clustering results. Jinxin Cao et al. [1] given a deep learning-based community detection method by taking both network topology and node content into consideration.

3   Description of Data Set

We used two types of data sets of 1199 iron and steel taxpayers. One is GSTR-1 data, and the other is the monthly GST returns data.

3.1   GSTR-1

GSTR-1 is a monthly financial statement that should be submitted by every taxpayer. In this statement, the taxpayer has to provide complete details about every sales transaction done in the corresponding month. GSTR-1 is the monthly financial statement upon which the entire compliance structure in GST is based.

   Table 1 is a sample of this data set. Every row in Table 1 corresponds to one sales transaction. Every row contains information such as seller details, buyer details, invoice number, invoice value, rate of tax, the quantity of goods sold, *etc.* The data set we have taken contains fifteen million rows. The size of the data is 1.2 TB. Figures 2, 3 show the distribution of values of sales transactions and tax on those transactions.

Table 1. GSTR-1 DATA

S. No.	Month	Seller	Buyer	Invoice number	Amount (Rs)
1	Jan 2018	A	B	XY123	12000
2	Feb 2018	B	D	ZU342	18000
3	Jan 2018	B	C	UX5434	14000
4	July 2018	C	D	YS8779	15000
5	Mar 2018	D	A	ZX7744	12000

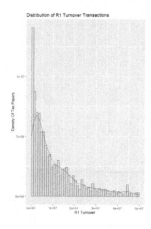

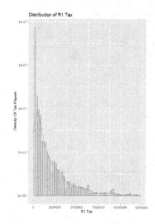

Fig. 2. Distribution of values of sales transactions

Fig. 3. Distribution of tax on sales transactions

3.2 GSTR-3B

GSTR-3B is a monthly self-declaration that has to be filled by the taxpayer. It is a simple return in which a summary of outward supplies along with Input Tax Credit is declared, and payment of tax is affected by the taxpayer. The taxpayer does not need to provide invoice level details in this form. The taxpayer provides only a summary of inward supplies and outward supplies of the corresponding month.

Table 2 is a sample of GST returns data. Each row in this table corresponds to a monthly return by a taxpayer. *ITC (Input tax credit)* is the amount of tax the taxpayer paid during purchases of services and goods. The *output tax* is the amount of tax the taxpayer collected during the sales of services and goods. The taxpayer must pay to the government the gap between the *ITC* and *output tax*, i.e., output tax - ITC. The actual database consists of much more information, like, tax payment method, return filing date, international exports, exempted sales, and sales on RCM (reverse charge mechanism). Figures 4 and 5 show the distribution of liability and input tax credit.

Table 2. GST returns data

S. No.	Firm	Month	Purchases	Sales	ITC	Output tax
1	A	Feb-18	180000	220000	20000	26000
2	D	Sep-18	200000	280000	5000	9000
3	E	Oct-17	400000	480000	40000	48000

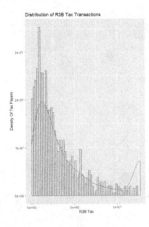
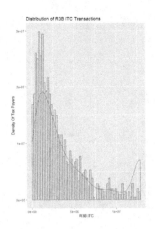

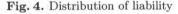

Fig. 4. Distribution of liability   **Fig. 5.** Distribution of input tax credit

4   Autoencoder

Autoencoder is an artificial neural network that is trained to encode/transform the input data to an efficient latent representation (output of bottleneck layer) and then decode/transform the latent representation to a representation (output of output layer) that is close to the input data as much as possible [15]. Autoencoders are preferred over PCA because an autoencoder can learn non-linear transformations with a non-linear activation function (manifold learning). An autoencoder consists of two neural networks (encoder and decoder) connected back to back.

The encoder takes a data point X as input and translates it to latent variable Z, which is in a lower-dimensional space. The decoder takes Z as input and translates it to X' such that X' will almost look like the input X. However, it might not be possible for the encoder to encode all information in X because the dimension of X is bigger than the dimension of Z. Therefore, if Z captures more information from X, then X' will be almost equal to X. The loss function of the auto-encoder measures the information lost (*reconstruction loss*) during the translation $X \to Z \to X'$. The most common loss functions are

- Sum of squares with the assumption that output follows Gaussian distribution: $(X - X')^2$
- Binary cross-entropy with the assumption that output follows binomial distribution: $(-X * log(X') - (1 - X) * log(1 - X'))$.

Low dimensional embedding Z could be used for several downstream tasks. We could use the embedding (features extracted) in other machine learning algorithms like clustering or classification.

4.1   Variational Autoencoders

The main characteristic of the variational autoencoder is that the latent space (output space of bottleneck layer) is *continuous* and *complete* [8].

- Continuous mean that two close points in the latent space should give almost the same output once decoded.
- Completeness means that for a point sampled from the latent space should give meaningful content once decoded.

The main idea of a variational autoencoder is that the encoder translates the input X to a probability distribution, most commonly a multivariate Gaussian, rather than to a point. And then, a random sample Z is taken from this probability distribution as a low dimensional embedding of input X. The decoder took Z and translated it to X', which almost looks like the input X. The loss function of a variational autoencoder is the sum of two components. One component is reconstruction loss, which is the same as the autoencoders, and the other is a latent loss. The latent loss measures the deviation of the multivariate Gaussian distribution generated by encoders from the standard normal distribution. This is computed using *Kullback-Leibler* divergence $1/2 * (1 + 2 * log(\sigma) - \mu^2 - \sigma^2)$, where μ, σ are mean and standard deviation of the multivariate Gaussian distribution generated by the encoder.

4.2   Graph Autoencoders

Graph autoencoder can reason about graphs. Since graph-structured data are irregular and each node in a graph has a different number of neighbors, it is not possible to apply the idea of autoencoder in a straight forward manner [7,11,14].

Let G be an undirected graph with n vertices, and matrix A be the adjacency matrix of G. Let matrix X be an $n * k$ feature matrix of input graph G. The ith row of the feature matrix X gives the feature vector of the vertex v_i. The encoder takes adjacency matrix A and feature matrix X as inputs and generates the latent features matrix $Z = h(A' * X * W)$ as follows:

- Matrix $A' = D^{-1/2} * A * D^{-1/2}$, where D is a diagonal matrix with the value of ith diagonal element is equals to the row sum of ith row of A.
- Matrix W be a $n * l$ matrix to be computed by a learning algorithm to generate good $n * l$ latent features matrix Z. The ith row of the feature matrix Z gives the latent features vector of the vertex v_i.
- The non-linear activation function is denoted by h.

The decoder takes Z and translated it to $\tilde{A}$ that almost looks like the input A.

5   Methodology

The objective is to identify malicious taxpayers who manipulate their tax return statements to minimize the amount of tax they have to pay to the government. We applied the following method on 1199 Iron & Steel taxpayers.

- **Step 1:** Using monthly returns of 1199 iron & steel taxpayers, computed correlation and ratio parameters for each taxpayer. The result is an 1199 × 9 matrix, where each row corresponds to a taxpayer.
  These correlation and ratio parameters are explained in Subsect. 5.1 and 5.2. The result of this step is the 1199 × 9 matrix, where each row corresponds to a taxpayer. Figure 6a shows the distribution of correlation parameters, and Fig. 6b show the distribution of normalized ratio parameters using box plots.
- **Step 2:** Encoded this nine-dimensional data to four-dimensional data using variational autoencoder. The result of this step is an 1199 × 4 matrix Z.
- **Step 3:** Constructed an 1199 × 1199 similarity matrix S. The value in i^{th} row j^{th} column is given by the equation $exp^{-(||x_i - x_j||)^2}$. Here x_i, x_j are i^{th}, j^{th} rows of matrix Z respectively.
- **Step 4:** Constructed an undirected graph G, where each vertex corresponds to a row (taxpayer) in S. Placed an edge between two taxpayers if the first taxpayer is among the 3-nearest neighbors of the second taxpayer or if the second taxpayer is among the 3-nearest neighbors of the first taxpayer. Let A be the adjacency matrix of the graph G. Matrix A is a 0/1 matrix of size 1199 × 1199.
- **Step 5:** Generated four latent features for each vertex of graph G using a variational graph autoencoder. The result is 1199 × 4 matrix E.
- **Step 6:** Performed KMeans clustering of rows (taxpayers) of the matrix E. *From the elbow curve in Fig. 7, we can conclude that there are eight clusters in the data. Figure 8 shows the cluster. Figure 9 shows the number of taxpayers in each cluster.*
- **Step 7:** Using the kernel density estimation, identified taxpayers at the boundary of each cluster for further analysis.

5.1   Correlation Parameters

In the Indian GST system, three types of taxes are collected, *viz.*, CGST, SGST, and IGST.

- *CGST:* Central Goods and Services Tax is levied on intrastate transactions and collected by the Central government of India.
- *SGST:* State/Union Territory Goods and Services Tax, which is also levied on intrastate transactions and collected by the state or union territory government.
- *IGST:* Integrated Goods and Services Tax is levied on interstate sales. The central government takes half of this amount and passes the rest of the amount to the state, where corresponding goods or services are consumed.

Table 3 gives the six correlation parameters used in clustering. These are derived from month-wise data in Table 2. Total GST liability is the sum of CGST, SGST, and IGST liabilities. Total ITC is equal to the sum of SGST, CGST, and IGST ITCs.

Table 3. Correlation parameters

S. No	Correlation parameters
1	Correlation of total sales amount and total GST liability
2	Correlation of total GST Liability and SGST liability
3	Correlation of SGST liability and SGST paid in cash
4	Correlation of total sales amount and SGST paid in cash
5	Correlation of total tax liability and total ITC
6	Correlation of total ITC and IGST ITC

5.2   Ratio Parameters

These three ratio parameters used in clustering are derived from month-wise data in Table 2.

1. The Ratio of *Total Sales* VS. *Total Purchases*: This ratio captures the value addition.
2. The Ratio of *IGST ITC* VS. *Total ITC*: This ratio captures how much purchase is shown as interstate or imports compared to total purchases.
3. The Ratio of *Total Tax Liability* VS. *IGST ITC*.

5.3   Clustering Taxpayers

Clustering is the most widely used data mining method [6,9,12]. In every scientific field dealing with data, people attempt to understand their data by trying to find clusters (groups) of "similar behavior" in their data. Given a set of data points $x_1, \ldots, x_n$ and some notion of similarity measure $s_{ij} \geq 0$ between all pairs of data points x_i and x_j, the objective of clustering is to segregate the data points into several clusters (groups), such that points in the same group are similar, and points in different groups are dissimilar to each other.

5.4   Identifying Suspicious Taxpayers

We used kernel density estimation [13], which is a common technique in nonparametric statistics for the approximation of the unknown probability distribution, for identifying taxpayers who are on the boundary of the corresponding cluster center. It is a method to estimate the unknown probability distribution of a random variable, based on a sample of points taken from that distribution. The formula to make a prediction for any point x is: $1/n \sum_{i=1}^{n} K(x - x_i)$, where $x_1 \ldots x_n$ are a sample of points taken from the distribution, and K is the kernel function. We had taken the Gaussian kernel. Then we further investigated those taxpayers who are on the boundary of the corresponding cluster [3].

6   Experimental Results and Case Study

The proposed algorithm is implemented using PyTorch, an open-source machine learning framework. Figures 6a and b show the distribution of correlation and ratio parameters. Figure 6c shows the distribution of the output of variational auto encoder. Figure 6d shows the distribution of vertex features. Figure 7 shows the elbow curve of the KMeans algorithm. Figure 9 shows the number of taxpayers in each cluster.

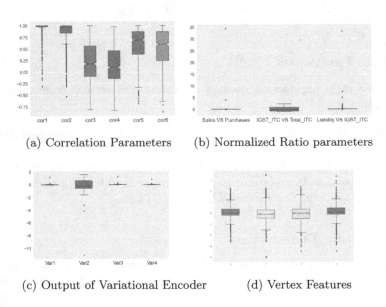

(a) Correlation Parameters   (b) Normalized Ratio parameters

(c) Output of Variational Encoder   (d) Vertex Features

Fig. 6. Illustration of correlation, ratio parameters, and output of encoders

6.1   Case Study

Figure 10 shows the sales and purchases of few suspicious taxpayers at the boundary of cluster seven. Amounts in Fig. 10 are in tens of millions. It is observed that they are not paying any tax. Their total ITC is 1860 million, and their total liability is 1780 million. Since the inverted tax structure is not applicable for steel & iron taxpayers and their ITC is almost the same or more than their liability, this is a clear case of fraud.

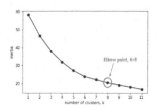

Fig. 7. KMeans elbow curve

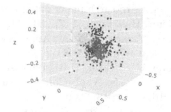

Fig. 8. Resultant clusters

C1	C2	C3	C4	C5	C6	C7	C8
115	122	259	204	143	90	153	113

Fig. 9. Clusters of eight groups

S No	GSTIN	Total Liability	Total ITC	Total Cash setoff
1	2	3	4	5
1	506CCJ6CCJ	2.20	3.18	0.27
2	506CCK6CCK	91.33	95.82	0.00
3	506CCK6CCK	19.88	20.81	0.00
4	506CMG6CMG	25.97	26.32	0.05
5	506CMP6CMP	21.69	22.03	0.31
6	506CHN6CHN	17.92	18.07	0.04
	TOTAL	178.99	186.23	0.67

Fig. 10. Case study

7 Conclusion

In this work, we analyzed the tax returns dataset of a set of taxpayers in the state of Telangana, India, provided by the commercial taxes department, the government of Telangana, India, to identify taxpayers who perform extensive tax evasion. We performed clustering analysis on the taxpayers over four latent parameters, which are derived from six correlation parameters and three ratio parameters. We used a variational graph autoencoder to derive the four latent parameters from these nine parameters. We identified possible evaders by identifying taxpayers located at the boundary of each cluster by using kernel density estimation. This idea can be applied in other nations, where multi-stage indirect taxation is followed.

Acknowledgment. We express our sincere gratitude to the Telangana state government, India, for sharing the commercial tax data set, which is used in this work.

References

1. Cao, J., Jin, D., Yang, L., Dang, J.: Incorporating network structure with node contents for community detection on large networks using deep learning. Neurocomputing **297**, 71–81 (2018)
2. Castellón González, P., Velásquez, J.D.: Characterization and detection of taxpayers with false invoices using data mining techniques. Expert Syst. Appl. **40**(5), 1427–1436 (2013)
3. Chandola, V., Banerjee, A., Kumar, V.: Anomaly detection: a survey. ACM Comput. Surv. **41**(3) (2009). https://doi.org/10.1145/1541880.1541882

4. Dani, S.: A research paper on an impact of goods and service tax (GST) on Indian economy. Bus. Econ. J. **7**, 264 (2016). ISSN 2151–6219
5. Issa, H., Vasarhelyi, M.A.: Application of anomaly detection techniques to identify fraudulent refunds (2011)
6. Maione, C., Nelson, D.R., Barbosa, R.M.: Research on social data by means of cluster analysis. Appl. Comput. Inform. **15**(2), 153–162 (2018). https://doi.org/10.1016/j.aci.2018.02.003
7. Pan, S., Hu, R., Long, G., Jiang, J., Yao, L., Zhang, C.: Adversarially regularized graph autoencoder for graph embedding. In: Proceedings of the 27th International Joint Conference on Artificial Intelligence, IJCAI 2018, pp. 2609–2615. AAAI Press (2018)
8. Pu, Y., et al.: Variational autoencoder for deep learning of images, labels and captions. In: Proceedings of the 30th International Conference on Neural Information Processing Systems, NIPS 2016, pp. 2360–2368. Curran Associates Inc., Red Hook (2016)
9. Rousseeuw, P.J.: Silhouettes: a graphical aid to the interpretation and validation of cluster analysis. J. Comput. Appl. Math. **20**, 53–65 (1987)
10. de Roux, D., Perez, B., Moreno, A., Villamil, M.d.P., Figueroa, C.: Tax fraud detection for under-reporting declarations using an unsupervised machine learning approach. In: Proceedings of the 24th ACM SIGKDD International Conference on Knowledge Discovery & Data Mining, KDD 2018, pp. 215–222. Association for Computing Machinery, New York (2018). https://doi.org/10.1145/3219819.3219878
11. Salha, G., Hennequin, R., Tran, V., Vazirgiannis, M.: A degeneracy framework for scalable graph autoencoders. In: IJCAI (2019)
12. Tian, F., Gao, B., Cui, Q., Chen, E., Liu, T.: Learning deep representations for graph clustering. In: Brodley, C.E., Stone, P. (eds.) Proceedings of the Twenty-Eighth ΛΛΛI Conference on Artificial Intelligence, Québec City, Québec, Canada,, 27–31 July 2014, pp. 1293–1299. AAAI Press (2014). http://www.aaai.org/ocs/index.php/AAAI/AAAI14/paper/view/8527
13. Tran, L.T.: The l1 convergence of kernel density estimates under dependence. Canadian J. Stat/La Revue Canadienne de Statistique **17**(2), 197–208 (1989). http://www.jstor.org/stable/3314848
14. Tran, P.V.: Learning to make predictions on graphs with autoencoders. In: 2018 IEEE 5th International Conference on Data Science and Advanced Analytics (DSAA), pp. 237–245 (2018). https://doi.org/10.1109/DSAA.2018.00034
15. Vincent, P., Larochelle, H., Lajoie, I., Bengio, Y., Manzagol, P.A.: Stacked denoising autoencoders: learning useful representations in a deep network with a local denoising criterion. J. Mach. Learn. Res. **11**, 3371–3408 (2010)
16. Şahin, Y., Duman, E.: Detecting credit card fraud by ANN and logistic regression. In: 2011 International Symposium on Innovations in Intelligent Systems and Applications, pp. 315–319 (2011)

Using Machine Learning for Risk Classification in Brazilian Federal Voluntary Transfers

Daniel M. Guilhon[1]([✉]), Aillkeen Bezerra de Oliveira[2], Daniel L. Gomes Jr[1],
Anselmo C. Paiva[1], Cláudio de Souza Baptista[2], Geraldo Braz Junior[1],
and João Dallysson Sousa de Almeida[1]

[1] Federal University of Maranhão, São Luis, MA, Brazil
{daniel.guilhon,anselmo.paiva,geraldo,jdallyson}@nca.ufma.br,
daniellima@ifma.edu.br
[2] Federal University of Campina Grande, Campina Grande, PB, Brazil
baptista@computacao.ufcg.edu.br

Abstract. Along with the re-democratization process in Brazil, states
and municipalities have started to rely on voluntary transfers of resources
through agreements with the Federal Government to execute their public
policies. To improve timeliness in the recovery process of default resource
usage, a classification tool is necessary to assign risk profiles of the success
or failure of these transfers. In this paperwork, we propose the use of the
eXtreme Gradient Boosting (XGBoost) algorithm using balanced and
unbalanced data sets, using Tree-structured Parzen Bayesian Estimator
(TPE) hyperparameter optimization techniques. The results achieved
good success rates. Results for XGBoost using balanced data showed a
recall of 89.3% and unbalanced data 87.8%. However, for unbalanced
data, the AUC score was 98.1%, against 97.9% for balanced data.

Keywords: Metadata · Voluntary transfers · Machine learning ·
XGBoost · Risk prediction

1 Introduction

In order to help Brazilian States and Municipalities to execute their public policies, the Brazilian Federal Government usually signs agreements with them to
enable voluntary transfers. Aiming at avoiding irregularities in spending these
voluntary transfers, Brazilian Audit Courts need to evaluate the execution of
these agreements and detect anomalies in order to prevent fraud as soon as possible. However, there are more than 140,000 signed agreements to analyze, and
a huge amount of public money involved.

One way of understanding voluntary transfers is to study it as a kind of credit
risk operation in the broad sense, a loan made by the Federal Government to
the states and municipalities. However, the results must be evaluated not only

© Springer Nature Switzerland AG 2021
A. Kö et al. (Eds.): EGOVIS 2021, LNCS 12926, pp. 167–179, 2021.
https://doi.org/10.1007/978-3-030-86611-2_13

from the financial perspective but also from the social benefits that the loan can produce. Credit risk assessment (a.k.a credit scoring) is the analysis of the risk associated with lending resources to companies and individuals and involves the use of risk management tools to evaluate the potential loss resulting from a borrower's failure to repay a loan or fulfill contractual obligations.

In this paper we propose a Machine Learning classifier to automatically predict risk classification on these agreements, aiming for scalability and timeliness.

The remaining of this paper is structured as follows. Section 2 discusses related work. Section 3 presents our methodology. Section 4 focuses on the results obtained. Finally, Sect. 5 concludes the paper and highlights further work to be undertaken.

2   Related Work

Several works approach assessing credit risk problems from different perspectives. According to [1] there is a method for assessing credit risk based on a continuous scale. For example, individual borrowing costs can be assigned to a person depending on the risk, rather than setting a standard loan price for everyone. [2] suggest classifying borrowers as "good payers", "can't pay", or "won't pay".

A literature review pointed out numerous computational learning techniques used for credit scoring [3]. An extensive benchmarking of the main credit scoring algorithms was carried out by [4].

According to [5], they developed models using Generalized Linear Models (GLM), Gradient Boosted Methods (GBM), and Distributed Random Forest (DRF), focused on the recovery of credit operations in a Brazilian bank. As a result, GBM presented the best performance.

Credit risk data generally shows a strong imbalance, an aspect that is widely discussed in the literature. There are more non-defaulter than defaulters borrowers. In cases where there is a large imbalance in the data, many models become biased towards the majority class. To mitigate this behavior, over-sampling (oversampling) or under-sampling (undersampling) techniques are often used. Among the oversampling techniques applied to the minority class, we emphasize techniques such as Self-Organizing Map-based Oversampling (SOMO) [6], and Synthetic Minority Over-sampling Technique (SMOTE) [6]. Among the under-sampling techniques applied to the majority class, some studies have compared k-Nearest Neighbours (kNN) [7,8] and under-Sampling Based techniques on Clustering (SBC) [9] with random subsampling. In their study, [10] also compared combined techniques of oversampling and undersampling with SMOTE to generate their training data, yielding promising results.

Recently, [11] proposed risk modeling using a gradient boosting algorithm, XGBoost, and hyperparameter optimization using the Bayesian Tree-structured Parzen Estimators (TPE) within the scope of credit scoring.

3   Methodology

Our methodology is based on the CRISP-DM and it is composed of four steps: data extraction; data selection and pre-processing; execution and optimization of hyperparameters of the chosen classification algorithms, and results assessment. In the following sections, we further detail each step of our methodology.

3.1   Data Extraction

The dataset used in this work is related to the celebration and monitoring of the transfer agreements publicly available for download at the Brazilian "Plataforma +Brasil" web portal[1].

This dataset is composed of 22 tables, but the agreement, proposal and proponents tables are the most suitable for the accountability process. Among the 212 features that exists in these three tables, we extracted only the most important ones for our study, because many of the available data are internal administrative information, such as the identification of the various actors in the process, and others refer to the internal phases of execution of the transfer instrument, such as project stages and description of the items of each phase.

3.2   Pre-processing and Selection

The voluntary transfers database contains 172,366 agreements. Many of them are still in the initial stages of execution or are in an accountability analysis stage. For conducting the experiments, we used only a subset of such agreements. During the pre-processing step, we performed a data cleaning process. We removed the records with end dates prior to the agreements start dates, empty values, and negative values. As a result, and supported by the experience of the technical auditor, we extracted the following information: Proponent Federation Unit; Proponent's municipality; Ministry; Executing agency (grantor); Modality; Bank account status; Project situation; Number of additive terms and extensions; Start and end dates of the agreement; Month of the instrument signature, and Agreed values. These features were, then, encoded using a one-hot encoding scheme.

The set of transfers used as success and failure are those in which the accountability analysis stage (internal control) has been completed. Positive cases are those in which internal control has disapproved the accounts. In these cases, the expression of internal control was "rejected imputability", "defaulting" or "contractual termination". On the other hand, the negative cases are those that were approved and the expression of internal control was "approved liability" or "approved liability with reservations".

After the data cleaning step, we gathered 53,581 voluntary transfers. We observed that 51,353 have opinions for the approval of the accounts (negative)

---

[1] http://plataformamaisbrasil.gov.br.

and 2,228 for the disapproval (positive). Hence, it is evident the great imbalance in our dataset.

We also ran a transformation process, aiming to generate extra features, regarding the case with information on amendments and consortia, such as the number of agencies in the consortia, it's value range, or the number of days since the signature. Another necessary transformation concerns the values of the agreements, which have a large variance. There are instruments of transfer from 2,000 to 170,000,000 (BRL - Brazilian Real). In order to avoid a bias, we normalized these values, making the values of all agreements in the range between 0 and 1.

Although one of the techniques used in our methodology (XGBoost), which uses gradient descent, does not suffer from problems related to vanishing gradients [12], the other two techniques logistic regression models and artificial neural network - MLP can suffer from gradient problems [13]. Hence, we normalized non-categorical data, such as amounts, number of extensions (additive terms), and number of consortium parties using the Min-Max [14] standardization technique, with min $= 0$, max $= 1$, $min_{new} = 0$, and $max_{new} = 1$, using the equation below:

$$\hat{x}_i = \frac{x_i - min(x_i)}{max(x_i) - min(x_i)} * (maxx_{new} - minx_{new}) + minx_{new} \tag{1}$$

For the remaining features, as they are categorical variables, we used one-hot encoding, which uses a sparse vector of dimension "d". This dimension is the number of values that the variable can assume. For example, for the feature "modality", which can be "AGREEMENT" or "CONTRACT", our representation would be a 2-dimensional vector, which would assume the values [1, 0] for "AGREEMENT" and [0, 1] for "CONTRACT".

Besides, we transformed the celebration and accountability dates into a difference of days between the beginning and end dates of the agreement. Thus, we added the following features: Total percentage agreed, percentage of counterparty, and percentage disbursed; Whether the instrument is derived from amendment; Difference, in days, between start and end of the term, original and modified, when applicable; Number of proposing members, when dealing with consortium.

3.3   Algorithms Execution and Optimization

We used three supervised classification techniques: Logistic Regression, MLP, and XGBoost to implement our credit score classifier. We implemented the classifiers using the Python programming language, along with the Scikit-Learn and the XGBoost libraries, which implement the tree boosting algorithm. We also used Hyperopt [15], for the hyperparameter optimization.

To perform the experiments, we used a 10-fold cross-validation method. Therefore, for each execution, the data for each segment was distributed according to Table 1.

Hence, training and testing were done in ten iterations. The evaluation metrics were obtained in each iteration. At the end of the iterations, the average and standard deviation were calculated, so that we can further evaluate the model.

Table 1. Data distribution proportion for training and testing.

Data	Positives	Negatives
Train	2005	46,217
Test	223	5,136

This entire process was carried out to obtain a model of risk classification to voluntary transfers. After each execution, searches were performed in the hyperparameter search to optimize the model. In the XGBoost classifier the hyperparameter optimization was performed using Hyperopt. The values of optimization parameters were set according to Table 2.

Table 2. Hyperparameters search space used in Hyperopt.

Hyperparameter	Domain
eta (Learning rate)	$0.025 + (n-1) * 0.025, n = [1..10]$
MXD (Max depth of trees)	$1 + (n-1), n = [1..14]$
MCW (Min child weight)	$1 + (n-1), n = [1..10]$
SS (Subsample ratio of training instances)	$0.7 + (n-1) * 0.05, n = [1..7]$
gamma (Minimum loss reduction)	$0.5 + (n-1) * 0.05, n = [1..11]$
CST (Subsample ratio of tree columns)	$0.7 + (n-1) * 0.05, n = [1..7]$
alpha (L1 weight regularization)	$1 + (n-1), n = [1..11]$
lambda (L2 weight regularization)	$1 + (n-1) * 0.1, n = [1..11]$
SPW (balance control of positive and negative weights)	$50 + (n-1) * 10, n = [1..16]$

As our dataset is highly imbalanced, we used stratification before being divided into segments, so that each folder is a representative of the whole set. Hence, each segment contained the same proportion of positive and negative cases.

In addition to the test with the highly imbalanced dataset, which can cause a certain bias in the classifier, sampling methods were used to deal with the imbalance, therefore, avoiding a bias. We performed the tests with SMOTE to generate new positive synthetic samples, as well as the NearMiss method of undersampling to reduce the number of negative samples. We also used combinations of methods to tackle the problem of imbalance.

3.4   Model Validation

We used accuracy, precision, sensitivity, specificity, and f-measure metrics for evaluating the models. We aimed at methods that had a good ability to correctly classify the disapproved accounts (sensitivity) and, at the same time, to be able to identify the approved accounts (specificity).

Every accountability should receive an opinion for its approval or disapproval. Thus, as it is a binary classification problem, we considered account disapprovals to be events of interest, therefore, classified as positive. For the other cases, approval of accounts, the negative value was attributed. Therefore, the TP, FN, FP, and TN measures have the following interpretation:

- True Positives (TP): refer to cases in which the audit analysis was for the dis-approval of the accounts, positive class, and that the model correctly classified as positive, that is, disapproval;
- False Negatives (FN): refer to the cases in which the audit analysis was for failure, that is, positive class, but the model mistakenly classified it as being of the negative class (approval);
- False Positives (FP): refer to cases in which the audit analysis was for the approval of the accounts (negative class) but incorrectly predicted as of the positive class;
- True Negatives (TN): refer to cases in which the class is negative and were correctly predicted to belong to this class, or approved accounts.

4   Results and Discussions

Table 3 shows the results obtained in the tests with imbalanced data and standard hyperparameters, and we highlight that the XGBoost obtained a sensitivity rate of 0.878.

Table 3. Metrics using unbalanced data without hyperparameter optimization.

	ACU	SEN	ESP	PRE	F-measure	AUC
XGBClassifier	0.952	0.878	0.956	0.510	0.645	0.979
LogisticRegression	0.919	0.710	0.930	0.345	0.464	0.937
MLPClassifier	0.961	0.485	0.986	0.641	0.552	0.936

After performing the hyperparameter optimization of the three chosen learning algorithms we obtained a significant improvement in the results, which are presented in Table 4.

Table 4. Metrics using unbalanced data with hyperparameter optimization.

	ACU	SEN	ESP	PRE	F-measure	AUC
XGBClassifier	0.965	0.805	0.973	0.606	0.692	0.981
LogisticRegression	0.891	0.924	0.889	0.302	0.455	0.961
MLPClassifier	0.967	0.523	0.990	0.721	0.606	0.973

Again, the XGBoost achieved better results, mainly concerning the f-measure metric. The most influential features were the modality and those that identify the agreeing parties or its binding ministry. These features are highly relevant to the model, which achieves an information gain by decreasing the entropy of the set. Along with the municipality code, these features have relatively low granularity, which can lead to overfitting of the model. When we removed these features, the result obtained by XGBoost reached an accuracy of 0.955, sensitivity of 0.733, specificity of 0.967, precision of 0.533, f-measure of 0.617, and AUC of 0.968.

Although we have 53,000 observations in our dataset, only 2,000 are positive cases, and 1,269 of the 5,570 Brazilian municipalities appear in the dataset. Brasília, Rio de Janeiro, and Recife municipalities concentrate a large part of the positive cases, resulting in 293 cases. In addition, 374 municipalities have more than one disapproval, and 227 only have two disapprovals. More than half of Brazilian municipalities do not have disapproval accounts statistics. Thus, we did a modification and maintained the model without this information for classification. This modification in the model must be evaluated as new municipalities with disapproved accounts appear, which will allow us to test the model already trained with information from a municipality that has not yet participated in the training.

The hyperparameter that most influenced the model was the maximum tree depth (MXD). Figure 1 depicts the low dimensionality [16], despite the number of hyperparameters to be optimized. Some hyperparameters have a high rate of variation, but without significantly impacting the model performance.

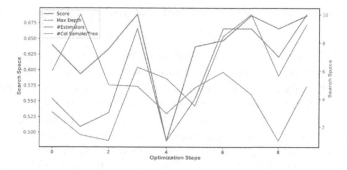

Fig. 1. Hyperparameter optimization of the model.

We used the area under the ROC curve (AUC) metric to perform objective comparisons between classifiers. The AUC is interpreted as the probability that a classifier will give a random positive sample a greater score rather than a random negative sample. Figure 2 compares the ROC curve of the three classifiers with optimized parameters. We noticed that XGBoost has the best relationship between True Positive Rate and its trade-off with the False Positive Rate.

We also analyzed our classifier by checking the cumulative frequency distribution of positive and negative cases, as shown in Fig. 3. The decision threshold was 0.5, and the cases of the probability distribution for positives that were below 0.5 are false negatives, and for negatives that are above 0.5 were false positives. Visually, we noticed what would happen with the cases of false positives and false negatives in case we change the classification threshold.

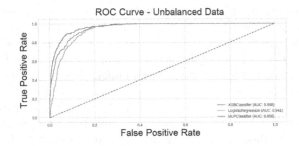

Fig. 2. Area Under Curve of the classifiers for imbalanced data.

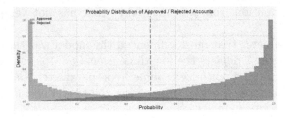

Fig. 3. Cumulative frequency distribution of positive and negative cases.

There is still another issue to be addressed. Note that the purpose of using a voluntary transfer risk classifier is to ensure greater timeliness in the analysis of possibly default agreements. The sooner a problem is detected, the greater the chance of recovering the public financial resources provided. Hence, the increase in the number of accounts analyzed by the Court of Audit prevents flagrantly reprehensible accounts from sifting through the containment of waste of public resources even if they do not result in disapproval of the accounts. Therefore, considering Fig. 3, if the threshold were decreased to 0.4, we would have a greater number of cases with false positives, however, we would also have an increase in cases with true positives, and this could achieve the proposed objectives.

Increasing the false positive rate, reducing the classification threshold and accuracy will cause an increase in the sensitivity rate, as this is the ratio of true positives to all positives. In this sense, the analysis of the Accuracy × Recall curve can be more interesting, especially when evaluating binary classifiers with high imbalance between classes.

Figure 4 shows the decreasing precision as long as the rate of true positives (sensitivity) increases. Adopting an appropriate decision threshold requires an analysis of risk appetite, which must be undertaken by the entities that will use these measures. In the "Mais Brasil" platform, the automated analysis must go through a process of assessing risk tolerance limits with the publication of the respective regulation. Thus, the Court of Audit will define how many accounts it would be willing to analyze to be more timely in the account analysis process.

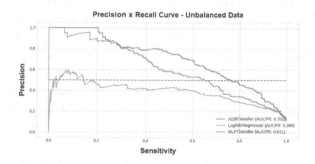

Fig. 4. Precision and Recall Curve of the classifiers for imbalanced data.

We carried out experiments on the performance of the three models using a balanced dataset. Three methods were adopted. We used rebalancing in three proportions: 10 × 1, 5 × 1, and 1 × 1. We used SMOTE methods to randomly generate new positive samples, NearMiss to eliminate negative samples, and we also used a combination of these undersampling and oversampling methods. Table 5 summarizes the results obtained by the methods.

We observed that the best results were obtained with the rebalancing using the combination of the SMOTE and NearMiss methods, with proportion of 1 × 1. It is interesting to observe the precision reduction in the models as we reduced the number of negative cases (NearMiss) in the rebalancing. In a scenario of a high dimension of features, as observed by [17], k-NN classifiers based on Euclidean distance seem to benefit more from the use of SMOTE, proportionally to the use of more neighbours. If we consider that the transferring agency needs to define the risk threshold to accept the accounts, the best indicator that captures this variation is the AUC. The AUC result obtained by the best model was 0.979. This result did not exceed the best result obtained by the best model with imbalanced data and optimized hyperparameters, which reached the value of 0.980.

Table 5. Comparison of model results with different methods of resampling.

Rate	Method	Model	ACU	SEN	ESP	PRE	F-M	AUC
10 × 1	SMOTE	XGBoost	0.967	0.775	0.977	0.636	0.699	0.977
		LR	0.894	0.929	0.893	0.307	0.461	0.961
		MLP	0.966	0.584	0.986	0.677	0.627	0.970
	NearMiss	XGBoost	0.932	0.782	0.940	0.404	0.533	0.963
		LR	0.930	0.855	0.934	0.401	0.546	0.964
		MLP	0.960	0.565	0.981	0.604	0.584	0.954
	SMO + NM	XGBoost	0.967	0.779	0.977	0.639	0.702	0.978
		LR	0.901	0.924	0.900	0.324	0.480	0.963
		MLP	0.967	0.553	0.988	0.704	0.620	0.970
5 × 1	SMOTE	XGBoost	0.967	0.737	0.979	0.641	0.686	0.978
		LR	0.896	0.920	0.895	0.312	0.466	0.961
		MLP	0.965	0.592	0.984	0.662	0.625	0.968
	NearMiss	XGBoost	0.855	0.805	0.857	0.226	0.353	0.918
		LR	0.874	0.824	0.877	0.258	0.393	0.927
		MLP	0.923	0.626	0.939	0.347	0.446	0.915
	SMO + NM	XGBoost	0.968	0.744	0.980	0.659	0.699	0.978
		LR	0.905	0.920	0.904	0.333	0.489	0.963
		MLP	0.964	0.565	0.985	0.658	0.608	0.968
1 × 1	SMOTE	XGBoost	0.970	0.626	0.988	0.726	0.672	0.979
		LR	0.902	0.920	0.901	0.325	0.480	0.962
		MLP	0.965	0.565	0.986	0.673	0.614	0.968
	NearMiss	XGBoost	0.690	0.893	0.680	0.126	0.221	0.859
		LR	0.256	0.798	0.228	0.051	0.096	0.520
		MLP	0.237	0.737	0.211	0.046	0.087	0.480
	SMO + NM	XGBoost	0.970	0.626	0.988	0.726	0.672	0.979
		LR	0.902	0.920	0.901	0.325	0.481	0.962
		MLP	0.966	0.546	0.987	0.691	0.610	0.967

A current problem when we are dealing with highly imbalanced data is that the accuracy does not reflect the quality of the classifier. In the present case, positive observations represent about 5% of the complete dataset. A model that classifies any sample as negative would still have an accuracy rate of around 95%. In the tests with the original imbalanced data, the best model slightly exceeded this result, reaching a 96.1% accuracy rate. The best model for the balanced dataset, with a 1 × 1 ratio, reached an accuracy of 97%, a slight improvement that was not achieved in other metrics that better capture the characteristics of the imbalanced dataset.

A crucial factor for the false positive was the feature value "Account Status" as "Registered", which is the value whose concentration of positive cases is higher, as shown in Fig. 5. Specialists in the business domain who can even propose improvements in the way of approaching the topic can analyze and validate this and other rules.

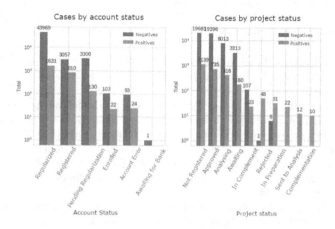

Fig. 5. Analysis of impacting features in forecasts.

5   Conclusion

This work presented a methodology for classifying voluntary transfers in risk profiles using XGBoost, comparing its results with other techniques used in the credit scoring domain, such as Logistic Regression and Multilayer Perceptron. The dataset we used had a high imbalance between the number of approved and disapproved accounts. Data rebalancing techniques, such as SMOTE and NearMiss, were used to verify the impact of imbalanced model training.

The results obtained proved the effectiveness of the proposed methodology, with good advantage for the use of XGBoost without major impacts, even with the use of imbalanced data. After optimizing the model hyperparameters, the results achieved were 96.63% accuracy, 84.73% sensitivity, 97.6% specificity, 79.37% precision, f-measure of 86.10%, and AUC of 98.0%. The results presented for the classification of risks of voluntary transfers are quite promising because they present high and consistent values.

As further work to be undertaken we would mention: qualitatively increasing the features used by the model, such as the inclusion of data from social indicators, such as human development Index (HDI), political parties, and Governance indicators of the agencies. Another important research is on introducing Natural Language Processing (NLP) techniques on information related to both objects agreed on the instruments, as well as those contained in the accountability report presented. Additionally, as some of the authors work directly with these audits, future work will assess the impacts of the absence of certain model variables in new observations, in order to determine their effectiveness.

References

1. Romanyuk, K.: Credit scoring based on a continuous scale for on-line credit quality control. In: 2015 IEEE International Conference on Evolving and Adaptive Intelligent Systems (EAIS), pp. 1–5 [s.n.] (2015). https://ieeexplore.ieee.org/document/7368796
2. Bravo, C., Thomas, L.C., Weber, R.: Improving credit scoring by differentiating defaulter behaviour. J. Oper. Res. Soc. **66**(5), 771–781 (2015). https://doi.org/10.1057/jors.2014.50
3. Dastile, X., Celik, T., Potsane, M.: Statistical and machine learning models in credit scoring: a systematic literature survey. Appl. Soft Comput. **91**, 106263 (2020). http://www.sciencedirect.com/science/article/pii/S1568494620302039
4. Lessmann, S., Seow, H.-V., Baesens, B., Thomas, L.C.: Benchmarking state-of-the-art classification algorithms for credit scoring: an update of research. Eur. J. Oper. Res. **247**, 124–136 (2015). https://www.sciencedirect.com/science/article/pii/S0377221715004208
5. Lopes, R.G., Carvalho, R.N., Ladeira, M., Carvalho, R.S.: Predicting recovery of credit operations on a Brazilian bank. In: 15th International Conference on Machine Learning and Applications (ICMLA) [S.l.]. IEEE (2016)
6. Douzas, G., Bacao, F.: Self-organizing map oversampling (SOMO) for imbalanced data set learning. Expert Syst. Appl. **82**, 40–52 (2017). https://www.sciencedirect.com/science/article/pii/S0957417417302324
7. Chyi, Y.-M.: Classification analysis techniques for skewed class distribution problems. Department of Information Management, National Sun Yat-Sen University (2003)
8. Mani, I., Zhang, I.: KNN approach to unbalanced data distributions: a case study involving information extraction. In: Proceedings of Workshop on Learning from Imbalanced Datasets, vol. 126 [s.n.] (2003). https://www.site.uottawa.ca/~nat/Workshop2003/jzhang.pdf
9. Yen, S.-J., Lee, Y.-S.: Cluster-based under-sampling approaches for imbalanced data distributions. Expert Syst. Appl. **36**(3, Part 1), 5718–5727 (2009). http://www.sciencedirect.com/science/article/pii/S0957417408003527
10. Sun, J., Lang, J., Fujita, H., Li, H.: Imbalanced enterprise credit evaluation with DTE-SBD: decision tree ensemble based on smote and bagging with differentiated sampling rates. Inf. Sci. **425**, 76–91 (2018). http://www.sciencedirect.com/science/article/pii/S0020025517310083
11. Wang, Y., Ni, X.S.: A XGBoost risk model via feature selection and Bayesian hyper-parameter optimization. arXiv e-prints, arXiv:1901.08433 (2019)
12. Xia, Y., Liu, C., Li, Y., Liu, N.: A boosted decision tree approach using Bayesian hyper-parameter optimization for credit scoring. Expert Syst. Appl. **78**, 225–241 (2017). http://www.sciencedirect.com/science/article/pii/S0957417417301008
13. Ioffe, S., Szegedy, C.: Batch normalization: accelerating deep network training by reducing internal covariate shift. arXiv preprint arXiv:1502.03167 (2015)
14. Singh, B.K., Verma, K., Thoke, A.: Investigations on impact of feature normalization techniques on classifier's performance in breast tumor classification. Int. J. Comput. Appl. Found. Comput. Sci. **116**(19) (2015)

15. Bergstra, J., Komer, B., Eliasmith, C., Yamins, D., Cox, D.D.: Hyperopt: a python library for model selection and hyperparameter optimization. Comput. Sci. Disc. **8**(1), 014008 (2015). https://doi.org/10.1088%2F1749-4699%2F8%2F1%2F014008
16. Bergstra, J., Bengio, Y.: Random search for hyper-parameter optimization. J. Mach. Learn. Res. **13**, 281–305 (2012)
17. Lusa, L., et al.: Smote for high-dimensional class-imbalanced data. BMC Bioinform. **14**(1), 106 (2013). https://link.springer.com/article/10.1186/1471-2105-14-106

Author Index

Printed in the United States
by Baker & Taylor Publisher Services